# Travel and Tourism Marketing Techniques

## Second Edition

## Robert T. Reilly
*University of Nebraska at Omaha*

DELMAR PUBLISHERS INC.
MERTON HOUSE TRAVEL AND TOURISM PUBLISHERS

**Delmar Staff**
Publisher: Laurence Stevens
Managing Editor: Barbara Christie
Production Editor: Eleanor Isenhart

For information, address Delmar Publishers Inc.
2 Computer Drive West, Box 15-015
Albany, NY 12212

Printed in the United States of America
Published simultaneously in Canada
by Nelson Canada,
a division of International Thomson Limited

10  9  8  7  6  5  4  3  2  1

**Library of Congress Cataloging-in-Publication Data**

Reilly, Robert T.
  Travel and tourism marketing techniques.

  (Travel management library series)
  Includes index.
  1. Tourist trade.  2. Marketing.  I. Title
II. Series: Travel management library.
G155.A1R457    1988    380.1'4591    87-31242
ISBN 0-8273-3300-5
ISBN 0-8273-3301-3 (instructor's guide)

# OTHER BOOKS IN THE TRAVEL MANAGEMENT LIBRARY SERIES

LEGAL ASPECTS OF TRAVEL AGENCY OPERATION, SECOND EDITION

COMPLETE GUIDE TO TRAVEL AGENCY AUTOMATION, SECOND EDITION

LEGAL FORMS FOR TRAVEL AGENTS

GROUP TRAVEL OPERATIONS MANUAL

GUIDE TO STARTING AND OPERATING A SUCCESSFUL TRAVEL AGENCY, SECOND EDITION

THE TRAVEL AGENCY PERSONNEL MANUAL

HANDBOOK OF PROFESSIONAL TOUR MANAGEMENT

FINANCIAL MANAGEMENT FOR TRAVEL AGENCIES

CORPORATE AND BUSINESS TRAVEL

BUDGETING FOR PROFIT AND MANAGING BY GOALS

GUIDE TO TRAVEL AGENCY SECURITY

THE DICTIONARY OF TOURISM, SECOND EDITION

CAREERS IN TRAVEL AND TOURISM, SECOND EDITION

A TRAVEL AGENCY POLICY AND PROCEDURES MANUAL

# CONTENTS

# PREFACE

All facets of the travel agency business are important—the staffing, the selling, the budgeting—and the advertising.

Ideally, the travel manager would be able to employ the services of a professional advertising agency; practically speaking, however, this is seldom possible. Most managers must settle for what they can create themselves, or for what they can obtain from the media. That's why a book on advertising for travel agencies seemed imperative. If managers are to be responsible for this facet of the business, they should know as much as they can about the subject.

Advertising principles remain much the same over the years, but the techniques and the audiences may be different. That's why a periodic revision of a text like this is necessary. This edition updates materials; expands the section on marketing; and adds new material on hotels, cruise lines and airlines, state and local tourism agencies, and other topics. Travel trends and statistics have also been changed to reflect the latest available figures.

This text, however, is merely a beginning. The wise manager— and student—keeps abreast of advertising as a live form, noting the routine and the exceptional advertising in the travel field, and saving samples that merit imitation.

Because of the growing number of colleges and universities that offer courses or degrees in travel management, the publishers opted for a textbook that would have equal value for the professional travel employee as well as for the student. While the questions and exercises may seem more appropriate to a campus atmosphere, they also serve as a checkpoint for those in the travel business who want to improve their skills.

Advertising, then, is a practical endeavor. It needs to be implemented in order to be learned. This text opens the door—but it doesn't furnish the room. The development of successful marketing and advertising techniques remains up to the individual.

Robert T. Reilly
University of Nebraska at Omaha

# ABOUT THE AUTHOR

This text is a revision of the first of two texts Bob Reilly has written for the travel industry and is the tenth book published by the author. The others, fiction and nonfiction, cover a range of topics, from the Indian Wars to public relations. Many of his books have Irish themes, including *Come Along to Ireland,* which combines a tour through Ireland with glimpses of that country's history and culture, and *Red Hugh, Prince of Donegal,* which was made into a Walt Disney film in 1966. Reilly has also published more than 500 articles in a variety of national magazines, writes poetry, scripts films and television shows, and has produced material for Mike Douglas, Fred Waring, and Capitol Records.

A native of Lowell, Massachusetts, Reilly now lives in Omaha, Nebraska and is professor emeritus of journalism at the University of Nebraska at Omaha, where he taught courses in advertising, public relations, and advanced writing.

The author spent thirty years in the advertising-public relations field before returning to teaching in 1972. During these years he worked on travel accounts in Boston and Omaha, served as public relations director for Creighton University, and was a partner in the state's largest home-based advertising-public relations firm.

Reilly has traveled widely, leading tours to Ireland and the British Isles, touring the South Pacific on various film assignments, and serving with the infantry in Europe during World War II. He has visited virtually all of the United States as a public speaker.

Reilly has a master's degree from Boston University, where he also spent two years toward his doctorate in English.

He has been a consultant to the Ford Foundation, provided counsel to numerous commercial and nonprofit agencies, and once lost a close race for Congress.

His honors include a number of foundation grants; the Fonda-McGuire Best Actor Award at the Omaha Playhouse (1954); Hall of Fame Award from the American College Public Relations Association (1965); Boss of the Year Award in Nebraska (1969); Midlands Journalist of the Year (1977); and the Kayser Chair at the University of Nebraska at Omaha in 1979.

Reilly is listed in *Who's Who in Advertising; Who's Who in Public Relations; Who's Who in the Midwest; Contemporary Authors; The Dictionary of British and American Writers; Dictionary of International Biography; The International Writers and Authors Who's Who;* and *Writers and Photographers Guide.*

# 1

# MARKETING IN A TRAVEL CONTEXT

Any company or individual who seeks to interest others in a product or service must be aware of marketing theory and practice. Regardless of the inherent value of the item, there are certain steps that must be taken in order to bring the product to the consumer.

You can't rely on luck, good will, or the law of averages to provide customers for travel services. Even when you have an exceptional tour to sell, this tour must be promoted. That's doubly true of regular travel services, which tend to be similar in nature and price.

Because of competition for attention, the wise travel manager must become familiar with all aspects of marketing. Researchers tell us that the average consumer is assaulted by more than 500 advertising messages daily: radio, television, newspapers, billboards, bulletin boards, magazines, shop windows, and so on. Of these 500 messages, the average person sees fewer than 10 percent. To half of these, he or she reacts negatively.

That means that, out of 500 chances, you have a 5 percent chance—or probably less—of capturing favorable attention. The more one knows about the whole process of marketing, the greater the chance of success.

## ELEMENTS OF MARKETING

Marketing includes

❑ The product or service itself
❑ Method of distribution
❑ Location
❑ Method of pricing
❑ Means of promotion

1

❏  Personal selling
❏  Advertising

## The Product or Service

First, you must have a good product or service that fills a need or creates a demand. If the product or service is not any good, or if it fails to provide satisfaction, no amount of promotion or advertising can sustain it for long.

Many corporate giants who failed to do the proper market research have paid for their mistakes. Campbell Soup failed with its "Red Kettle" brand; Ford launched and recalled the Edsel; and our top manufacturers of television sets concluded Americans did not want small-screen TV, until the Japanese showed them otherwise. Occasionally, it takes a while for a product or concept to catch on but, generally speaking, a reluctant citizenry can't be coerced in a competitive environment.

The travel field is no different. Some hotel ideas that work elsewhere—like the rented cubicles in Japan—may not suffice in the United States, because cultural differences affect consumer expectations and satisfaction. Our idea of a vacation may not be the same as in other countries. When New Yorkers eat out, their demands and expectations will be different from those of Parisians. Trying to force choices on consumers rarely works.

Tour operators must determine that the package they offer is one that generates maximum interest. Resorts have to ascertain that their amenities match the desires of their target audience. Travel agency managers should stand back and analyze their operations. Do they meet a proven need? Do they offer a superior product? Is there anything wrong with the items they are promoting? Besides this consideration of consumer services, the agency also has to examine itself as a product, scrutinizing the staff, the overall efficiency, and the profitability. Poor management, inadequate financing, inferior location, ineffective image, and faulty planning are also product errors and should be corrected before moving to any promotional phase.

It's a truism that good advertising only calls attention to a bad product. If a restaurant, for example, hasn't worked out the kinks in its operation and hasn't yet developed an acceptable cuisine, this is no time to buy space and time in print and broadcast media. An influx of customers will only result in a devastating word-of-mouth campaign against the restaurant. It will take months, perhaps years, to recover.

Airplanes obviously don't take off until all systems are perfect. Hotels, motels and resorts shouldn't welcome guests until they have a spotless facility and a flawless staff. And travel agencies shouldn't get over their heads in services unless they are able to handle them well.

## Distribution

This aspect of marketing may be more of a problem for a manufacturer who makes a complicated piece of machinery that must be transported great distances, or bakes a product with short shelf life, or produces an item with nationwide demand. The marketing manager must work on ways to transport the product to the consumer. This may include a decision on trucks versus trains versus airplanes, or it may encompass the question of selling via mail versus direct selling versus the use of dealers or distributors.

Travel suppliers also have certain unique distribution problems. Airlines, for example, try to select routes that promise an adequate

**Fig. 1–1   In the travel and hospitality industries, marketing means all those things relating to the delivery of individuals to a destination, plus arrangements for accommodation and entertainment once they arrive.**

return on investment and try to avoid those that are not cost effective. Cruise lines and motor coaches function similarly. Tourism bureaus have to be conscious of the market they can realistically serve, and hotels must project their occupancy rate based on an intelligent analysis of potential guests.

Travel agencies also have certain distribution problems. The travel manager must consider means of reaching potential customers within a geographical area where the delivery of services is both possible and practical. It's unlikely, for example, that an agency can count heavily on drawing clients away from Agency B if Agency B is doing a good job and is more convenient to the client.

## Location

More pertinent to travel agencies is this factor of *place*—having the service available *where* the customer wants it. This is, of course, particularly true of firms that provide services that are duplicated elsewhere. You might go out of your way to patronize a place with something genuinely unique but, if a travel firm is both competitive and more convenient, it has an edge. That's why intelligent research, which includes checking on things like traffic and need and parking and competition, precedes the location of any travel firm.

Some marketing texts list *place* as one of the elements of marketing, along with the *product, promotion* (under which they group advertising and public relations) and *pricing*. These "Four P's" of marketing are seen from the consumer's viewpoint.

## Pricing

With deregulation, this element of marketing became even more important. Although some of the chaos of the earliest days of deregulation has passed, there remain wild variations in the pricing of air travel, and the travel agent is often faced with a few hundred different options to a major destination, each with a variant price tag, and, perhaps, each with its own set of restrictions.

Hotels, too, keep an eye on competition and try to bring their room charges into line. Special weekend packages are popular, along with all sorts of combinations, from free champagne to free car rental. In some cities where hotel costs are notoriously expensive, like New York, London, and Paris, some hotels make their main theme a cheaper range of room rates.

A high percentage of prospective tour members are shoppers. They look for the most competitive price, sometimes ignoring what that price covers. That's one reason cruise lines have a number of accommodation options, allowing them to reach prospects with different tastes and different incomes.

Much of the pricing in travel agencies has been traditionally dictated by supplier costs. Airline tickets, hotel rooms, package tours—these arrive with basic price tags. Even when an agency builds its own tour, much of the price represents standard supplier charges. There are variations. Anticipated volume can lower costs, as can the ability of the travel manager to promote a better basic arrangement. The desire to make more money can, of course, increase costs.

Like advertising agencies, travel agencies in the past have wrestled with the low margin of profit. Because of this factor, and because of changes contemplated by governing bodies, new methods of securing revenue may be added. Smaller travel agencies are fearful these trends could drive them out of business, since larger agencies, for example, perhaps those with a number of branches, may contract for an entire plane and thus be able to compete unfairly with the smaller agencies on a volume basis.

Fig. 1–2  Pricing is a vital part of the travel scene.

There may be other innovations that could be developed, such as a different commission schedule, add-on charges for certain services, and so on.

Travel, however, will always be competitive. Not only will people gravitate toward the more economical offering (other things being equal), they will also resent an agency that seemed to overprice a trip. That's why pricing should receive high priority in the travel business, with both profit margins and competition receiving consideration. Even clever and continuous advertising can't save an overpriced offering.

Another pricing factor is the problem that consumers may not understand what travel agencies do and what their services cost. A significant majority of Americans still think they will be facing a number of extra charges when they use a travel agency. While this practice may change in the face of inflationary costs, extra charges are currently a rarity. Most travel agency services are free. Customers need to know how agencies are compensated, what services they can perform, and what these services mean to the client in terms of convenience and economy. A number of travel agencies have mounted promotional campaigns addressing this point, but the misconceptions persist.

As changes in the service and revenue phases of travel agencies take place, such information must be speedily and continually disseminated.

## Promotion

Ways to promote travel will be covered in detail in a later chapter. All that needs to be mentioned here is that there are many methods of selling merchandise or services. Advertising and salesmanship are merely two routes.

Two cars per family, fast foods, health spas—these and hundreds of other concepts have been sold as the result of publicity and promotion. Look at all the newspaper and magazine columns that promote—often by brand name—certain foods, flowers, movies, plays, books, sports events, medicines, and travel.

Demand for travel space to places like Australia often stems more from information people get from publicity rather than from advertising. Conversely, coverage of terrorist acts in Europe may curtail travel. The media certainly influence travel decisions. Cruise lines will readily credit the popularity of shows like "The

Love Boat" for the upsurge in interest, and a spate of films on India a few years back helped expand American tourism to that country.

Most promotion is carefully orchestrated and involves far more than publicity, which is simply the placement of news and feature material in the mass media.

## Personal Selling

This could take several forms, the most common of which are over-the-counter selling and the practice of calling on prospective commercial clients. To these might be added phone solicitation and the use of social occasions to subtly introduce the subject of travel services.

Individual salesmanship is important. Advertising and sales promotion alone rarely sell travel. They are more likely to provoke interest, to stimulate inquiries. At that point, the expert salesperson takes over and closes the sale. That's why intelligence, experience, perseverance, and a grasp of human psychology are indispensable for travel counselors. The able salesperson can turn mild curiosity into a solid booking; can make a customer out of a walk-in spectator; can extend a trip or services on that trip; and can save a wavering prospect.

The person who makes calls on large institutions, like corporations, universities, hospitals, and other major employers, must know his or her business thoroughly, must be able to deal with all types of people, and must be committed to an extra dimension of service at all hours of the day and night.

Weak salespeople are a drag on any company. Clients who arrive as a result of advertising, promotion, or word-of-mouth appeals can be quickly turned away by the salesperson's lack of enthusiasm, inattention, rudeness, ignorance of travel needs, inefficiency, or failure to provide real service.

## Advertising

Since this is the principal subject to be covered by this book, this topic need only be defined here. Advertising includes all of the messages in print or broadcast media that are purchased by the travel firm and whose content is controlled by that firm. This involves everything from a small two-inch advertisement in the Sunday travel section to the printed brochure mailed to prospects.

The inexperienced manager may think that advertising can do it all. Not true. The reason for listing all of the aspects of marketing is to emphasize that each of them has a role in the successful conclusion of any travel transaction.

In short, you must have something the client wants; you must be able to deliver it; it must bear an affordable and reasonable price tag; it must be communicated to the public in an interesting and appealing manner; and it must be clinched by some personal selling or service.

## PRODUCT VERSUS SERVICE

Selling a tangible item is different from selling a less tangible service. Marketing and advertising specialists are generally better at moving merchandise than they are at promoting services. For one thing, they've had more experience in selling products and have been able to gather more data. Learning how to properly market services is still a relatively new science.

For another thing, there are more variables in services. When you manufacture a product, you can exercise a considerable amount of control over it, virtually all the way to the consumer. With services, you rely more on the individual abilities and personalities of people. Many times, particularly with similar services—like banks and restaurants and hotels and travel agencies—you are really selling people. People are harder to control than products. They have their good and bad days; they can be superbly efficient or miserably inept. Therefore, when you make advertising and promotional claims about your service, you feel less secure than you do when making them about a tangible product.

For instance, your ads tell readers how easy it is to get a loan at a certain bank, but, when they go there, they find it nearly impossible to qualify. Your travel ads refer to fast, congenial, knowledgeable people, but the customer finds long lines, delays, brusqueness, and insufficient information.

Another difference between products and services is that, while both are sometimes bought for emotional reasons, services are more frequently purchased emotionally. Emotion figures heavily in advertising. Items like cosmetics (male and female), clothes, and even large items like houses and cars are bought, at times, for emotional reasons. With travel, except for business and other necessary travel, the reasons are virtually always emotional. The consumer tries to match his or her perception to the ability of the professional to satisfy it. Unless there is a perceived compatibility, the prospect will go elsewhere.

Service doesn't have the staying power of many products. When you've returned from a tour, you can't hang that warm feeling in your closet or play it on your stereo. There are lasting effects but they are more difficult to define.

While you may stockpile products, you can't do the same with services. That's what makes travel work such a problem. There are certain peak times of year when the travel industry could use more personnel, but the load the rest of the year might not support this. The only real inventory you have in the travel business is staff. A related concern is the fact that travel managers can't anticipate demand as well as some other product-centered industries, so, when a surprise pressure arises—like when the local university makes it to the NCAA Final Four in basketball—the overburdened agency or airline may either neglect some regular customers or turn away the new business. Both of these solutions are negative.

Salespeople for services have to be better than those who pitch products. They are not order takers, for the most part; they have to stay with the prospect longer; and they must know how to turn a visitor into a client.

Finally, the long-range effects of travel sales are hard to measure. Many who supply travel services never hear again from the clients. They also have a more difficult time focusing on the positive and negative aspects of their work. Clients, too, can't really measure most travel experience. It's not like knowing your car still runs or your electronic school courses brought you a job.

What this means for the travel business is that those selling services need a great deal of research into what people like and dislike about specific services; why they choose one over the other; why they change from one to another; and what they perceive to be the difference.

You can sometimes recover fairly rapidly from a bad product by removing it from the marketplace, by redesigning or repackaging it, by repricing it, or by moving it aside with an acceptable substitute. With services, this is much more difficult to do. A bad experience with a service leaves an impression that's hard to turn around, especially if the consumer has an alternative.

Travel agency managers know that a client whose travel plans have been messed up, perhaps without any fault being laid at the agency door, will start looking around for another agency. The bank customer who fails to get that loan and succeeds elsewhere will probably boycott the first bank forever, regardless of advertising.

That's why it's important to have good people (who are, after all, your link to the consumer), to train them well, to monitor their performance, and to reward excellence.

## MARKET PROBLEMS OF THE TRAVEL BUSINESS

While this topic will be discussed more fully in the next chapter, it's well to reflect here that, even among services, the travel business is a little different.

Perhaps, as with so many things, money is the bottom line. Many services that travel agencies perform are unprofitable. There are the people who drop by to chat, or to pick up brochures; there are those who make dozens of costly itinerary changes and then scrap the idea of the tour; and there are a number of client services whose profit margin is too low for any real agency benefit.

When you consider that many of the nation's advertising agencies argue that they can no longer make a living on the basis of fifteen percent commissions, you realize how narrow the gap is between financial success and failure in the travel business, where the commissions average ten percent.

**Fig. 1–3  With hundreds of Honolulu hotels to choose from, all aspects of marketing enter the promotional and decision-making processes.**

Money also has something to do with the number and kind of people you employ to give service, and the length of time you can expect to have them with you. Money affects the office surroundings, even the kind of image you are able to project through your advertising and direct mail.

## EXTERNAL PROBLEMS

Travel agencies also differ from many other service firms in that, even when they manage situations properly, they remain at the mercy of other individuals and circumstances.

If a bank handles a new account correctly, chances are no external event will erode customer satisfaction. If the postal clerk is courteous and helpful, the patron feels good about this contact. A clean, attractive hotel, with genial and efficient staff members, can control a majority of the factors included in a traveler's stay. Oh, the mail may take longer than you anticipated, and there could be a noisy party next to you in the hotel, but those risks are minimized.

With a travel agency, events are less certain. Because travel agencies broker for other services, the dangers multiply. A beautifully conceived tour, economically priced and well-led, can still experience surly waiters, governmental red tape, airline delays, and distasteful companions. There may be transportation strikes, inconvenient bank holidays, student riots, and miserable weather.

Airlines, too, can be victims of weather and other problems which cause delays and cancellations and, as a result, anger customers. Even tourism bureaus may have a carefully planned event go awry because of a sudden storm or the errors of local political leaders.

## PEOPLE AND MONEY

Ultimately, staffing and financing affect performance. Travel personnel have to know what customer service is, what customer needs are, and how to relate to customers one-on-one.

Travel firms almost always have less personnel than the volume of business requires, meaning that they work long and full hours. This places an extra burden on all of the personality traits which must be part of effective customer relations.

Unlike banks, which have both more personnel and more money for advertising, the travel industry rarely ventures into image ads, which don't sell anything directly but which attempt to create a favorable opinion. Travel agencies are also short of funds to underwrite research, to attract advertising agency attention, or to take advantage of advertising opportunities.

# TIMING

Perhaps one final difference between service and product advertising is that product ad philosophy generally advises pouring additional dollars into promotion when the product is selling well. The "strike while the iron is hot" syndrome is at work here. With service industries, this may not be true—particularly in areas like travel. If a motel chain has no rooms to sell, it is unlikely to beef up its advertising campaign. If the travel agency (happy thought!) has filled all tours to capacity, it is not likely to increase advertising expenses.

# DO THE BEST YOU CAN

Most astute agency managers can't really afford to do the best they know how: they merely do the best they can. They adapt the research that is available to their own situation, using common sense in applying it to their market. They use all the services supplied by carriers, hotel and motel chains, tour operators, and others. They read their professional travel publications and keep up on trends. They review advertising by competitors and by similar agencies in other areas and imitate what they can afford to imitate.

In short, they husband the dollars that go into advertising and promotion, carefully allocating each hard-earned dime.

Every segment of the travel industry can, however, develop a marketing plan. This is true for the small agency as well as for the large cruise line.

# THE MARKETING PLAN

Marketing plans differ for certain types of businesses, depending on things like size and relative strength and the nature of the business. Even within the travel field, the plans will be diverse. However, there are some standard concerns we might list. These are the elements that would fit many marketing programs within a service industry like travel.

1. *The Current Situation Must Be Defined and Analyzed.* The travel firm needs to review its position in the market and determine how it reached this plateau and where it wishes to go from here. That means knowing such things as:

   a. What the travel industry is doing within the framework of the particular area served by the individual company. What are the trends, the problems, the competition? The manager should have a clear picture of the general conditions before narrowing the focus.

   b. Past sales records should be checked for patterns. If these totals can be further refined—vacation, commercial, travel tours, for example—this should be done. The firm needs to know where the strengths and weaknesses are and where the firm is headed.

   c. Some concept of market potential must be posited. Within the bounds of realism, what results might be expected if things are handled properly? Are there any trends that will influence these results?

   d. The analysis should include a study of *how* sales are made. Can responses be tracked to a particular form of advertising, or promotion, or personal selling? Are they seasonal? Have any of these factors changed in recent years? What do we know about the buying habits and attitudes of prospects? Can we break down this information by type of travel interest? And what about our own sales methods and promotional campaigns? Have they been effective? Can we improve on them?

   e. How well can we identify the best customer? What sort of profile can we draw in terms of age, income, occupation, geographical location, and other considerations? Besides these demographic factors, what psychographics can we come up with—facts on the attitudes and behavior of these individuals?

   f. What about a review of past advertising and promotional campaigns? What was the strategy? Did it work? What was the ratio of expense to return?

   g. What about the travel service itself? Is the product right, correctly and competitively priced, efficiently delivered? Are there ways we could improve on these elements?

2. *Problems and Opportunities Should Be Identified.* Once information has been collected, it's necessary to analyze it, consider various alternatives, and make a decision. Research can reveal problems but it can also uncover opportunities.

   The manager is really asking what problems seem to be hampering growth or financial success, and how these problems may be turned into realistic opportunities.

   Operations may have to be modified or enhanced. New markets may need to be found or old ones expanded. More efficient methods of conducting the business may need to be developed.

3. *Goals and Objectives Need to Be Spelled Out.* Based on as much research material as can be afforded, the travel firm should develop some assumptions about the future in terms of changes in client needs; economic patterns; state of the industry; changes in the way the service is promoted or distributed; and changes outside the firm's control, like deregulation, inflation, or political problems in destination areas.

   From these assumptions, some preliminary marketing objectives must be formulated, establishing goals that are realistic, concrete, and measurable.

   Once the primary objectives have been established, then the travel firm outlines a strategy to reach these objectives. Perhaps this calls for additional staffing, more of the budget committed to advertising, a move to a new target audience, a reshuffling of duties, or a restructuring of the organization.

   Finally, this strategy and its objectives must be shared by all divisions within the firm. Again, in a very small agency, people will need to wear many hats, but, in a larger company, there would be objectives for the promotional areas, the financial areas, for market research, personnel, customer service, and others.

4. *Establish Priorities and Set Deadlines.* After deciding on objectives and the strategy necessary to reach them, planners need to go into more detail about how these things will be accomplished. The outline must be fleshed out. Priorities need to be addressed, realistic deadlines assigned, audiences clearly defined, messages devised and produced, salespeople trained, and so on. Everything required to accomplish the goals must be spelled out, step by step. Even alternatives must be built in, just in case the initial activities don't work.

5. *The Marketing Plan Should Be Monitored and Evaluated.* Planners in the travel firm have to determine in advance what they will be looking for in terms of success, and how and when they will review the programs to see how they are doing. There may well be periodic and departmentalized review, along with a full-scale evaluation of progress measured against planning. If changes need to be made, it's back to the drawing board and the process is repeated.

There are, of course, other ways to plan. Each travel organization may wish to make its own adjustments. However, the research, planning, implementation, and evaluation phases are common denominators.

Although much of this text deals with the advertising and promotion aspects of marketing, it is well to remember that the other elements in marketing cited earlier—the product, pricing, and place—all require attention and analysis. No marketing plan is complete without considering *all* the things that are part of it.

## CHAPTER HIGHLIGHTS

❏ Marketing includes the product or service, method of distribution, location, pricing, advertising, promotion, and personal selling.
❏ The product or service must meet a felt need.
❏ Travel services have to be channeled effectively and efficiently.
❏ Prices for travel services should be current and competitive.
❏ Proper promotion can have a major impact on travel prospects.
❏ Personal selling is often the final and most important step in marketing travel services.
❏ Advertising is a principal mass communication means of alerting prospects to the potential service.
❏ Selling a service is different from selling a product. The service is less tangible, less durable, more varied, can't be stockpiled, requires capable salespeople, and has results that are difficult to measure.
❏ The travel business has its own unique set of problems, some of which are external (like weather) and some internal (like narrow margins of profits and low salaries).

❑ Every segment of the travel industry should have a travel plan. This plan involves defining the current situation, identifying problems or opportunities, setting goals and objectives, implementing activities, and evaluating results.

■          ■          ■

## ❑ *EXERCISES*

1. Using the travel section of a metropolitan newspaper or the information contained in brochures featuring similar tour destinations, compare prices and details of these tours.
2. Select three print ads from a travel magazine and write out for each who you feel the "target audience" is (the specific group to whom the ad is directed), the main theme, and the plus and minus features of the particular offering.
3. List five things you believe are effective in salesmanship, especially in the selling of a service, and five things you feel turn off prospects.
4. Besides advertising, what other aspects of radio and television may influence the travel prospect? Which of these do you feel are planned and which are just part of the media?

## ❑ *CASE PROBLEMS*

*1. Assume you are the manager of a new hotel in your area, a hotel that features individual suites for all guests, including bedroom, kitchenette, bath, sauna and sun deck. The lowest priced suite is $150 per person per night and the highest is $300 per night. Breakfast is complimentary and there is a pool and other amenities. Your chef formerly ran the kitchen in one of the finest New Orleans restaurants and is famous for his Cajun and Deep South recipes, a cuisine not that familiar to diners in your community. This new hotel has a location that is close to the interstate highway system but some distance from main residential and shopping areas. Given these few facts and what you know about your general area, list some of the considerations you would include in your marketing plan.*

*2. Your travel agency is part of a holding company that owns a brokerage service, a chain of clothing stores, a frozen food manufacturing firm, a publishing house that specializes in business texts, and a home computer company. As manager of the travel firm, you are meeting with the chairperson of the holding company, your ultimate boss, and you're discussing the marketing plan for the upcoming year. This CEO tells you that selling travel is no different from selling suits, dresses, convenience chicken dinners, bonds, or books. You disagree. What points would you make to convince your boss that travel presents a different marketing challenge?*

# GATHERING MARKETING DATA

Many of the marketing skills that work in other businesses will also work in the travel business. Research, testing, good salesmanship, innovative promotion, and superior products work anywhere. Larger travel operations may be able to implement these areas to their fullest, but the smaller travel agency has to rely more on available data, common sense, and the example of others.

Regardless of size or the nature of the function, every travel business must conduct some sort of introspection. No firm can survive on guesswork. Some form of research should support every decision made.

There are two ways to gather data: informally and formally. Formal research involves the conducting of a survey; informal research includes all other forms of information gathering, from use of the library to chats with travel professionals.

## FORMAL RESEARCH

Generally, travel agencies do not do much formal research. To produce a professional survey result is complicated and expensive. However, airlines, cruise lines, hotels, tourism bureaus, and other arms of the industry may develop survey data, and even the smaller travel units may try a simpler and limited survey. There are *four* ways to sample individuals being surveyed.

1. *Accidental samples,* where individuals are selected merely because they happen to be at a particular place at a particular time. Shopping mall surveys are one example, and this category might also include individuals who happen to walk into a travel agency. Obviously, this technique is hardly scientific.

Mall traffic may overrepresent older and younger citizens, could have a geographical bias, or even an economic bias. For some sorts of general data, accidental samples may be interesting and informative. They could, for example, provide suggestions for problem areas to be studied or even provoke comments that would work in promotional copy. However, these samples are hardly reliable when predicting trends or behavior.

2.  *Quota samples* try to match the percentages in a total universe (which could be a city, a state, a country, or even a limited area within a city) with the percentages in the survey. If 11 percent of the people within a city were over 65, for example, that percentage should be matched in the survey sample, meaning that 11 percent of the people surveyed should be over 65. You could also select along income levels, sex, ethnic background, religion, or other variables. Obviously, the number of variables must be limited and there are also restrictions on how far you can extend the results achieved.

3.  *Purposive samples* have more application in travel, since they deal with groups with known characteristics—a list of former passengers or clients, for example. Again, the findings are not really random nor can they be assumed to represent any group beyond that surveyed. Therefore, they could be misleading. Besides compiling your own list to survey, you might also buy a list, subscribers to travel magazines, for example, or people who have applied for passports. When you have a good idea of the profile of your best customer, this is not a bad way to proceed.

4.  *Probability samples,* which are used by the major polling firms, are truly random and depend on no other factor except where a person happens to live. The principle behind this is that, since you can't contact everyone in the particular universe, you work on a smaller number, randomly selected, with each person in the universe having an equal chance of being interviewed.

    To achieve a confidence level of 97 percent, for example, meaning that your results shouldn't vary more than 3 percent from what they would be if you could sample everyone in the universe, you should have a randomly selected population of about 1500 persons. Once the sampling error goes beyond 5 percent (or the confidence level less than 95 percent), many companies will not accept the research results.

**Fig. 2–1  Computers make information gathering much simpler.**
(Courtesy of Leslie Associates, Inc.)

For travel industry members, only the larger units would engage in this sort of research. Perhaps an airline, for example, wants to know what its image is among college-age men and women, or a cruise line wants to discover reasons why individuals have never taken a cruise.

## Formulating the Questionnaire

Before anything is done, those conducting the survey need to know what they want to find out. Are they trying to determine reaction to a well-publicized crisis, checking on the tolerance of prospective passengers to a rate increase, or attempting to find out what alternative times of year people would like to travel to Europe? Once this has been decided—and it isn't always easy—the next step is to devise a series of questions that produce the objective response you need, without confusing, misleading, or directing the respondent.

There should be enough questions to gather the information you require, but no more than that. And there should be sufficient alternatives to accommodate a wide range of opinion. Positive and negative replies may not be enough; those surveyed may be undecided, or they may prefer a questionnaire that permits them to display the intensity of these feelings, using terms like "strongly agree" or "somewhat agree."

## Methods of Surveying

With probability sampling, professional help is certainly advisable, and it might also be desirable with other forms of surveys. There are research firms that specialize in this work and, if you want to be able to trust the results, these firms add a dimension of credibility.

Many travel firms use a mail questionnaire, and there is nothing wrong with this. A mail questionnaire allows the respondent to peruse exhibits, study questions, and devise thoughtful answers. However, it can be costly, and it is difficult to tell the source of the replies. For instance, you may hear only from those people most interested in the issue and not from a true cross-section.

Personal surveying is also expensive, but it does allow the interviewer to make some judgments about the respondent and about the quality of the answers.

While the telephone is a major research instrument, it also has its limitations: the annoyance factor, the limitations on length, the impossibility of showing things to the respondent, and the inequitable distribution of telephones. But it is fast, good for short questionnaires, easy to randomize, and generally reliable.

## Evaluation

However the survey is conducted, once the results are in, someone has to evaluate them. What does it mean when 43 percent of the respondents say they have no opinion abut a certain international exposition? Does it mean that these people don't know about the event or that they don't care about the event? What does it mean when you find twice as many women as men reacting negatively to hotel services? Someone has to analyze and refine these answers, measuring them against other responses or other surveys, and then advise the travel firm as to the probable conclusions.

# INFORMAL RESEARCH

Because of the complex nature of *formal* research, most travel businesses rely more on *informal* research.

Chief among the tools in conducting informal research are the various publications that feature data of interest to the travel firm. These include books on travel, trade journals, business directories, federal publications derived from census data, digests of consumer information, studies produced by members of the travel industry, periodicals from related fields like advertising and marketing, and a number of other printed sources.

Other means of gathering information include visits with professional travel personnel, either singly or in groups; attendance at appropriate seminars and classes; an analysis of consumer and trade news; and even a thoughtful scrutiny of material available at the travel firm.

The point is that you seek out data to support decisions, doing the best you can with the time and resources available.

## WHAT SORT OF DATA ARE YOU LOOKING FOR?

The travel professional may be interested in all sorts of data, depending on the nature of the problem or responsibility. Managers will be looking closely at profit margins and at examples of efficiency. Those in commercial sales will be interested in the impact of the new tax laws on business travel, in the increase in female corporate travelers, and in the range of incentives available to certain levels of commercial passengers. Hotels may be researching convention potential or competitive room rates or the array of amenities offered by other hotels. Airlines are interested in passenger demographics and federal regulations and scheduling efficiencies—perhaps even long-range weather forecasting.

There are some subjects that interest almost every professional in the travel industry. Managers want to know who the prospects are and what they want, and they want to know what trends are likely to affect their business.

## WHO ARE THE PROSPECTS?

The first thing you have to realize in marketing any product or service is that not everyone is a real prospect. What you try to do is locate those individuals who constitute the more likely prospects. What you aim for is a market segment.

Three things characterize a market segment:

1. *Ability to pay.* In travel as in other areas, the ability to pay is not related solely to income size. Studies show that people who are making identical incomes make purchases based on the way they view that income. Some feel the present salary is at peak and that it will decline in the future. These people make poor travel prospects. A second group feels this salary will remain about the same. This group has only fair prospects. People in the third group see themselves moving up, and they make the best prospects, even though they are holding paychecks identical to groups one and two.

    It's obvious, however, that a person making $25,000 a year, regardless of how he or she feels about that income, is not a prime prospect for an $8,000 luxury cruise.

2. *Ability to make a buying decision.* You want to reach the person who has the largest say in selecting a product or service. Men usually exert a larger influence in buying insurance, for example, while women are most likely to have the deciding vote in home furnishings. Perhaps both carry equal weight in purchasing a car or home. College-age students affect the choice of university, even when parents are footing the bills, and children have a lot to say about things like breakfast cereals, fast food restaurants, and toys. In this chapter we'll examine the buying decisions involved in travel.

3. *Ability to derive satisfaction from the product or service.* The best prospects have to be able to enjoy what they have purchased, either directly or indirectly. A housewife may enjoy a beef roast herself or may get vicarious pleasure out of serving it to her family or guests. A father may detest rock music but may feel good about selecting a record album his teenage son admires. With travel, the purchaser usually anticipates personal happiness, but the individual could also be traveling to please a spouse or could be underwriting a trip for a son or a daughter.

These three elements can be found in the prime prospects. The problem is to locate these individuals, and that's where research is valuable.

## RESEARCHING THE PROSPECTS

It's both economical and efficient to have some solid evidence about travel prospects. This allows the agency or carrier to focus its promotional campaign on certain segments that promise the best return. Research should help the travel manager determine who these people are, where they live, what their concerns are, and where and when they want to travel. To gather this information, many travel agencies do periodic surveys of their clients, or they may expand the list by adding others who fit the typical travel profile.

Even if the small travel agency doesn't have the money or staff to undertake even a limited survey, it can always hitchhike on existing information and use studies compiled by other travel entrepreneurs. The agency must, however, be careful about applying all data from another situation to its peculiar situation.

A midwestern travel agency analyzes its client list. It discovers its best prospect may be a bit older than the normal traveler, that this person is married, and is probably either retired, in a business/ clerical post, or a member of a profession. Income levels range widely, but the average income of members is slightly higher than that of the public at large.

The American Automobile Association (AAA) asks its members, among other things, what attracted them to use their travel services. It finds that experience, the reputation for providing fun at a reasonable price, the insurance aspects, and the choices of many types of tours are among the answers. Favorite months to travel were summer and early fall, with winter travel picking up. These conclusions, which should be tested periodically, help AAA plan its tours and its advertising.

## Why Do People Travel?

While the principal reasons for travel are fairly uniform, the order of their importance will vary from region to region, and among age groups and income levels.

Adventure, business, a change of climate, visits with family and relatives, education, shopping, genealogy, antidote to boredom, a chance to meet people of the opposite sex, the availability of exotic cuisine—these are among the top reasons cited in surveys.

Those seeking adventure are easier to sell (though they may be hard to please) than those who are generally reluctant to leave home. As men and women age, women remain more adventurous in terms of travel.

Obviously, appeals to those seeking education are different from those to individuals looking for companionship. Certain resorts, for example, may deliberately cater to the latter, while certain European tours may be aimed at the former.

**Fig. 2–2 Focusing on the
trend toward more unique
travel experiences, this ad
carves out its own adventurous market segment. (Courtesy of Exploration Cruise
Lines)**

## What Travel Elements Concern People?

Just as research can dig out positive appeals to prospects, it can also
discover negative factors that may impede sales. Knowing this, carriers or resorts or agencies may write copy or develop sales tracks
that respond to these fears.

Travel to Europe fell off in the summer of 1986, largely due to
the concern about terrorist attacks. Americans viewing this nation's
media were convinced travel was not safe and they put off trips they
had planned. Virtually every hotel in Europe was hit by cancellations.

Safety is one obvious concern. When someone puts out money for
a trip, perhaps a once-in-a-lifetime trip, that person doesn't want to
worry about a volatile political situation.

Travelers who respond to surveys also admit to uncertainties about food, water, language barriers, money exchange, clothes, climate, pace of the trip, and the accommodations they'll find. They want to know if they will really enjoy themselves and, if on a tour, what sort of people they'll be with.

Many Americans want to take their own country with them. This means the travel salesperson must *sell up* their travel, providing this type of person with better facilities at a higher cost in order to ensure satisfaction. This is one specific way that recognizing tourist concerns affects sales.

## WHAT POLLS TELL US ABOUT TRAVEL

Some travel information may be compiled simply by processing sets of existing figures. Computers make this much easier and infinitely faster.

The top tourism destinations of 1985, for example, were compiled from a list of air departures. Mexico ranked first that year, followed by Great Britain, West Germany, the Bahamas, Japan, Jamaica, Italy, and France.

In the same year, *Travel/Holiday* magazine, in its annual poll, found that the favorite tourism spots within the continental United States were in the South, followed by the Middle Atlantic region (including New York and Washington, D.C.) and the Pacific Coast. This same poll, conducted by mail among subscribers, asks respondents to rank airlines, cruise lines, hotels, trains, tour companies, and rental cars. In 1985, Delta and Air New Zealand led in the domestic and foreign airline categories; Princess Cruises, Royal Caribbean, and Royal Viking lines tied in the cruise category; Tauck and Maupintour were winners among tour companies; Westin took honors both inside and outside the United States among hotel chains; and Hertz placed first among rental cars in foreign countries.

*Travel Weekly,* which bills itself as "The National Newspaper of the Travel Industry," issues many special sections during any given year, covering topics like economic forecasts, business travel, promotion, trends, and other areas. In several of its 1986 publications, survey results showed the following:

❑ Travel agencies rose from fewer than 8,000 in 1970 to nearly 28,000 in 1986.
❑ March, June, and September were the highest volume months in travel agency sales.

❏ Better than half the agency dollar was spent on salaries and about 5 percent was committed to advertising and promotion.
❏ While ownership of travel agencies was pretty well divided between men and women, some 81 percent of agency employees were female.
❏ The world's busiest airport in 1985? You guessed it—Chicago's O'Hare.
❏ The total number of summer vacation trips taken by Americans in 1985 was 282 million, just under 1981's 286 million.
❏ New Yorkers greeted the largest number of foreign travelers (almost 8 million) followed by Florida, California, Hawaii, and Texas.

In its "Economic Survey" issue (1986), *Travel Weekly's* correspondents were predicting a 4-5 percent increase in travel, but that was in January, before the terrorism scare. Statistical information in this issue showed travel agencies having an increasing impact in the sale of airline tickets, a weaker dollar serving as a spur to domestic travel, and an increase in commercial and government accounts.

Typically, business travel accounts for little more than half of travel agency volume, and business clients are regarded as the most loyal clients. One could also read from the statistics that the larger travel agencies were getting an increasing share of market while the midsized agencies saw their volume decline.

Evidently, the travel, leisure, and recreation areas will remain healthy. A United States Department of Labor study projects a 27 percent increase in the job market for these services by 1995.

And you don't have to be a major trade or consumer publication, or a federal agency, to collect data. Estes Park, Colorado, which subsists primarily on tourist dollars, worked with the University of Colorado to fashion a profile of an average tourist to this Rocky Mountain community. They found, for example, that the average visitor stayed one to three days, spent less than $500, probably drove there, and that advertising about Estes Park may have reinforced their decision to go but they had already strongly considered that possibility.

## OBSERVING TRENDS

Surveying, compiling, and analyzing data to determine what has gone on or is going on is helpful, but the wise manager always wants to have an idea of what the future holds. Since, like the weather, nothing is certain, even with extensive market research, planning must automatically include an awareness of the present business and cultural environment and a projection about where these trends will take us. Promotion can't be built on assumptions or data alone. External factors always have the potential of changing things. The effects of events like the energy shortage or the terrorism scare are examples; they alter our carefully researched plans.

Some trends exist within the travel industry, while many more are at work outside the field that have the potential to influence various aspects of travel.

Within the travel industry, for example, a 1986 Lou Harris survey isolates items such as the increase in cruise bookings, now representing some 14 percent of travel agency revenues; the strength of repeat business travel bookings, with almost 75 percent of this business coming from previous customers; the dominance of computer-

**Fig. 2–3  While some tourists prefer first class hotels, others may opt for bed and breakfast accommodations.**

ization, with 90 percent of the retailers being automated and with a third of them handling their accounting in this fashion. Harris also showed that travel agents continue to have an influence on customers, with about half of the vacationers stating they seek advice of these agents, and with almost a third of them admitting they are sold on a cruise even though they hadn't contemplated taking one.

Other internal trends reveal commercial travel on the rise, increasing as much as 60 percent in one year on the east coast, and a slight but steady gain in group bookings in 1986. Among specialty vacations, golf, skiing and honeymoons were the leaders, with gambling, scuba diving, and tennis following. Statistics for 1986 showed a slight decrease in air travel, even though this area still represented almost two-thirds of travel agency revenue, and a dollar increase in hotel bookings that remained about 10 percent of agency volume.

In trade journals and elsewhere, the travel industry planner can also find statistics on employee satisfaction, salaries, car rentals, attitudes toward rebates, and about any other subject that would be of interest.

Outside the industry, there are also trends that show up in travel sales or behavior. Some of the obvious travel-related trends might be

❑ The notion of entitlement, that one *deserves* a vacation.
❑ Delayed parenthood, meaning that younger couples are available for travel.
❑ Longer life span, resulting in the "graying" of the population.
❑ Increased education levels, which may influence tour choices, but will certainly influence income and expectations.
❑ Crisis orientation and concern about spurious terrorism attacks.
❑ Affluence, especially among the young and among people once thought of as middle class.
❑ Independence, leading to the selection of less structured tours.
❑ A more casual attitude toward sex, which affects everything from advertising to hotel bookings.
❑ Growing complications, resulting in a more impersonal environment, and affecting the way agencies do business as well as the individual's desire to get away from it all.
❑ More careful, even cynical, consumers, who will read details critically and demand better performance.

Even factors like the changing attitude toward orthodoxy in religion will have an impact on travel decisions like tours to Europe's shrines. The continued growth of women in the work force also affects both business and vacation travel. More leisure time, a more casual lifestyle, and the emphasis on dieting and fitness all show up as influences in the travel business.

All of these trends dictate what is to be carried in the promotional message. Because of both economic concerns and consumerism, for example, ads must work harder. Readers are more sophisticated and they will regard exaggerated claims and promises with suspicion. They want more facts, less showmanship. That doesn't mean that advertisements must read or sound like catalog copy, but it does warn the writer that he or she must stay within the bounds of credibility.

It's also important to remember that trends change and what was true in 1987 may not be true in 1990. Conclusions have to be reviewed regularly to spot subtle shifts.

## DETERMINING MARKET SEGMENTS

The more personal you can make an advertising message, the more successful you will be. If you could gather all of the best prospects for a particular kind of travel in one room and expose them to a message aimed directly at them, this would be a much more efficient way of approaching sales than placing an ad before an audience of half a million readers, most of whom won't even see it.

Unfortunately, you can't do this. Advertising remains largely a mass media game. However, you can target in on audiences more through direct mail. And even in mass media advertising, you can present information in a way that seeks out the best prospects. Let's look at a few special groups.

1.  *Working women.* Nearly two out of every three women are employed outside the home, and they constitute approximately half of the total labor force. Working women, on the average, are better educated than nonworking women, are younger than their nonworking counterparts, watch less television, but read more magazines. These facts would affect the media decisions of an advertiser desiring to reach the working woman. Nearly 10 percent more working women take vacations than do housewives, and they are more likely to travel by air. The households in which they live also have higher median incomes.

Advertising must be attuned to this profile, considering in its approach the fact that portraying women only in home or play situations is no longer realistic—or relevant.

2. *Youth market.* Just four decades ago, it was the rare young person who could contemplate a trip to Europe. That pleasure was reserved for the rich. Today, because of increased mobility, more available resources, and the desire for travel, young people form a special audience for travel. Their needs differ from those of their parents. They are likely to stress economy and will put up with more discomfort. They are also likely to opt for travel on their own, seek out places where they will encounter other young people, and look for entertainment that is compatible with their age.

   Some travel agencies specialize in youth travel, and there are any number of brochures directed to the younger set.

3. *Honeymooners.* Partly as a result of couples marrying (or remarrying) later in life, the traditional honeymoon destinations have been supplemented by other choices. Hawaii and the Caribbean remain strong, but cruises, once almost ignored by honeymooners, are now a major option, and those marrying older frequently settle on Europe, especially London or Paris. Travel agents also note that honeymooners may later book a return to that same romantic spot.

   Promotional material for honeymoons may be a little more daring than other appeals and could feature couples curled up on a lonely beach or sharing a heart-shaped tub in the Poconos. But other, more adventurous, honeymooners may be intrigued by pictures of a safari or cycling trip through Germany.

   While resorts and cruise lines make a pitch for honeymoon business (and one resort even offers discounts for every month booked in advance), most travel agencies do little to attract altar-bound couples, relying instead on walk-in traffic.

4. *Singles.* This has always been a good tour market, especially in terms of female travelers. In fact, there is a whole new marketing world for singles, in everything from food to apartment rentals. One enterprising new company, Travel Share International, was formed to provide members with bimonthly lists of other members with whom they might pair up for travel, since a main complaint of single travelers is that they have no one to share the experience with.

Promotional appeals to singles are heavy on the idea of having fun, meeting other people, and touring in safety.

5. *Senior citizens.* With the increase in the number of individuals over 65, and in improved health care, older Americans have become an even more important travel segment. The tour member heading for Europe has been categorized as a widow in her sixties and, indeed, there seem to be an abnormal number of package tour members who fit that description. Women do live longer than men and, in the over-65 group, this imbalance shows only 70 men for every 100 women.

The basic pattern for older people is one of geographic stability, more concerns about travel, desire for warmer climates, and, for a majority of them, the necessity to practice economy.

Many carriers and hotels feature discounts for seniors. Some airlines offer elderly Americans a yearly air pass good for unlimited travel at one set fee. Others promote discounts up to 65 percent, if specific conditions are met. Cruise lines reduce fares for those booking early or late, and hotels may offer their own senior cards or accept those from major senior clubs.

*Modern Maturity Magazine* conducted its own survey among its senior citizen readers and discovered that 78 percent of the respondents had taken one or more domestic trips during the past 12 months and that almost half of the respondents had traveled outside the continental United States. Although the family car counted heavily in stateside travel, rental cars and charter buses figured in the foreign travel and about 8 percent of the seniors opted for a cruise. These travelers averaged more than $1000 on their most recent trips, made good use of traveler's checks, and favored motels over hotels. Canada, Western Europe, Hawaii, Mexico, and Great Britain were the top nondomestic destinations.

Other studies point to better health for those 55 and older, discretionary income higher than that of the average American (people over 50 control half of the nation's discretionary income), and a strong desire to travel. On a per capita basis, older travelers are the most lavish spenders, stay longer at destinations than younger counterparts, and travel more frequently. They are also good bets for off-season travel.

Noting the trends in senior travel, at least one agency, Grandtravel of Maryland, specializes in package tours for grandparents and their grandchildren, blending attractions to appeal to young and old, from games and music to lectures and visits to historical sites. Planned by psychologists, teachers and travel counselors, these trips, to places like Disney World, the Grand Canyon, Africa, and Ireland, even build in time for each age group to share with peers.

6. *Minority citizens.* Some advertising executives claim that audiences like the black consumer market are virtually untapped. Blacks make up 11 percent of this nation's population, have approximately $80 billion in spendable income, and are showing a greater financial growth rate than the economy as a whole. These facts don't obscure the high unemployment rate among black Americans and other minorities, but they do indicate that there is a potential here that has scarcely been reached. Like many minorities, blacks have their own media, which often give advertisers an effective entry into this market.

   Jewish Americans are generally better educated than the average prospect, read more extensively, have higher disposable incomes, and travel more. A number of advertisers have been able to target this group. American Airlines, for example, produced a pocket-sized paperback entitled *Tourist's Guide to Jewish History in the Caribbean.*

   Spanish-speaking citizens also form a significant proportion of our population, and advertising programs are being designed to meet the needs and aspirations of various groups within this category. These programs realize that even the shared language has different shades of meaning for Mexicans and Puerto Ricans, for example. Orientals have occasionally appeared in ads; the American Indian rarely. When a particular minority can't identify with the advertising campaign, it's at least a partial failure for that minority.

7. *Foreign visitors.* It took a number of years for travel promoters to realize that foreign visitors had different scenic interests than Americans. They have beaches in Europe, and mountains, and lakes. What they wanted to see were signs of the Wild West, or the skyscrapers of New York, or the wonders of Disneyland.

   America has also been slower to accommodate visitors in terms of the language barrier, but this is being handled more expertly now, with linguists available as greeters at many of the international airports and seaports.

**Fig. 2—4   Various groups may also promote their own tours, catering to a homogeneous membership.** (Courtesy of American Association of University Professors)

8. *Miscellaneous.* Any number of other groups may be viewed as special market segments.

There are those interested in adventure. In 1986, about 300,000 people tried whitewater rafting in Colorado. Thousands more rode camels in the Middle East, scuba dived off the Great Barrier Reef, or joined safaris in Kenya. A fast growing area of the travel business, adventure tours bring in about $13 billion annually and represent between 5-10 percent of the United States travel market.

There is incentive travel, offered as a reward to those who perform well in sales or other departments. Also, there are educational tours for youth and adults, the former gaining college credit and the latter combining business with pleasure and a possible tax deduction. Skiers trek from their hometowns to Aspen, Squaw Valley, even Sarajevo. And some cruise lines have added casinos to their ships, to attract the casual or serious gambler. There are golfers, camera buffs, museum patrons, theater fans, lovers of the occult, and dozens of other market segments that can be wooed.

## COMMERCIAL ACCOUNTS

Not much media advertising is directed at commercial accounts. Most of this business comes as a result of personal selling, direct mail, phone calls, or referrals. These accounts sometimes make up as much as two-thirds of the business in agencies located in metropolitan areas. While they can be lucrative, they also come equipped with their own set of problems. For one thing, commercial accounts expect a lot of service. A number of large companies began with an in-house person handling travel, then switched to using an agency when they found this more efficient and economical. Some firms prefer the in-plant service and make all of their own travel arrangements. Still others combine both in-plant and travel agency service.

What companies find attractive about the agencies is their ability to simplify most transactions, their delivery of tickets, single billing, convenience, saving of executive time, and, in some cases, the broader experience represented by the counselors.

Among the complaints about commercial accounts are computer malfunctions; errors in charges; less interest than an in-house person, which results in failure to go the extra distance to get reservations or make changes; difficulty in reaching the agent by phone; and failure to follow up on travel requests.

Travel agencies of any size find it profitable to assign one or more individuals to these commercial accounts, rather than to leave such service to whoever happens to be staffing the desk or answering the phone. Mailings to these accounts are also designed differently. They focus less on romance and color, and more on facts and figures.

Handling commercial accounts is becoming more competitive and more complicated. In addition to the assumption of error-free service, the client may also be looking at some dollar return based on volume. Without the advantage brought about by modern technology, much of this service would be impossible or, at least, unprofitable. Travel agents and carriers continue to wrestle with appropriate commissions for different types of commercial operations. There are also legal problems and potential legal problems, from charges of kickbacks to suits involving failure to perform promised services.

Hotels and motels institute numerous features to appeal to the corporate client, from all-suite units to homelike condos, and from a selection of meeting rooms and business accessories to all-female floors for the business woman.

Even airlines may equip charter flights with conference areas and air-to-ground telephones.

## SUMMING UP THE RESEARCH AND PLANNING PHASES

As mentioned earlier in this chapter and in the previous chapter, success in the travel business doesn't depend on luck; it depends on planning. You gather data as outlined here, and use it to develop goals and strategies.

Obviously, each situation is different. Besides concerns about stabilizing or increasing revenues, a travel firm may be thinking about expansion, acquisition, or merger. It may wish to focus on sales growth, or profit margins, on cost effectiveness of delivering services or on ways to improve its market share.

In addition, each company is positioned differently. One may be a market leader, another a market challenger, a third a follower (who doesn't want to risk confrontation), and a fourth could be satisfied with its own separate niche in the market. Each, then, would have a different strategy. One may succeed by emphasizing full service, while another narrows the scope of its potential clients, focusing, for example, on cruises.

Regardless of size or mission, experts contend that any company succeeds or fails depending on its ability to stay close to its customers. The various members of the travel industry have to know the client, know the competition, must meet customer needs more cost-effectively, and must constantly strive to be the best in their field.

All of these steps underline the need for research and planning, and for a system of evaluation to keep tabs on how well you are meeting your objectives. These steps also support all promotional efforts, giving the creative people a basis for copy and the media people a design for their purchases.

## CHAPTER HIGHLIGHTS

❏ Every travel business must do some form of research.

❏ Formal research involves the conducting of a survey, with the sampling technique being accidental, purposive, based on quotas, or based on probability.

❏ To properly poll respondents, the survey designers must know what they want, must ask the right questions in an objective way, must use an appropriate survey method, and must spend time on evaluation.

❏ There are many informal ways to gather data, from research into printed materials, interviews, seminars, and analysis of existing data.

❏ While research needs and goals differ, in the travel industry most managers are interested in data on prospects and on industry trends.

❏ Even the small agency can develop a client profile, determining who their prospects are, why they travel, and what their concerns are.

❏ Various polls provide information on favorite destinations, agency growth, numbers and kinds of trips taken, commercial versus leisure travel, and other travel topics.

❏ Other trends also affect travel, such as the notion of entitlement, the aging of the population, higher educational levels, affluence, independence, and the growth of women in the work force.

❏ Whenever possible, market-conscious managers segment their prospects, designing programs to appeal to groups like honeymooners, singles, senior citizens, working women, young people, ethnic groups, and foreign visitors. They also attempt to reach special clients like adventure types and corporate travelers.

■            ■            ■

## ☐ EXERCISES

1. Besides the trends mentioned in the text, list five other trends you feel will have an impact on travel and explain why.
2. Find five ads for travel that you feel appeal to certain specific segments of society. Explain why.
3. Conduct a brief informal survey among relatives and friends, resulting in 10 completed responses. Try to determine what they look for in hotel or motel accommodations. You draw up the list: price, location, service, decor, amenities, comfort, and other facts. Tabulate the results. This could be done as a class project, with the results compiled and evaluated.
4. Find 3 articles in newspapers or magazines (including trade magazines) that you feel should be read by those in the travel profession. These do not have to contain world-shaking news but should have some information that would be of value to the professional. Bring these articles to class.

## ☐ CASE PROBLEMS

*1. As a representative of your peer group, you have been asked to submit your ideas on a two-week educational tour that might appeal to college students. This tour will take place between December 26 and January 10, during the break between semesters. Three hours of college credit will be offered for the completed experience. Submit a memo to the University Travel Coordinator (who works out of the Office of the Academic Vice President) with your suggestion for a destination, appropriate stops in the itinerary, educational aspects, special features, and approximate cost. You might also add your thoughts on marketing this tour, including a theme and means of disseminating the information.*

2.  *The time is now mid-November and you find that, despite your marketing efforts to students, you have only 22 solid bookings. These bookings are sufficient to assure the trip will go and will break even, but you would like to have 35 or 40 persons on the tour to make it a real success. Are there any additional things you might do to woo students? Assume the school approved opening this tour to alumni, how would you reach them? How would you vary the message to this group? Would you make any changes in the itinerary (but not major changes)? What sort of problems might you anticipate in mixing the groups?*

# THE ROLE OF ADVERTISING
# IN MARKETING

As outlined in the first chapter, advertising is merely one of the elements in the marketing mix. It is, however, the focus of this text, along with other promotional efforts. This is not to downplay the importance of elements such as salesmanship, place, price, or product. Salesmanship deserves a book by itself. For a high percentage of those in the travel field, product and price are not items over which they have much control. For travel agencies, prices are primarily dependent on the rates set by suppliers and, except for their own agency image, the product is also developed by external sources. Even larger travel units, like airlines, face federal restrictions and, in this era of deregulation, they also face the realities of competition and cost.

Advertising and public relations become the areas in which the travel industry, viewed as a whole, may have the most input. These are also areas where even the smallest travel unit can make an impact. Consequently, it makes sense to learn as much as possible about how these skills work.

## WHAT IS ADVERTISING?

There are many definitions of advertising, some of them humorous, some cynical, some only partially accurate. Perhaps any definition will limp a bit, but here's a working description.

*Advertising is a paid form of presenting goods and services to the public, using the mass media rather than personal selling, and carrying the signature of an identifiable sponsor.*

Perhaps we should emphasize that advertising is a paid form of presentation, as distinct from publicity, which is an unpaid form of presenting products, services, and ideas.

41

**Fig. 3–1 Every form of advertising tries to sort out its target audience.**

Keep in mind that, while the ad replaces the salesperson for the more distant audience, it still relies on many of the selling points and techniques employed by salespeople. It tries to put into a limited space or time block what a good salesperson might say to a prospect.

It is important, too, to recall that the sponsor is identified. This is not really a news item, nor is advertising normally bipartisan. It strives to deliver a message—the message of the sponsor who paid for it.

Of course, advertising can be "news." That's one of the ways in which it works. A travel ad can communicate a new fare, new schedule, or new tour offering.

Besides presenting news, advertising can also:

❑ Remind you of a product or service. This works well in travel, where repetition about a trip may eventually sink in. An individual advertisement may trigger thinking about some place a reader intended to visit.

❑ Convey information that will make the product or service better known. This may not be news, but it is of interest. The more people know about a subject like travel, the more likely they are to consider a trip.

❑ Enhance the image of the service or product. Good writing and strong illustrations can make travel even more appealing. Copywriters who can come up with prose that "sings" are invaluable.

❑ Close the sale. Well, perhaps advertising doesn't really close many travel sales but it can make it easier for the salesperson to get a chance for the clincher. Good ads can stimulate readers to action, get them to mail a coupon, or write for a brochure, or visit the travel office.

Many consumers, and some businesspeople, don't fully appreciate advertising. They consider it a necessity perhaps, but they don't grasp its long- and short-range potential. Advertising does many things that the casual observer never realizes.

Ads don't merely sell products or services, they accomplish a variety of tasks. They get people to switch brands ("Would you rather have. . . ."), or they solidify brand loyalty ("If it doesn't say. . . ."). They may try to correct confusion about a brand, or get you to use a familiar product in a new way (like baking soda in your refrigerator) or to buy more at one time ("Don't run out of. . . .") or to extend the buying season—as tour operators have been able to do. They turn a minus into a plus ("We try harder.") or explain a problem or enhance the image of an entire industry, as an American Society of Travel Agents (ASTA) campaign attempted to do for travel agents.

Keep in mind that you are directing ads to certain groups of people for certain reasons. Casual readers who don't understand a sophisticated ad in *The New Yorker* don't worry the people who created that ad; they are after sophisticated readers and buyers. People who never intend to go to Mexico can complain all they want about your ad for a Mexican vacation; you're not writing for them.

This fact also tells us something fundamental about human behavior.

## UNDERSTANDING HUMAN BEHAVIOR

Every good travel counselor knows there is a certain amount of psychology in selling. Advertisers understand this, too. Not only must you know who the prospects are and where they are, you should also know how they tick.

For example, needs and wants differ among individuals. This may be the result of age, taste, income, family size, background, station in life, and other factors.

Not too many years ago a winter vacation was something only very wealthy people could afford. Or so the others thought. Today winter vacations are commonplace, and some people state that they positively need them because of the pressures of their work.

Air conditioning has become a virtual necessity in most states, and two-car families are the norm. Even the agreed-upon necessities, like food, shelter, and clothing, are subject to the whims of the purchaser.

There are diet foods, health foods, people who think steak is the ultimate, others who lavish money on gourmet meals. There are those who fancy jeans, those who prefer three-piece suits, and those who will pay anything for a fashion first. The choice of a home has something to do with income, family size, proximity to work, personal taste, even the image you want to convey.

Travel is affected by all of these variations, based on individual preferences. Time of year, locale, group or individual, city lights or solitude, luxury or economy—all of these factors will strike people differently.

# MOTIVATION, PERCEPTION, AND LEARNING

Psychologists tell us that the three things fundamental to an understanding of human behavior are motivation, perception, and learning.

*Motivation* deals with our inner drives and urges, the reasons we behave as we do, the things that move us toward goals.

There are primary motives, like pain avoidance, self-preservation, satisfying of hunger and thirst, and secondary motives, like the desire for security or success. Obviously, the travel industry is concerned only with the secondary motives.

Think of the reasons people travel and their motivations for spending the money on a trip. They could be after pleasure, amusement, a chance to talk about the trip later, an opportunity to satisfy their curiosity, an improvement in health, a degree of comfort, or an educational experience. Each trip, in fact, probably stems from a combination of motives. Good salespeople try to ferret these out, to learn why a person wants to go to a certain place and travel in a certain way.

Primary motives may assert themselves on occasion. If, for example, the prospective traveler saw some physical danger in an otherwise attractive journey, he or she may be motivated not to go on that trip. However, the secondary motives, largely emotional, dominate in selling.

*Perception* deals with the way we see things. We may be subject to the same external stimuli as others, but our backgrounds and personalities cause us to interpret them differently. Perception has a great deal to do with our taste for certain things, including travel. In a way, this is good, because not everyone is turned on by the same destinations.

Some people, when they think about Paris, envision romance and springtime and Edith Piaf singing "La Vie En Rose." Others think of traffic and high prices and surly waiters. Ireland is hospitality to some and rain to others. Cruises may appear relaxing or boring.

Often, we see what we're looking for. Our preconceptions cause us to selectively perceive. That's why consistency and repetition are important in travel advertising. Last month your prospect wasn't even thinking about a vacation, let alone going to Mexico. This month he begins looking ahead and decides he wants to travel south of the border. Your ad for a Mexican vacation has been running for six weeks, but he didn't see it until this week—because now he's looking.

Experience brings about the third behavioral trait: *learning.* This is a relatively permanent change in our thinking and conduct. After taking a lot of overexposed photos, we learn how to do a better job with our camera. After being served several poor meals, we decide to boycott a restaurant.

Travelers also store up these conclusions about themselves and about certain sites. They learn to pace themselves on walks, or to eat lightly at noon, or to drink more moderately, or to count their change. Those who work in the industry also amass experiences, so they can counsel others on the best times of year to go certain places, what to wear, and what hotels offer the best value.

## EMOTION VERSUS INTELLECT

Are ads written to appeal to the emotions or to the intellect?

Both.

Even in travel, where the "product" is highly emotional, there are numerous intellectual or rational appeals. Trade magazine advertising directed to travel agents talks about commissions and repeat business because a specific resort or tour will leave customers satisfied. Even consumer ads may be heavily rational, saying little about the sandy beaches and concentrating on the low, low price.

Most consumer travel advertising, however, speaks to the senses. At least that's true for all but the smallest print ads. Copy conjures up images of fun and excitement and relates to the emotions of the reader. Photography depicts happy people in exotic or joyful or restful situations. The aim of these ads is to have readers place themselves in these locales.

There is also an emotional response to some elements of the travel industry. People may feel safer on airlines with well-publicized names, unless the publicity has been negative. Some state tourism bureaus have to work hard to dispel a false impression of their state. Even travel agencies may reflect, by the way they look and the way their employees behave, a negative or positive image. Even the printed materials that come from these agencies create a concept of those operations.

## PERSUASION AND REINFORCEMENT

Advertising is criticized for many reasons. Television viewers dislike the interruptions; motorists complain about highway signs; economists state that advertising interferes with the normal course of supply and demand; readers, listeners, and viewers protest that advertising is degrading, immoral, or just plain dumb.

Above all, advertising is feared because it persuades.

This fear is foolishness. Persuasion is the civilized way to accomplish things. The alternatives are force and payment. Persuasion is the art of bringing the other person to your point of view. We do it all the time, from our childhood years through old age. As we mature, our arguments on our own behalf become more sophisticated, combining what we know about the audience with what we know about the subject.

That's also what advertising tries to do.

Advertising, however, tries to persuade a mass audience, so it assumes some general psychological responses. Cruise lines showing passengers lined up on deck chairs normally select tanned and well-proportioned figures rather than pale overweight subjects. The assumption here is that readers would rather look at the former. Advertising also assumes that a catchy headline, a familiar face, a compelling illustration, or a bargain price will attract attention.

# The Real Experience

## Its pleasure speaks to all the senses

Some hotels are just there; they could be anywhere. But each Westin hotel in Mexico gives a special feel for the place it's in.

Their location, architecture, ambience, amenities, cuisine and service are all created to please and satisfy all the senses.

For reservations or more information call (800) 228-3000.

Acapulco • Las Brisas • **Cancun** • Camino Real • **Guadalajara** • Camino Real **Ixtapa** • Camino Real • **Manzanillo** • Las Hadas • **Mazatlan** • Camino Real **Mexico City** • Camino Real • Galeria Plaza • **Monterrey** Ambassador • **Puerto Vallarta** • Camino Real

THE PEOPLE AND PLACES OF WESTIN.
*Caring·Comfortable·Civilized.*
**WESTIN**
HOTELS & RESORTS
MEXICO

**Fig. 3–2  Much travel advertising and promotion has emotional appeal.** (Courtesy of Westin Hotels & Resorts/Mexico)

Advertising does try to convert others to a viewpoint. As an advertiser, you feel you have the best hotel in Houston. You're certain travelers will love this tour of the Greek Isles. You think your city is underrated as a tourist attraction, so positive convictions have to be captured in copy and illustration and conveyed with the same sort of excitement and enthusiasm you feel.

The reinforcement merits of advertising come about in several ways. Repetition is one way. Reaching the prospect with exactly the right message is another. What happens here is that a person, inspired by an ad, tries the product or service advertised. That person is satisfied with the experience, and so is likely to repeat it and likely to see the advertisements that offer something similar from the same supplier. That's why readers return to favorite authors, gourmets to favorite restaurants, and travelers to agencies that have met or exceeded their needs and desires.

## PSYCHOLOGICAL APPEALS OF ADVERTISING

Built into most advertising are appeals that focus on some psychological trait, appealing to the motives mentioned earlier, and drawing upon what the advertiser knows are basic behavioral patterns.

❑ *Advertising that emphasizes peer identification or snob appeal.* Clothing, cars, or brands of liquor comes into mind here. Both motivations could also be at work in booking travel. Young people want to go "where it's at" or older adults look for locales that will impress their friends.

There is, in fact, a whole genre of tourism titled "luxury travel" that caters to individuals who may spend a minimum of $1,000 a day per couple. One three-week luxury tour of Europe, complete with chauffeured Mercedes, *haute cuisine,* and the most glamorous of hotels and estates, averaged out to more than $55,000 per person. A $5,000 a day stay in San Francisco's Fairmont Hotel buys a suite with a spectacular view, 24-karat gold bathroom fixtures, a library, game room, a living room, three bedrooms and four fireplaces.

❑ *Advertising designed with a cultural trend in mind.* You notice this in the type of art used, in headlines that take off on current slang, in ads that use celebrities who are popular, or that feature themes that are popular, such as tours to Dracula country, an appeal to a search for roots, or headlines like "Sail on Our Love Boat."

❏ *Advertising that stresses saving money or time, that promises entertainment, or a chance to meet the opposite sex.*
❏ *Advertising that appeals to health, physical or mental comfort, good food or drink, or concern for your family.*

Think of the travel ads that rotate around these themes: the get-away-from-it-all sun havens, the tours that take the worry out of traveling, the cuisine offered by airlines, the series of television commercials that urges the businessman to take his family on his business trips for just a little more.

Sometimes these categories naturally fit the travel being advertised; sometimes you dig out these ideas as additional reasons for traveling.

# ADVERTISING BY TYPE

There's another major way to classify advertising—by noting what it sets out to do and where it appears. There are a dozen generally accepted classifications of advertising, but only a few really pertain to the travel industry.

## Institutional Advertising

These ads sell ideas. They are the image-making ads that companies are using in greater numbers, partly because of consumer movements, and partly because, with the clutter of advertising, it's important to make known the company behind the product. These ads may tell the public what the firm is doing to help society (note the environmental ads) or they may merely use the firm's name as sponsor of an ad about some national problem (drugs, voting, drunken drivers).

## Commercial Advertising

This is advertising directed to middlemen, to the business people who will eventually sell to the consumer. You see ads for products or services (like desks, copy machines, and tax preparation) for use by businesses; or the merchandising of products or services to those who will sell them to others (everything from precooked fried chicken to Christmas cards), and professional ads directed at professional people (like physicians and dentists and lawyers) asking them to recommend products and services to clients.

All three of these categories affect travel, although the second one is rare. Agencies do use both routine office furniture and some specialty items, like brochure racks; and trade magazines like *Travel Weekly* and *The Travel Agent* contain ads that appeal to agents, as professionals, to recommend certain tours, locales, resort hotels, carriers, and other competitive services to their clients.

## Consumer Advertising

This category is, of course, the most common, the one we generally associate with advertising. It has three main divisions, all of which embrace travel advertising. These are: mail order, national, and local or retail advertising.

*Mail order advertising* is not the same as direct mail. Mail order advertising sells things through the mails, directly. You see these ads in hundreds of different magazines, where you are directed to fill out a coupon and enclose ten dollars and you'll receive a monogrammed T-shirt. Or you may be given an address to which you post your check for assorted cheeses.

Travel isn't sold this way, although travel accessories and travel books may be. Returning a coupon to receive a brochure is not the same thing, because the brochure is not an item of sale, it's an introduction to a personal sale.

Tour operators, airlines, hotel chains, and resort areas use national advertising in their campaigns. As normally defined, national advertising doesn't mean simply that the ads are seen nationwide; it means that you are pushing a brand name or a general service, and you are not particular about where the customer purchases it. Advertising for beer and cigarettes and cosmetics falls into this area. So do ads for Holiday Inns, American Airlines, Maupintours, and those ads that promote trips to specific states or countries, like "Mexico— The Amigo Country."

*National advertising* affects travel agencies in a number of ways. These ads provide referrals, inspire curiosity, and may even direct the reader to see the local travel agency. Local agencies may also tie into such ads by putting their names at the bottom as the local contacts.

National advertisers buy schedules in the various media (principally newspaper, magazine, and television) to call attention to travel offerings. They may use the network on television, for example, or they may select fifty cities in which they want the spot to run. They may also specify billboard locations across the country, aiming for areas where the best prospects live, or they may pick radio stations that cover target markets.

*Local or retail advertising* is what virtually every travel agency uses, even when it is part of a larger geographical chain. This form of advertising specifies the supplier, asking that the consumer shop at a certain place of business. It isn't a matter of asking the reader or viewer to buy herbal shampoo; this form of ad asks him or her to buy herbal shampoo at Walgreen's Drug Store, at 16th and Douglas Streets.

Similarly, tours by major tour operators share space in local ads with trips organized by the local agency. Both of these may be joined with information on popular resort areas, like Hawaii or Las Vegas. The clincher is an appeal to visit this agency, or to call for information, or to return a coupon for further details.

As we'll note in the next chapter, local or retail print advertising is usually not commissionable, meaning that advertising agencies cannot earn 15 percent from newspapers for placing local ads. That's why most retail newspaper ads are done by travel agency personnel.

Radio and television advertising, even on the local level, is generally commissionable, and may involve an advertising agency. Printed materials, like brochures and newsletters, although not commissionable, may still be turned over to a specialist, with the travel agency paying this person or firm a fee for services.

## Cooperative Advertising

Cooperative—or co-op—advertising is the name given to ads that are jointly sponsored by two mutually interested parties. Newspaper ads for new cars, for example, may be a collective venture in which the manufacturer and the local dealer share costs. Clothing stores also avail themselves of matching funds and other services from brand name suppliers.

Travel agencies, too, can look for help in a variety of ways.

- ❏ Carriers, resort hotels, tour companies, and other travel-oriented suppliers may make available newspaper mats or glossy proofs which can be incorporated into the agency's print ads, or which may be used as ads themselves, with the agency adding its name at the bottom.
- ❏ These same firms may also furnish items such as radio commercials on tape or cassettes, television spots on videotape, slides, scripts which may be worked into agency broadcast commercials, films for special showings or for television pro-

**Cartan Escorted**

# EUROPE
## WONDERLAND
## HOLIDAY

**FULLY ESCORTED
13 HOTEL NIGHTS
IN EUROPE**
Selected Saturday
Departures.
Visits London 3 nights,
Amsterdam 2 nights, Co-
logne 1 night, Mainz 1 night,
Lucerne 2 nights, Besancon
1 night and Paris for 3 nights.
24 meals plus tax and waiters' tips. 11 Sightseeing Trips
by Deluxe Air-conditioned
Motorcoach. All airport
transfers, handling and tips
for 2 pieces of luggage.
Total cost per person sharing
twin including airfare $000.

**YOUR NAME
ADDRESS
PHONE NUMBER**

## Cartan's

# MEXICO
**ESCORTED**
**ROMANTICA—MEXICO
CITY, IXTAPAN, TAXCO
AND ACAPULCO**
**FULLY ESCORTED**
9 Hotel Nights in Mexico
Selected Sunday Departures.
Visits Mexico City for 3 nights
at Fiesta Palace, 1 night at Spa
Ixtapan, 1 night in Taxco at De
la Borda and 4 nights in Aca-
pluco at Condesa del Mar.
4 Sightseeing trips by Deluxe
Air-conditioned Motorcoach. 7
meals including tax and waiters' tips. All transfers in Mexico, handling and tips for 2
pieces of luggage.
Total cost per person sharing
twin including air fare $000.

**YOUR NAME
ADDRESS
PHONE NUMBER**

## Caravan
Africa
1978

# Africa

### Free! Beautiful New Brochure

Thrill to wild game viewing, tribal
dancers, etc., on East Africa Safari
or Cape to Kenya tour. 3 weeks, all
expense, all meals, escorted, best
hotels, $1875 to $1995 per person,
double occupancy, plus air.
**Frequent departures.**
For your free copy write or phone:

**Fig. 3—3   Tour operators and other suppliers provide materials for
co-op advertising.** (Courtesy of Cartan Travel Bureau)

grams, posters for display, brochures, brochure shells into which travel agencies may insert copy for tours they originate, point-of-sale materials like counter stands and model airplanes, even giveaway items for clients and prospects.

❑ Suppliers of travel services may also agree to participate in a proposed advertising campaign, supplying part of the money to pay for the advertising. The amount they will commit depends on such considerations as the amount of space or time they get in the ad, the extent to which they feel they need the business, the way in which they view the travel agency, their own budget allocations, and other factors.

❑ Occasionally, local and state governments will share the costs of tourism promotion with business developers and hospitality firms.

The travel agency manager should discuss these co-op opportunities with the airlines, hotel chains, tour operators, resort managers, and others who might share an interest. Find out what their policies are, what they can supply in the way of materials, and what their requirements are for allocating matching funds.

## THE ETHICS OF ADVERTISING

This subject needs airing because of the many complaints about the advertising profession. As in all fields, there are those in advertising whose ethics may be marginal. These people generally don't last. Most practitioners are as ethical as those in any line of work.

Advertising gets blamed for the low moral tone of the nation and for persuading people to buy things they don't want with money they don't have. It is also attacked for debasing our cultural standards, increasing the cost of goods, dictating television programming, establishing public taste, and deliberately misleading the consumer with false product claims.

Let's look at these criticisms very briefly.

There may be some truth in the complaint that advertising has adversely affected our culture. Certainly, language has been altered, with superlatives losing much of their impact because of overuse. A number of television commercials, too, seem to take a low view of the intelligence of viewers. At the same time, advertising has also helped to popularize various art styles, to pioneer television techniques, to promote thousands of good causes, and to raise awareness in a variety of social and cultural areas.

Advertising doesn't increase the cost of goods. True, the cost of advertising must be included in the price charged for any product or service but, without such advertising, how would the public know of the item's existence? Most selling is a volume business, and volume can only be achieved through advertising. Volume is one of the factors that can actually lower the cost of goods, rather than increase it. The travel agency or hotel that waited around for the public to discover its wares would be in for a long wait.

Television programs are retained or retired because of viewers, not advertisers. A program that attracts a large audience will also be supported by advertising, regardless of the sponsors' personal views about content (except where such content conflicts with their own goals and philosophy). If an inane and repetitive situation comedy stays on while your favorite symphonic program disappears, that's because the former, whatever its relative merits, simply has more people watching. The advertising dollars follow audiences.

Similarly, advertising follows taste in other things rather than establishing taste. Unfortunately, advertising was not in the vanguard of the fight for minority rights (although it has an exemplary record as an employer of minorities); it followed trends. Black people began appearing more often in commercials at about the same time white Americans were becoming more sensitive to the evils of discrimination. In general, ads react to trends, extending them perhaps, but rarely creating them.

Finally, good advertising doesn't make false claims. This practice doesn't work over a long period of time, is unethical and immoral—and also illegal. Sometimes advertisers do exaggerate, often because they think superlatives make for strong ads. They're wrong. Credibility is to be preferred over extravagance.

## LEGAL CONSIDERATIONS

Some critics think advertising gets away with murder. Actually, advertising is a highly regulated business. Some ad execs have groused that major conglomerates withhold millions in taxes and get a slap on the wrist but, when an advertiser punches holes in a can of radiator stop-leak, the government jumps all over him. One of the reasons for such vigilance is that advertising is highly visible and any lapses are certain to be noticed. Another reason for the number of cases involving advertising is that there is a considerable body of law affecting the practice.

Most complaints against advertising stem from false and misleading claims. A prohibition against such claims came into law in 1938 when the Wheeler-Lea Act substantially amended the earlier (1914) Federal Trade Commission Act that regulated unfair competition. "Unfair or deceptive acts or practices in commerce" were viewed as giving an edge to the violator, thus making them illegal.

This concept has been refined and expanded through the years in a series of laws and court cases that cover packaging, labeling, the distribution of obscene material through the mails, the use of false statements about competitive products and services, and other matters. Even the location of outdoor advertising is rigidly controlled, particularly along the interstate system.

Some areas of the law covering advertising are vague. In the past, advertising was excluded from the interpretation of First Amendment protection as freedom of speech. Courts looked upon it as commercial, rather than an expression of opinion or protest, or a means of communicating information. This view has softened somewhat. Advertising that expresses political opinions, for example, is considered protected and, if there is any trend, it is moving toward a liberalization of the coverage afforded all advertising.

Another grey area is the question of libel and slander. In the past two decades, judgments expanded the definition of who was a public figure, a person whose activities were inherently newsworthy. These individuals were—and are—entitled to less protection under the laws of libel than private citizens. The principle is that these men and women—political leaders, entertainers, socially prominent citizens—are in the public eye and reporting about their foibles, even in a critical way, is acceptable. The reporter or advertiser had to be careful, however, about separating the public figure's public life from his private life.

How could travel advertising run afoul of these laws? For one thing, if photos of any recognizable individuals (and this doesn't mean prominent, but merely identifiable) are used in ads, written permission must be obtained. The same thing pertains to the use of a person's name in any sort of endorsement copy.

Obviously, too, you cannot merely appropriate a photo or a piece of artwork without clearing it with the owner. You must secure a written permission and pay whatever fee is agreed upon. If you purchase a photo for use in an ad, that doesn't mean you can later use this photo in a brochure or newsletter, unless the permission you obtain covers all uses. (In cases where photos are supplied by airlines or hotels, along with approval for use, travel agencies need no further okay.)

Travel advertising has to be as factual as any other advertising. The copy must fairly represent the actual tour and the price structure must not be misleading. You couldn't, for example, advertise an "All-Expense" tour and then indicate in the small print that this covers only transportation to and from the destination and some hotels. Nor would you be allowed to show photos of first-class hotels but put the tour members in third- or fourth-class hotels.

You can't use a "bait and switch" technique, advertising a terrific travel bargain, then, when the customers arrive, telling them this trip is sold out, and selling them on a more expensive vacation.

You can't subvert competitors by spreading false rumors about their methods or their lack of solvency or their treatment of other clients. This goes back to the original principle of unfair competition.

In terms of cooperative advertising, a supplier is supposed to make available to all agencies, large or small, the same sort of participation. Just because one agency does a large volume of business and the other a small volume, the supplier can't offer the first agency 80 percent of costs for an ad campaign and the second agency only 20 percent. All middlemen must be treated equally.

The media are generally aware of these legal problems and will often counsel an agency in the event of some questionable copy or practice. However, the travel firm shouldn't automatically count on this. It should police its own advertising, making certain it is in conformity with both legal and ethical standards.

In addition to federal laws governing advertising, there are also state laws. Not every state has such legislation (most of which is based on the Printers Ink Model Statute, drawn up in 1911, revised in 1945) and less than half the states have what is called effective legislation.

Besides these major legal concerns, there are also some less likely, but also important, considerations:

❑ The use of obscenity (which may be broadly interpreted by each community) in copy or illustrations can get you into trouble.
❑ Infringing on another's copyright, by stealing a slogan or identifying logo or other copyrighted item, could lead to legal action.
❑ Participation in a lottery, such as the offering of a free trip, could be dangerous. To constitute a lottery, there must be three elements present: prize, chance, and consideration. If

any of these three is missing, the contest is not a lottery and, therefore, may not be legal. If you offered a trip for two to Hawaii, based on the drawing of numbers, and open to anyone, whether or not they ever did business with you, this would be considered a lottery. If you limited the contestants to those who had traveled with you, or who purchased an airline ticket, or who performed some task (even a visit to your office, as interpreted in some states), you could be in violation of the lottery restriction. In addition to watching your own possible offerings in this area, be careful about tying in with any other companies who plan to use you as a supplier of the trip in return for advertising and promotion.

❏ Remember that the consumer and the competition have access to corrective and counter advertising, forcing a statement that amends an earlier ad, or securing space or time to express a point of view counter to the advertiser's. This time, however, is no longer a legal right under the Fairness Doctrine.

## AD PRINCIPLES ARE PRETTY CONSTANT

Styles change in advertising. Television effects become more sophisticated and copy matches the jargon of the day. There are new media choices and fresh combinations of media. The basics, however, stay the same. People, who are the targets of advertising, change very slowly and, in some respects, change very little. That's one reason why advertising is such an important phase of marketing.

## CHAPTER HIGHLIGHTS

❏ Advertising is one element, but an important element, in the marketing mix.
❏ Advertising accomplishes many different tasks, some of which are not obvious to all consumers, especially those who are not targets of that particular message.
❏ Creating effective advertising requires knowledge of psychology and human behavior. And this means a grasp of the effects of motivation, perception, and learning as they apply to communication.
❏ Advertising employs appeals to both emotion and intellect. It seeks to persuade and to reinforce decisions.

❏   Among the psychological appeals of advertising are those that capture snob appeal, peer identification, cultural trends, health, pleasure, and other needs and wants. All of these have some association with travel.

❏   Advertising can also be classified by type: institutional, commercial, consumer, national, mail order, local or retail, and cooperative.

❏   Along with ethical considerations involving truth and taste, advertising must also comply with a considerable number of legal restrictions, from libel to copyright and from misrepresentation to unfair competition.

■          ■          ■

## ❏   EXERCISES

1.   Bring to class 10 print ads for travel that appeal to different psychological traits. Label each.
2.   Bring to class a national and a local ad for the same travel item (a tour to the same destination, for example) and compare the approaches in both ads.
3.   Bring to class two print ads for travel or hospitality that you consider offensive, misleading, or otherwise unappealing (to you).
4.   Describe a television commercial for travel, restaurants, or hotels that you feel does an effective job. Explain why you feel this way.

## ❏   CASE PROBLEMS

*1. The Smithsonian Institution sponsors walking tours to various places in the world, including the Lake District of England. They say the walking averages about 8 miles a day with frequent rests, and, while you have to be in decent shape, this isn't terribly demanding. Let's assume they want to recruit more tour members from the 55 and older group but are finding some resistance and fear about the demands the tour might place on them. If you were assigned to write copy for a print ad directed to this group, what would you want to know? In 100 words or less, write the kind of copy you feel would allay the audience's concerns, but don't put in anything that isn't true.*

*2. As a travel agency manager, you are bidding for a major tour to be underwritten by a large insurance company for its top producers. There will be at least 500 bookings and the tour package involves all costs of a 5-day vacation in Acapulco. This would not only be a nice piece of business but could also provide a foot in the door for the insurance firm's on-going commercial travel. Consequently, you bid the tour as low as possible, barely covering expenses, and showing virtually no profit. You discover, however, that you have been substantially underbid by another agency whose reputation within the advertising fraternity is nil. This particular agency has lost its accreditation, has gone bankrupt twice, has been denied credit by several of the major airlines, and has been suspected for some time of using unethical practices to garner business. At the moment, it is operating through a national tour operator who does hold a legitimate accreditation.*

*What should you do? Forget about it and figure you were just outbid? Blow the whistle on the agency by reporting all to the client? Mobilize your fellow agents against this agency? What? (Remember the legal implications of any action you initiate.)*

# THE ADVERTISING AGENCY

No profession's image has been as distorted by the mass media as has advertising's. The ad agency executive is depicted as a flashy, ulcer-prone, unscrupulous entrepreneur who fawns over clients, plots against his own colleagues, and espouses even the shoddiest ideas if they sell merchandise. He arrives late to work, takes three hours for martini lunches, and spends enormous amounts of time losing to client-golfers on the nation's courses.

Every stereotype has some exemplars, but most people who work in advertising are not only creative but also intelligent, productive, and diligent. They are used to pressure and committed to a life of deadlines. Unlike some other professionals, their efforts are publicly displayed and their results are obvious and measurable.

The advertising agency is largely a product of this century, although its roots go back to pre-Civil War days when space brokers would purchase several pages of a newspaper and then resell this space to advertisers at a profit. Just over 100 years ago, N. W. Ayer & Son agency began the practice of lining up clients who agreed to buy space through their agency. Ayer would then contract with the newspaper for this space.

A natural consequence of this arrangement was that clients began to request additional services from Ayer—things like copywriting, layout, and artwork. From this model, today's agency was born.

## AGENCY SIZE

There are some 4,000 advertising agencies in the United States, and they range from firms that employ thousands of people to those that have only a handful of employees. Size, however, is determined not by personnel, but by billings. Gross charges for all agency activities are totaled and that dollar figure is used to measure ranking among the nation's advertising firms.

Firms like J. Walter Thompson and Young and Rubicam consistently make the top of lists. Billings might exceed a billion and a half dollars and income might go as high as $250 million. The ten top agencies in the United States list incomes of between $60 million and well over $100 million for domestic sales alone.

These agencies, of course, are the exceptions. They handle the large cruise lines and hotel chains and major airlines and international tourism accounts. They buy space in the slick magazines and time on network television. Sophisticated research and marketing services are included, plus a wide assortment of creative options. These advertising giants are located on either coast, and in a few inland cities like Chicago, Detroit, Atlanta, and Dallas. While one of their branches might work with a travel agency, such an alliance is unlikely. Most travel agencies, if they have professional help, are clients of smaller ad firms.

Most ad agencies, in fact, are small businesses. A majority bill less than a million a year, making their income between a hundred and a hundred and fifty thousand dollars each annually. Many agencies bill substantially less than this—perhaps half a million or even a quarter of a million dollars. Some are "ma and pa" shops that operate out of an individual's home, cutting down on the overhead, and may feature a single employee, often an older executive who wants to taper off, or a younger one who wants to build his own clientele. The fact is, many advertising agencies are modest operations, just like many travel agencies.

## WHAT CAN AN AD AGENCY DO?

Obviously, the larger the agency, the more services there will be available on the premises. A full-service agency is expected to provide media services, marketing advice, research, copywriting, art services, public relations, production capabilities, and other specialties. Smaller agencies may not have research and marketing experts and may also try to double up on public relations activities. Even smaller agencies may merely provide ideas, writing, and make media placements, contracting out the other specialties, such as artwork and production.

Clients with considerable money to spend (like the large suppliers and hotel chains) are likely to announce the availability of their account and to conduct a competition for their business. They invite agencies to submit bids, supporting their request to handle the account. These presentations can be expensive, embodying everything from agency and personnel data to a full-blown campaign plan, with film, slides, layouts, and pages of market research. The advertising agencies must be sure they are competitive, that they can handle the account, and that they can afford to go head to head in the bidding. The tourism client may select an agency on the basis of numerous factors, ranging from quality and reputation to the chemistry between personnel.

When the modest-sized travel agency seeks help, it's unlikely there will be any expensive extravaganza. The agency may search the Yellow Pages for appropriate advertising contacts or may ask for suggestions from friends, colleagues, or the media. They could also work through national directories or local professional advertising guilds. From one of these sources, a meeting is initiated. Of course, the advertising firm could also be soliciting business and may call on the travel agency. One way or the other, the two entities get together.

Keep in mind that a majority of travel agencies would not be considered major prospects by advertising professionals. The typical commissionable expenditures would be far too lean to generate any ad agency excitement. Then, too, the ad agency may already have a travel or tourism account that could product a conflict of interest, so the travel firm's approach is turned down.

Let's assume there is a match. The travel execs like what they see of the advertising firm and these professionals decide to accept them as a client—either because of current budget, potential, or their interest in this specialized form of promotion. The two parties may sign a contract, although most agencies have only a short-term agreement that may be cancelled by either party after sufficient notice, or both may also settle for a verbal pact. With larger agencies and larger accounts, there's a difference. In these cases, the commitment is deeper and the dollar outlay greater, so the security factor is more important.

In either situation, however, one or more individuals would be assigned to the account, acting as liaison between client and ad firm, helping see client needs and ideas through the creative and campaign phases.

## THE CAMPAIGN

Here is where differences are most apparent. A hotel chain advertising nationally, or a state trying to lure tourists, would allocate hundreds of thousands of dollars and would consider all media as part of the advertising mix. The campaign should be one that adapts easily to various applications and must have a broader view of audience potential. A single print ad or TV commercial might match the total annual budget of a small travel agency.

But the less affluent travel firms should still expect the advertising agency to develop some intelligent campaign tactics, designed to meet the needs and finances of the client.

This campaign would focus on a theme, involve some print and broadcast ads, perhaps, and direct mail and other media. The agency would show some sample ads or scripts and also present a recommended budget that would spell out its choices of media, programs, broadcast dates and times, and other items. The travel agency always has the right to turn down the campaign, suggest alterations, or trim the budget. It's their money that's being spent!

When they've agreed upon the creative work, expenditures, and general use of media, the agency goes ahead and completes the production of the print ads or the radio and television ads, contacts the media to reserve space, keeps track of the costs, and submits a bill. In a sense, the ad firm serves as a bank, since the media know and trust the agency and see it as a guarantee of payment. They may not be as familiar with the travel agency credit record.

## WHAT DOES THIS COST THE TRAVEL/TOURISM CLIENT?

It could cost nothing extra, depending on a number of things. Advertising agencies are something like travel agencies; the majority of their income comes from commissions from the media they use, just as travel agency income comes from commissions from suppliers of services.

If the medium chosen allows the advertising agency the usual commission, the only other costs a client may incur are those associated with the production of the advertisement. (That assumes, of course, that the travel firm has not requested some special sort of services or that the advertising agency does not have an alternate form of billing.) If the medium does not permit advertising agency commissions—and newspapers usually do not when the client is local—then the travel agency will likely be requested to pay the equivalent of the commission to the advertising firm. A cruise line placing print ads in newspapers across the country would normally be buying commissionable space, but a local agency, advertising in its hometown paper, would earn a lower rate and this rate would not be commissionable. This explains why many travel agencies handle their own advertising direct with the newspaper, while farming out the radio and television advertising, which is routinely commissionable, to an advertising agency.

## HOW DO AGENCIES MAKE THEIR INCOME?

There are two principal sources of income in the advertising profession—commissions and fees.

Commissions usually amount to 15 percent of the money expended in the media and, with the exception noted above, are paid by the media to the agency. Let's say, for example, the travel firm plans to spend $1,500 for radio during a given time period. If they go directly to the radio stations, they will pay $1,500; if they go through an advertising agency, they will also pay $1,500, but the radio stations will bill the agency for $1,275 (which is $1,500 less 15 percent). The advertising agency keeps the remaining $225. Commissions form the greatest proportion of any agency's income.

It's easy to see why major travel accounts are much more profitable to the advertising agency. A travel ad placed in the *Des Moines Register* may cost only a few hundred dollars and may result in income of $50 for the advertising agency—*if* the client agrees to pay this. The same-sized ad in a national magazine may cost $20,000 and return $3,000 to the advertising agency. Yet the production and creative time are similar.

Fees are also charged for various services. If the client wants public relations help for news releases, feature stories, special events, or other activities, he or she may pay an hourly fee (anywhere from $25 to $60 an hour and up), a monthly or annual retainer, or a set price agreed upon for a specific assignment. Fees might also include charges for research, for photography and artwork, or for manual chores, like preparing mailings, which are turned over to the agency.

There are some additional ways in which agencies may earn money. Collateral materials—printing, photography, artwork, and the like—may be marked up 17.65 percent. If the photographer charges $100 for photo services, the agency will bill the client for $117.65. Why? Because the agency personnel also spend time meeting with the photographer, accompanying him, reviewing his work, deciding on usage and so on. Why 17.65 percent? This is a figure arrived at by calculating the equivalent of 15 percent of gross.

A final, though minor, source of income stems from agency discounts that are sometimes allowed if bills are paid within a specified time limit, normally 10 days. This may amount to 2 percent of the net charge. Reputable advertising agencies will pass along this discount to the client if the client also pays within this 10-day period. If the client chooses not to do so, then the advertising agency may pay the bill and pocket the 2 percent commission. This may raise a few questions:

❑ *Why are the media willing to pay commissions to advertising agencies instead of retaining the 15 percent themselves?* The media assume that they are going to get material that is in a more professional state, that payment is assured, that direct contact with the client is unnecessary, that time is saved in meetings and in billing. They may also see the advertising agency as a source of new business, since agencies locate and convince clients about media placement.

❑ *Why don't most newspapers pay commissions then?* They do pay commissions on national advertising, ads like those for Marriott or TWA that are national in scope. Travel agencies would generally be looked upon as local clients within that newspaper's community and they therefore earn a lower local rate, which presumably saves the client some money but cuts out the advertising agency. Agencies don't like this practice but can do little about it. If a travel agency wants to employ an advertising agency to create and place local newspaper ads, they must be prepared to pay an add-on cost for this service.

❑ *Do radio or television stations ever work directly with the travel agency?* Do they rebate the commission an ad agency would get? Many stations work directly with clients. Generally, however, their creative efforts can't match those of ad agencies, although there are exceptions. Some also rebate part of the costs to a travel agency client, but most media would find this unethical. There should be no under-the-table deals.

❑ *How can a client be sure in advance about ad agency charges?* Ask! Most agencies will spell this out anyway, and a good number have printed standard operating procedures that are given to clients. There should be no secrets and no surprises.

Finally, on the subject of money, if we take the hypothetical case mentioned earlier of the $1,500 expenditure for radio that results in a profit of $225 to the advertising agency, the client should realize that this is hardly a windfall. It would barely pay a week's wages for a secretary in many agencies. That's why large agencies can't even bother with such accounts. Their people are so high-salaried, they would lose money on such transactions.

So why would they bother with a travel account at all? Perhaps the billings are substantial enough to whet their interest. Perhaps there are attendant public relation fees. Perhaps they just like the variety of working with different accounts, and travel agencies are generally considered one of the more "fun" accounts. Perhaps, too, they see some growth potential in a small account and want to get in on the ground floor.

It should be noted that some advertising agencies are experimenting with different methods of compensation, feeling that the straight 15 percent commission doesn't allow for the variables of the business. It may take as much time, for example, to prepare a full-page ad for a trade publication like *Travel Weekly* as it does for *Newsweek* but the commission on the former would be a few hundred dollars and, on the latter, $6,000 or more. Spot television costs more to buy than other media in terms of time, so clients who use a disproportionate amount of TV are more expensive to handle. Travel agencies, of course, are familiar with this. Some money comes relatively easily, some breaks out at a nickel an hour.

Again, if the agency suggests another form of payment—such as an hourly basis for its work and keeping the agency commission—the client must approve.

## WHAT SHOULD A TRAVEL CLIENT LOOK FOR IN AN ADVERTISING AGENCY?

First, compatability. Do they like these people? Can they work with them comfortably? Travel execs should arrange to meet with agency personnel, particularly with those who will be assigned to an account. Does the style of this agency fit the travel firm's philosophy?

Second, the client should take a look at the agency size to see if they are going to get sufficient attention. If they are a minor concern, they can't count on much service.

Third, does the agency understand the travel business? Having previous experience in this field would be a plus but, if the personnel don't have that, have they worked on similar accounts, or do they grasp the peculiar nature of tourism work? Even without such foreknowledge, the agency might still function very well, but some familiarity is a big timesaver.

Fourth, what do other clients say about the agency? Are they satisfied? Would they recommend it? Prospective clients can request a list of the agency's current clients and make a few phone calls. Also, does the agency have any clients who would be direct competition—another travel agency in the same market, for example?

Fifth, what type of people does the agency have? Are they creative, innovative, dependable? Do they have sufficient depth so that the travel firm isn't left stranded when its account executive is ill or out of town?

Sixth, what kind of services does the agency offer? Are these what are required? How will it charge for them?

Seventh, is the agency's credit rating good? Does it pay its bills? Is it stable? Does it have a good reputation with the media and with other advertising agencies?

Eighth, prospects should ask to see some examples of the agency's work, particularly work that is similar to what the travel agen-

**Fig. 4—1  Advertising agencies are able to provide services the average travel or hospitality firm cannot supply.** (Courtesy of Bill Ramsey Associates, Inc.)

cy is looking for. They might even ask agencies to compete by making presentations based on campaign needs, as do major clients. If the proposed budget is small, however, as most travel agencies' budgets tend to be, such a presentation might be an imposition. Perhaps a written statement of how the account would be handled would suffice.

There are other considerations, of course, from proximity to the makeup of the agency (an old conservative group or a young radical group?), and these must be sorted out according to the requirements of each travel agency manager.

# HOW IS AN ADVERTISING AGENCY STRUCTURED?

Agencies differ according to size, specialization, type of management, type of personnel, type of accounts, location, and other variables.

A moderate-sized agency—say, a $1,000,000 agency—would have the following departments:

- ❑ *Management.* Senior officers who may also handle some accounts in addition to running the business.
- ❑ *Account executives.* Those individuals who work directly with clients. Account executives may also do some creative work, particularly copywriting.
- ❑ *Creative department.* Headed by a creative director, this department pools the talents of writers and artists to develop campaigns and create advertisements.
- ❑ *Production.* There will be someone (or several people) in charge of print production, seeing that print ads and brochures are produced properly and on time. Another department might handle radio and television production, supervising the production of spots at local studios.
- ❑ *Media.* This person or department is responsible for knowing the pros and cons of the media, the top rated television shows, the best magazine markets, and so on. The media buyer deals constantly with media salespeople and can advise on the most efficient use of a given budget.
- ❑ *Traffic.* In this division, the print ads, tapes, and videotapes are recorded, mailed, and collected. This individual keeps tabs

on these items and sees that they get where they should go and get back again.

❏ *Accounting*. Because of volume, the number of suppliers, and employees who may be more creative than careful, this department is a busy one. All costs are captured here and billed out to the proper client.

❏ *Other*. Many agencies have public relations (PR) departments or some PR affiliation. Some have research capabilities, extensive marketing functions, even specialty areas like computer graphics, experts in humor, and composers. Like so many other factors in advertising, this depends somewhat on size, somewhat on demand, and somewhat on the availability of the proper personnel.

# WHAT IS THE TRAVEL/TOURISM CLIENT'S RESPONSIBILITY?

Clients are an important part of any advertising campaign. They should know what they want and know when they see it. That means they must do some thinking prior to the involvement of the ad agency, and they must then communicate clearly to the account executive what they have in mind. It is up to the agency then to express this idea creatively or to solve the problem effectively.

The travel client should have a reasonable system of campaign or ad approval, keeping the list of reviewers to a minimum. Circulating materials too widely merely causes confusion. Criticisms are most helpful when specific. Comments like "I don't know why I don't like it. I guess it just doesn't do anything for me," are not helpful. The creative people need to know where they have failed—if they have failed. Sufficient time should be given to meetings with ad agency personnel, especially when expenditures are significant. Good clients make the relationship pleasant. They suggest, they critique, they cooperate. They don't nag or nit-pick. This negative behavior discourages creativity and results in poor campaigns, in ads that are "safe" but ineffective.

The travel client is also responsible for paying the bills, and payment should be rendered promptly. Advertising agencies can't afford to carry IOU's too long. To keep the agency and the relationship strong, the travel client sees to this obligation.

# WHAT ARE SOME OF THE PITFALLS IN THIS RELATIONSHIP?

Client complaints about agencies include

- Lack of sufficient staff
- Inexperience
- Inflexibility
- Lack of interest in travel business
- Carelessness in meeting deadlines and other obligations
- Poor communication
- Lack of fresh ideas

Agency personnel sometimes find these travel client flaws:

- Expecting too much for too little money
- Lack of direction and communication
- Inconsistency of planning and funding
- Indecisiveness
- Too many critics involved
- Lack of candor
- Failure to have its own house in order

No relationship is perfect. The more communication clients have with agencies, the more they understand each other's problems, and the better the partnership will function.

A time may come when a client wants to change agencies. This could be because they've outgrown their current agency, because it has gone sour on the account, because it keeps changing personnel, because it ignores old clients in the pursuit of new business, because it won't listen to problems, because it can't handle finances, or because it can no longer deliver what is promised.

When this day arrives, the travel client must ask whether the rift is terminal or not. Can it be rectified with a change of personnel, or a change of strategy? They have lived with this agency for some time and know each other. Do they want to start over?

# WHAT ABOUT OPERATING AN IN-HOUSE AGENCY?

This is something like operating an on-site travel department, except that it entails even more headaches.

An in-house advertising agency is one in which the client, hoping to save agency commissions, decides to either handle advertising internally or incorporate as an agency, adding a couple of small accounts to their own account in order to qualify for agency status. To do this, there must be sufficient volume to make the move worthwhile. Some automobile dealers who spend thousands of dollars annually on advertising may strike out on their own, contracting out some services (like television production) and pocketing the savings on commissions—primarily in the form of lower newspaper rates.

Large cruise lines or hotel chains might also opt for this approach, but it really doesn't make much sense. They are exchanging a few dollars in profit for a decline in creative and professional expertise. Keep in mind that, in many instances, they are paying exactly the same price for commercials as they would if they went through an agency.

A combination of some travel agency involvement (in print and direct mail, for example) and some advertising agency contributions (in the electronic media, in creative services, and in other specialties) works for a number of medium-sized agencies, but may be beyond the small travel agency and of no interest to the large tourism accounts that can afford to attract the major advertising agency.

The next few chapters explain what advertising agency personnel do for the larger clients, while also providing tips to the smaller travel agencies that must handle most chores themselves.

## CHAPTER HIGHLIGHTS

❑   Advertising agency size is determined by the amount of billing done, and this makes the majority of agencies small businesses.

❑   Advertising agencies may perform a variety of services, with size again a factor, but almost all would offer creative talent, media expertise, and accounting.

❑   Major travel clients may put their account up for bids, while the smaller travel agency may have to seek out an advertising form when the need arises.

❑   All advertising should be part of a structured campaign, with specific goals and a realistic budget.

❑   Advertising agencies make most of their revenues from commissions paid them by the media, with additional income coming from specialized services, collateral charges, and discounts.

❏ Travel and tourism clients should be compatible with their ad agency; should look for agency travel acumen and experience; should expect creative expertise, service, and honesty; and should make certain their new partner has a decent reputation.

❏ Advertising agencies, in addition to creative and production services and media buying, may also offer PR help, marketing and research, and other benefits.

❏ Clients should know what they want, work with advertising personnel to achieve this, and should pay bills on time.

❏ When changing advertising agencies, travel/tourism clients should review all aspects of the relationship to be certain why it didn't work, if it can be fixed, and if a new arrangement will be better.

❏ Operating an in-house agency doesn't make much sense for most travel/tourism accounts.

■          ■          ■

## ❏ EXERCISES

1. Check with a local or regional travel agency to see how they handle their advertising and how they structure their relationship with an advertising agency, if they use one.
2. Check with a local or regional hotel to determine the same thing.
3. Go through the files of some advertising trade publications (like *Advertising Age* and *Ad Week*) and find a couple of stories involving ad agencies and travel/tourism clients. Report on them to the class.
4. Visit a local advertising agency, perhaps as a class, and have agency personnel explain why they feel a travel client would benefit from their services.

## ❏ CASE PROBLEMS

*1. Assume you are a medium-sized advertising agency making a pitch for a small 6-hotel chain in your general geographical area. Keep in mind that you do not have all of the resources of a large ad agency. What sort of presentation would you make?*

*What would be the focus of this presentation? Would you be able to include any campaign theme ideas?*

*2. As the manager of a small travel agency, you decide you want to put together a radio campaign that will be carried by two dozen radio stations in your section of the state. You have no advertising agency but decide to employ one to assist you in creative work, production, and media placement. How would you go about finding an agency? What would you tell the agency you selected so that it would understand your needs? What would you expect of it?*

# 5

# UNDERSTANDING MEDIA

The first thing to remember about the various advertising media is that no one medium is the perfect answer for everything. Television may be the darling of advertising agencies and the favorite toy of consumers—and a powerful advertising tool. That still doesn't mean it is within the reach of all those within the travel industry, or that it would be the right buy even if affordable. Like all media, TV has its strengths and weaknesses.

In this chapter we examine these strengths and weaknesses, along with use, adaptability to travel promotion, and cost.

## NEWSPAPERS

This medium is one of the oldest forms of mass communication and remains a prime outlet for advertising, especially for local agencies, local hotels and carriers with local schedules. Along with direct mail, newspapers are favored by travel agencies. These businesses claim these two media, plus word of mouth, account for better than two-thirds of their business.

Newspapers are the nation's largest advertising medium (although television may argue that more dollars are spent on producing and airing commercials) and more than half of America's retail businesses, like travel agencies, use newspapers. Even larger travel accounts are heavily into newspapers. Trans World Airlines spent nearly $21 million in newspapers in 1986; Pan American topped that figure; and People's Express, although struggling that year, spent nearly $30 million on newspaper advertising. Hotels and restaurants call newspapers their "bread-and-butter" medium, and praise the flexibility, variety, and response-generating advantages of the dailies.

The number of newspapers in the United States has declined steadily in the last 60 years, from a high of nearly 2,500 daily newspapers in 1915 to nearly 30 percent fewer today. The remaining newspapers, however, do a higher volume of advertising business than did the 2,500 newspapers years ago.

Studies show that newspaper readership is high, with around 80 percent of the people in the United States seeing a daily paper. Involvement is also high. Readers clip coupons, write letters to the editor, talk about items with friends, or respond to classified ads.

While local or retail advertising is the mainstay of newspaper advertising, national ads also figure strongly in total income. Of these national advertisers, the top three categories are automotive, foods, and transportation. Under transportation are listed airlines, bus service, trains, tours, and cruise lines. Hotels and resorts rank in the top ten among national advertisers.

Totals for all newspaper advertising amounts to about $24 billion a year, which makes this print medium a pretty healthy business.

What are the pros and cons of advertising in newspapers?

❑ For the national or even statewide advertiser, the ability to select markets based on geography is a plus. There are many towns and cities where the local newspaper really dominates. You can buy space in these papers without having to purchase papers in areas you don't want.

❑ Compared to magazines, for example, or billboards and other print media, the frequency of publication of the newspaper is a plus. A daily paper is usually described as one which publishes four or more times a week; a weekly comes out less than four times a week. In either case, the newspapers represent an opportunity to reach an audience many times during a limited period.

❑ It is relatively easy to change newspaper copy—compared to television copy, for example, or billboards, or magazines. In some areas you might even be able to change a word or a line between a morning and evening edition, and most changes can be made within a day. For special sections—like the travel section on Sunday—there is a longer lead time, perhaps a week or more.

❑ It is also easier to schedule newspaper advertising. You don't have to wait until a certain time segment opens up, as on television. Television and radio are locked into a certain number of commercial minutes per program hour. Newspapers have no such restrictions. If they secure an unusual amount of advertising, they merely add pages.

❑ Cost for newspaper advertising is relatively low—again compared to media such as magazines and television.

❑ Newspapers are used for reference; they hang around a while. Prospects may keep the Sunday travel section around until the next one is issued.

❑ Newspapers are a good medium for co-op advertising. It's easier to work with print in fixing costs and in altering copy and illustrations to fit your own needs.

❑ A plus for many products and services—but not necessarily for all segments of the travel industry—is that newspapers cover a wide economic range.

What about the drawbacks?

❑ There's a considerable amount of waste circulation. With fewer newspapers, each paper covers a wider geographical area. Many of the people who read the paper will not come to you simply because other suppliers may be closer and more convenient. You also reach such a broad spectrum of the public that you take in a great many people who are not prospects at all.

❑ When you advertise in a number of different newspapers, you may run up against the problem of different sizes. That makes it difficult—but not impossible—to design an ad that fits all newspapers.

❑ If you plan to use color, and this would be a consideration for very few agencies, newspapers, although improving steadily, are not as good as magazines or billboards in reproducing color.

❑ Advertising agencies cite the difference between local and national rates as a problem with newspapers but this should have little effect on travel agencies.

## DIRECT MAIL

Despite the seemingly continual hikes in postal rates, direct mail, sometimes called "the quiet medium," remains on the increase. It accounts for better than 10 percent of first-class mail, a third of the postcards sent, 85 percent of third-class mail, and 100 percent of fourth-class mail. In a quarter of a century, it's grown from a $1 billion per year business to one that claims more than $14 billion in revenues.

The largest users of direct mail are small businessmen, retailers, magazine publishers, catalogue companies, and pharmaceutical houses.

Small businesses, those doing an annual business under half a million dollars, account for two-thirds of the users of direct mail, and travel agencies figure heavily in this number. Tour operators also use direct mail and, to a lesser extent, so do hotels, cruise lines, tourism departments, and others. Any member of the travel industry that can target an audience has to consider the effectiveness of this medium.

There is an erroneous opinion that most people don't open direct mail, that they consider it junk mail and toss it without even opening the envelope. Not true. Three out of four people at least open the envelope, but 60 percent of these people merely glance at the contents. That's why you need a strong and attractive message to hold the reader's attention.

**Fig. 5–1  Direct mail pieces take many forms.** (Courtesy of Travel & Transport Inc.)

There are direct mail specialty houses that have the capability of designing mailing packages, recommending audiences, checking returns, and performing other duties. Some of their charges can be far above the budget of most travel agencies, but local sources, like mailing houses, might be worth investigating. Among other things, these mailing houses broker lists of individuals according to a multitude of categories. You can buy lists of people by location, income, occupation, age, and other variables. The cost is so much per thousand and good mailing houses update their lists regularly, catching changes of address, deaths, and other alterations.

The Direct Mail Advertising Association lists these reasons why direct mail works well:

1.  You can aim direct mail at a target audience better than you can with any other medium. If you have a special farm tour, for example, and you advertise in a regional newspaper or TV station, you will be addressing more nonfarmers than farmers. With direct mail, you can select out the farmers and mail only to them. There is far less waste circulation.
2.  Direct mail can be personalized more than any other medium. Many of today's mailing pieces are so well done, you can't even tell if the signature is genuine or printed. With banks of automatic typewriters cranking out thousands of mailing pieces daily, these, too, have a first copy appearance.
3.  There is no competition for attention as there might be in another medium—no TV or radio commercials butted up against your message, no cluster of billboards, no page full of ads. If the reader opens your mailing piece, it's the only thing he or she sees.
4.  There are far fewer restrictions on space and format in direct mail. Ads in magazines and newspapers are limited by things like page size and balance with editorial matter; with rare exceptions, television and radio have the 10-, 20-, 30-, and 60-second time limits. Direct mail can be any size and shape you want, as long as it conforms to postal regulations. Even when it doesn't, you can usually have your way by paying an extra fee.
5.  Production is more varied and flexible. You can use the kind of paper you want, insert little novelties, even have things pop up. And you can suit production to your schedule rather than tailoring it to that of the medium.
6.  It can be mailed according to your needs and schedule, so that it reaches the consumers almost exactly when you want it to reach them, providing the postal authorities cooperate.

7. Direct mail gives consumers their best chance to take action, by returning a postcard, or using a postage-paid envelope, or sending along a coupon, or bringing in something to be redeemed. Direct mail is an effective way to get people to write for brochures, for example.
8. If you want to check on results, direct mail makes this sort of research much easier. You can key envelopes in a certain way to check response from small or large groups.

Since no medium is perfect, what are the handicaps of direct mail?

1. It often has a poor image.
2. It can be quite expensive. All of the elements of direct mail—paper, printing, postage, and other items—have risen considerably in cost over this past decade.
3. There are relatively few people who really understand direct mail and who can get the most out of it.
4. There are many restrictive mailing regulations covering things like size, number per package, weight, and even width.

## TELEVISION

There are solid reasons for TV sales representatives to tout their wares. For one thing, people spend much more time in front of their TV sets than they do with their newspapers or magazines. The average household watches television seven hours a day. National manufacturers use it more than any other medium. Its total dollar volume for advertising exceeds that of any other medium. Television is big business for advertisers.

At least $20 billion a year is spent on television advertising, with three-fourths of that going to the networks and the remainder to local stations. To lure visitors to Florida in 1986, for example, that state bought nearly $17 million in TV time. That same year, TWA spent almost $10 million on spots in local markets.

In many ways, television would appear to be a natural for the travel industry. The ability to show and tell and put the prospect in the setting has to help. So does the excitement element of TV, and the association with entertainment. However, except for some local travel shows and some sporadic local campaigns, travel agencies don't use television much. The reasons are cost, lack of experience

**Fig. 5–2    Television is a popular but an expensive, sometimes complicated, medium.** (Courtesy of WOMT)

with the medium, and even tradition. Airlines, hotel chains, cruise lines, and other hospitality suppliers are better bets for TV buys.

Some of the good points about TV as an ad medium include

❑ It combines sight, sound, and motion. You can show the Hawaii tour, in color, play ukeleles in the background, show tourists enjoying a luau, even superimpose the dates and prices, if you want.

❑ Because the message is immediate, there is believability to it. People may not believe everything they read, but they believe what they see—or think they see.

❑ There are huge audiences for TV programs, often several people gathered around a single set.

❑ Because of the combination of sight and sound, there is a good opportunity for product identification.

❏ Television is popular. People go to it to relax and be entertained. Some of that pleasure can rub off on products or services advertised.

❏ There's a high impact to the message. As long as you are staring at the tube and paying attention, there's just one communication reaching you.

Disadvantages of television advertising include

❏ The message is restricted by time segments. If you have something that takes 2½ minutes to say, you have to cut it to a minute (unless you sponsor the whole show, but even then you have to cut to a standard time length). The most common length today is 30 seconds.

❏ The viewer has a hard time responding to the message. No coupons to clip, no return envelopes, and, since most travel agencies aren't open all night when viewing is heaviest, even listing a phone number isn't too helpful.

❏ It's also hard to arrange for time on TV. Many of the strongest time slots are already taken by larger advertisers. You have to take what you can get on the less popular shows and at less popular hours.

❏ Costs are very high for both time and production, with the latter being a major cost factor. Some commercials may come with a price tag of half a million dollars or more. And a one-minute spot in the Super Bowl telecast would more than match that figure in media charges. In a medium-sized local market, the best (or "prime") times are going to run from $300 to $500 for a 30-second spot. These may drop down to under $100 for some of the less popular times, when there are fewer people watching.

❏ There is considerable waste coverage. Think of the number of people who might see one of your travel spots compared with the number that would actually be prospects for that trip. The percentages would be overwhelmingly negative.

# RADIO

In the past ten or twenty years, radio has made a real comeback. Some media observers thought radio was washed up once television entered the scene, but radio found its own niche and has been doing well. A good part of its success stems from its role as "background" entertainment and information, a medium you don't have to watch or read to enjoy. The universal use of car radios has helped, as has the advent of FM radio, and the production of small transistorized radios. Its reach is everywhere.

If figures impress you, then consider that there are about 300 million radios in homes, 10 million in offices or plants, 100 million in automobiles, and some 40–50 million portable transistors. That's a lot of listeners.

Radio stations have also developed individual formats so that they can reach a certain type of audience. There are rock stations, country western stations, soul stations, all-talk stations, middle-of-the-road stations, classical music stations and so on. Of the approximately 7,000 radio stations in this country, about two-thirds are independent, and the remainder affiliated with networks.

Both radio and television salespeople will give the prospective advertiser a demographic breakdown, telling him or her how many and what kinds of people are watching different shows or listening at specific hours. By using this information, you can make some general selections by audience type—usually male or female—and by age groupings.

While television's prime hours are usually defined as being from 7–10 P.M. (with 6–7 and 10–11 P.M. carried as prime time in some markets and "fringe prime time" in others), the most popular (and most expensive) radio times are "drive times," those periods, morning and evening, when millions of commuters have on their car radios. Morning drive time is frequently more expensive than evening drive time.

Both television and radio also have terms to describe the range of their messages. They talk about "share of households using television" and "program ratings," which represent that program's share of all the homes having TV sets. There are various rating services to determine how many people actually are watching a certain program or station—as against how many could watch it because the signal reaches them. The most current way of measuring TV's reach is by using gross rating points (GRPs). One GRP stands for 1 percent of the homes with TV sets in a given area. If you wanted 70 GRPs a week, you'd have the choice of buying 10 programs with 7 GRPs each, or two with 30 and one with 10, or any other combination.

Radio stations often talk in terms of their coverage, which means their potential reach, which is based on the strength of their signal. (Some stations are purely local, with a range of about 25 miles; others are regional and may cover an entire state: a few are clear channel 50,000-watt stations that may reach hundreds, even thousands of miles.) They also talk about circulation, which is the actual number of people listening in a given time period. (TV may also use these same terms with the same meanings.)

Travel agencies are concerned about circulation rather than coverage, except in unusual circumstances. If you own an agency in Fort Worth, you couldn't care less if your local radio station's signal reaches Tulsa. You have no potential there. On the other hand, this sort of reach may have considerable appeal to a hotel chain or a state tourism bureau. The ability of certain stations to penetrate deeper into potential sales areas make them an economical choice.

What are the advantages of radio?

❏ You can select geographical markets and select different kinds of listeners.
❏ It's an intimate medium, and some products are sold best by this means.
❏ In some areas, where there is a single dominant station, you can really saturate the market.
❏ Radio is relatively inexpensive. Because sound has the ability to conjure up images, you can stage elaborate events with a little imagination and a few sound effects. A Strauss waltz puts the listener in Vienna; drums suggest Africa; a ship's whistle says "cruise."
❏ It is not too difficult to change copy. Given a willing radio station, you can alter a majority of spots the same day.

On the negative side:

❏ Radio has no visual appeal and will have waste coverage.
❏ No possibility of consumer referral to message.
❏ Messages are limited by restrictions of time.

## MAGAZINES

Some of the larger accounts in the travel industry are partial to magazines, especially those that have a proven relationship to their prime audiences. Tour operators may be seen in *The New Yorker* or *National Geographic,* while cruise lines are advertising in *Travel/ Holiday* or *Modern Maturity Magazine.* Few local travel agencies use magazines, except for occasional advertising placed in regional editions of national publications or in the growing list of city magazines.

Thanks to computers, it's possible for clients in many cities to buy a page in a special section covering only their limited geographical area. *Magazine Network,* for example, sells space in a combination of *Time, Newsweek, Sports Illustrated,* and *U.S. News and World Report.* Your ad appears only in the regional edition you want, so you get the prestige of association with a national publication, but at a fraction of the cost.

The big story in magazines over the past two decades has been the demise of many general circulation magazines (like the weekly editions of *Life, Look,* and *The Saturday Evening Post*) and the phenomenal growth of specialty magazines, catering to everyone from motorcycle riders to bottle collectors.

Travel is represented in this area by publications like *Travel/ Holiday, Tours & Resorts, Cruise Travel, Carte Blanche Magazine,* and *Diversion,* which contain a heavy sampling of travel prices. For the travel professionals, there are trade journals like *Travel Weekly, The Travel Agent, Business Travel News, ASTA Travel News,* and *Travel Age* with its regional editions.

Like newspapers, radio, and television, magazine information is carried in a set of publications called *Standard Rate & Data Service.* In these pages you get details of mechanical requirements, deadlines, and sworn circulation for the nation's major magazines. Data for purely local publications can be secured by calling the local sales representatives.

What are the advantages of magazines?

❑ Good selectivity of audience—next to direct mail—but this is more helpful to a national advertiser than to a local one like a travel agency (unless you buy the regional edition). If you had a farm tour in Oklahoma, for example, you could buy an ad in *The Oklahoma Farmer* and reach a fairly select audience. If you want to let travel agents know about new destinations for your airline or cruise line, you can appear in their trade journals. Adventurers may be selected out by ads in magazines like the *Smithsonian.*

❑ Magazines reach more affluent customers. That doesn't mean that everyone who reads magazines is rich, but the level of income is above average.

❑ Magazines have long lives and are often kept around for reference. If you miss the ad the first time, you may see it at a second reading.

❑ Magazines offer prestige to an advertiser. You can also derive a spin-off benefit from this by ordering copies of the ad (as it

"Appeared in_____ ") and mail these to prospects. You need editorial approval for this, however.

❑ Color reproduction, a facet that doesn't affect much travel advertising, is also good in magazines.

There are some drawbacks:

❑ Long lead time for advertising. Some national magazines want your ad three months ahead of publication. Even local magazines, like city magazines, may request six weeks to two months.

❑ If you advertise in more than one magazine, you take the chance of duplicate circulation. The same person sees your ad in two or three different magazines. This isn't all bad, of course, but it does cut down on the number of people you are actually reaching.

❑ Despite the advent of regional editions and inserts, magazine advertising cannot normally dominate a local market the way newspapers or radio can.

❑ Production costs can be high. This, of course, affects the larger, full-color ads, rather than the small black-and-white ads.

## OUT-OF-HOME MEDIA

This category is used to describe all those messages you see only outside the home: billboards, transit signs, taxi signs, and so on. The most common of these is the outdoor poster.

Like direct mail, the outdoor advertising media have taken a great deal of criticism, from both the government and private citizens. It's easy to sympathize with environmentalists who protest the marring of our landscapes, but outdoor media people feel the size of their operation is greatly exaggerated. They say that, if all the legitimate outdoor advertising billboards in this country were placed end to end, they wouldn't cover one runway at O'Hare Field. They also claim that, when photographers take those telephoto shots to show the clutter of signs, the majority of these signs are on-site signs, erected by the owners.

There are varieties of sizes in outdoor posters, generally from about 5 feet high and 12 feet wide, to 10 feet high and 23 feet wide. They also vary according to special features, such as painted versus posted, illuminated or not, or with or without moving parts. The more you do, the more the cost. A 30-sheet poster (10 feet x 23 feet), painted in full color, with a trivision panel that exposes three different scenes at intervals as a pyramidal device rotates on a pivot, and in a prime location, would cost considerably more than a junior board (5 feet x 8 feet), in 1 or 2 colors, in a less desirable location.

Cost is based on production and location. The wise advertiser drives to the location and checks which way the board faces and estimates the traffic flow and looks for obstructions.

Audience reach with outdoor posters is expressed in showings and gross rating points (GRPs). A "100 percent showing," for example, would be equal to the number of outdoor posters you would have to purchase in a city (or locality) in order to reach 100 percent of the car-owning households in a 30-day period. A GRP is reaching 1 percent of the population one time. A "100 percent GRP" would be equal to the number of outdoor posters you would require to yield a daily effective circulation equal to the population of the area.

One other term used by out-of-home media people is a rotary board or rotary (or rotating) plan. Under such a plan, an advertiser might buy a single board for six months but have it moved to a new location every two months. Or he might have three different boards and rotate them in different areas every couple of months. This is one way to achieve variety and exposure at a reasonable cost.

The advantages of outdoor posters are:

❑ Selectivity of geographical markets. You could locate a few boards in the area of your travel agency, or you could place them where you feel your best prospects will pass them. Airlines often employ billboards near the airport and outdoor advertising may direct travelers to hotels by strategic placement on highways or within cities.

❑ Large physical size. This, however, can be deceptive. On fast thoroughfares, distant posters are postage-stamp size, loom large momentarily, and are gone. Obviously, a location near a stop light is a prime site.

❑ There's a high repetitive value in outdoor posters. A commuter who travels the same route daily may see a specific poster 20 or more times a month.

❑ Costs for outdoor posters are relatively low, and color reproduction is good.

On the other hand:

❑ There's a lot of waste circulation. Many thousands of people drive by your sign who may never be your prospects.

❑ The message must be short. You can't use outdoor for lengthy or complicated copy.

❏ Billboards sometimes have a poor image, and there are not too many creative specialists who can handle them properly.
❏ Changing copy isn't easy; weather can deteriorate your lovely creation; and, even though you are on a good corner, you might be the bottom inside sign among four, and be partially obscured by a building.

# OTHER MEDIA

There are many other ways to advertise, some of which may be used by travel agents, and some of which would be unlikely tools. There are movie trailers, sky-writing, signs on bus benches, and messages on match boxes.

## Yellow Pages

Travel agents find this medium a must. Even when you have been advertising in other media, the prospective traveler may have no other reference material in front of him except for the phone book. You have to at least be listed and you should also consider a small space ad that is purchased on a yearly contract. These ads are sold by salespeople for the telephone company.

For purposes of commercial travel, you may also want to be listed in the city directory, or in other directories that have an audience that matches the profile of your best customer.

## Booklets and Brochures

Unless you can do a decent job with printed materials, it pays to employ someone who can. Sending out something that poorly represents any business only detracts from sales.

In addition to the usual collection of travel brochures, many travel agencies also issue quarterly newsletters or similar publications, and they may print up general brochures about their services. These are handy to have and should be kept current.

It isn't necessary that everything that is printed be full color and on slick paper, but it is imperative that it is neat, attractive, interesting, and informative.

The great value of printed materials is that the client or prospect has something to take away, something to savor, a reminder of the agency's presence. Like every other advertising tool, it seeks to re-

place the salesperson when personal contact is impossible or impractical.

## Point-of-Purchase Materials

These are signs, posters, easel-type cutouts, and other items that
serve as reminders in the travel firm itself. Virtually all of these are
supplied by outside agencies. Too many of them, however, are hap-
hazardly arranged, so that they merely clutter up the office decor.
Don't use too many; make them as compatible as possible; change
them periodically; make them work for you; and don't let them get in
the way of efficient salesmanship.

## Novelties

Businesses use thousands of giveaway items—pens, tie clips, matches, rulers, shoe horns, caps—all with some printed reference to the
company name. The trick is to find things that also remind the
recipient of the product or service.

**Fig. 5–3    There are many forms of advertising, from expensive TV
commercials to simple window cards.**

For the travel industry, items like calendars, flight bags, cards showing conversion rates of money overseas, pens and pencils, and other related novelties are used. Frequently these are handed out when the agency opens and may not be used in the future. Even calendars are used much more infrequently because of the high cost of paper and printing.

## Donation Advertising

Every small business is the target of appeals to advertise in high school yearbooks, college newspapers, opera or theater programs, anniversary editions of publications, and many other periodicals.

To most of these, the advertiser should be polite but negative. There are perhaps only two times when you should use such advertising:

1. When it reaches an audience you want to reach. Programs for various artistic functions may be good—opera, ballet, community theater, symphony—particularly where you have reason to believe that the people who attend these affairs are prime prospects. If you have special events that appeal to special audiences, finding the right vehicle is a plus—a golf club membership booklet for a golf tour, or a college directory for youth tours, or a Saint Patrick's Day dinner program for a trip to Ireland.
2. The other reason for considering such advertising is the possibility of good public relations. Even though it's unlikely you'll get any direct business from the ad, its appearance in a high school annual may enhance your image as a good citizen and lead to future contacts.

## A PROPER MEDIA MIX

This subject was mentioned in the first chapter in a slightly different way. There we had a look at the relative values placed on all marketing activities. For most travel agencies, however, these activities amount to advertising except for special events and newsletters, which are not far removed from advertising. Marketing strategies for larger travel organizations—like suppliers, carriers, the hospitality industry—would be much broader and would bring into play all of the normal marketing elements.

Within the advertising framework, you also try to effect a proper mix. Again, when you are dealing with budgets that are quite limited, this is not a great burden. Firms that spend millions on advertising have a lot of tough decisions to make as to where they'll place these dollars.

Smaller entities, such as travel agencies, resorts, theme parks, and travel divisions of companies, still perform a miniature version of this planning (as illustrated in Chapter 11), assigning dollar amounts to a number of promotional areas. Obviously, each type of situation and each size company or division faces different challenges and budgets; the object is to make whatever money you have work for you as efficiently as possible.

Even among the larger advertisers, the media mix varies from year to year, depending in part on the way their research tells them people are spending time with each medium. If there is any constant trend in this decade, it's toward more use of television, even among local advertisers.

In planning, the manager should sit down with staff members, and, if appropriate, consultants or ad agency personnel. All concerned then examine past performance, consider sales goals, the advantages of available media, and then put some price tags on potential packages. When the total cost seems in line, other internal opinions may be sought, plus the advice of media people who can update availabilities. Several revisions may be necessary.

## MOST PRODUCTIVE MEDIA

After that lengthy list of media pros and cons, it's worth repeating that most travel and hospitality firms find newspapers and direct mail their most productive means of reaching prospective clients although, with the larger companies, magazines and television may predominate.

Direct mail succeeds for all the reasons cited earlier, while, especially for travel agencies, newspaper travel advertising is aided by habit. People who are prospects turn to the travel section of the paper, just as movie patrons consult the entertainment section.

It would be a rash travel agency manager who would ignore these two media or award them a low budget position.

Airline packages to Hawaii, on the other hand, might opt for a television schedule in top markets, or could find their way into trade and consumer magazines. Network radio could also apply, with hotel chains like Marriott spending around a million dollars on this medium.

## MEDIA PLACEMENT

As noted earlier, advertising agencies have individuals who are specialists at media placement. Travel agencies may have to do placement on their own. However, there are guides.

Television and radio stations issue periodic breakouts of their audiences by age, sex, and other factors, and they also indicate listening and viewing audiences by program or time of day. You can go over these with station sales representatives, trying to match your needs with what the stations have available.

Once you agree on what you want and find they can supply it, they will issue a contract that spells out their obligation to air the commercials at a certain time and on certain days (or they may give you a range of times and days) and indicate your obligation to pay.

Newspapers also have their representatives and you can talk with them about how often you want to run ads, what size, and what location. You can learn a lot by listening to these reps and by observing what other agencies do in other papers in other cities.

If you want to buy billboards, the sign company will supply you with a list of available sites or, perhaps, with a map on which these sites are indicated. Get in your car and drive to these sites, looking at the exact locale where your message will appear.

Obviously, the people who sell time and space are in business to make sales, just as travel consultants are. That doesn't mean they can be expected to pressure you into an unwise decision. They'd like to make you happy because they are counting on repeat business. So, know what you want, but also pick their brains.

## MEDIA CHARGES

In general—but not always—you get what you pay for. If you want programs or publications with the largest audiences, you pay top dollar. If you opt for a smaller but exclusive audience, you also pay a premium. If you want a special place in the newspaper or magazine or a special location for the outdoor poster, you can anticipate an add-on charge.

Let's examine some of the ways the media charge.

## Newspapers

Newspapers charge by the line or by the column inch, although they also have some full- and half-page quotations in many newspapers.

There are 14 lines to an inch, meaning that, if you bought a 2-inch (1-column) ad and the rate charged was $2.10 a line, you would have 28 lines times $2.10, or $58.80.

If the rate quoted is a column-inch rate, that means you are billed on the basis of each inch in a single column in the paper. Take a look at your daily paper. You'll note that it has anywhere from 6 to 9 columns of type across the page. These columns, which are often about 2 inches wide, are used because, if the human eye had to scan across the entire page, reading the newspaper would be a laborious job. The 2-inch wide columns are easily and rapidly read by a subscriber.

Take your ruler and measure up 4 inches on a single column. That's a 4-inch ad—an ad composed of 4-column inches.

You could also use 2 columns of 2 inches each to get a 4-inch ad but this preference would have to be spelled out. Most newspapers won't allow you to buy wider than you buy high. For example, you couldn't buy a 3-column × 2-inch ad; they'd insist it be at least 3-column × 3-inch ad.

If the charge per column inch is $21, that means a 4-inch ad will cost $84.

There are extra charges assessed for preferred position (such as on the run-over news page, or the society page) and for extra color (one or more). Run of Paper (ROP) is cheaper and means the ad may be placed anywhere the newspaper decides.

The reason some papers charge more for exactly the same space as another paper is simply because they have more readers—their circulation is larger.

To review, then, the factors that affect cost on newspaper ads are size, circulation, position, and color.

If you have the newspaper perform other services, such as allowing you the use of their artwork, doing the layout, or setting the type, they may also bill you for these items.

## Magazines

Magazines charge much like newspapers, but with some differences.

Instead of dealing in column inches or lines (although magazines may do this, too), the magazine typically sells a portion of a page:

full, half, quarter, sixth, eighth. You have a limited amount of lee-way in the way you can set up your space on the page.

Because you are dealing in huge circulation figures when you get to the top national magazines, like *Reader's Digest, TV Guide,* and *Time,* you shouldn't be surprised to find that the rates are considerably higher.

Perhaps a full-page black-and-white ad in your daily paper runs $1,500–$2,000 (much less in smaller towns, higher in the largest cities). The same ad (but smaller to fit the format) in a magazine like *Time* would run you twenty times that much. If, however, you bought the *Magazine Network* mentioned earlier, settling for regional circulation, you might find the newspaper and magazine costs not too far apart.

Magazines also charge for position. The back cover, center spread, and inside front and back covers are generally the highest-priced. Premiums may also be charged for pages adjacent to a popular columnist or section, or the page adjacent to the index.

Color would be another factor, and so would any other extraordinary instructions, like tipping in a coupon, or arranging a special fold.

The magazine would not normally provide any of the services a newspaper might—no artwork, layout, typeset. You supply them with the ad ready to run.

## Direct Mail

There are a number of costs attached to direct mail, depending on how extensive the mailing is and how sophisticated the methods used.

To begin with, you have the cost of printing the materials to be sent—the mailing package. You might have a brochure, a letter, and a return card, plus an envelope to contain these elements. Type must be set for these, photos taken or illustrations obtained; you decide on weight of paper, colors to be used, the way the brochure lays out, and any other mechanical factor. Each of these decisions involves financial considerations.

You need a list of people to whom the mailing will be sent. If you use only the list of your clients, no problem. If you need to buy a list from a list broker, you are talking about another $35-$50 per 1,000 names depending on the value of the particular list. These names can be furnished on labels, or envelopes addressed, or a straight printed list. In the case of a travel agency, for example, you might

**Fig. 5–4 There are hundreds of helpful directories that provide lists of vacation or commercial prospects.** (Courtesy of American Directory Publishing Co. Inc.)

buy a list of individuals who live near your office, or who are in a certain income bracket, or who have traveled in the past three years.

Then there is the handling of the mailing. If you turn this over to a mailing house there will be a charge for their efforts of sorting, labeling, stuffing, tying, and so on.

Finally, there is postage, both the cost of mailing, either bulk or first class, and the cost of return cards or envelopes.

Even when you do all of the handling yourself, you have to figure in the value of employee time.

You may, of course, be able to use a brochure supplied by a resort or carrier. If so, that cuts back on printing charges. Any savings you can realize makes the mailing that much more efficient.

People new to direct mail methods always want to know what percentage of return is a good one. This is impossible to say, since it depends on so many external elements. If, for example, you represent a tour operator and you buy a "cold" list of 50,000 names from a travel magazine subscription list, you would be happy with a return (or sales) of anything over 1½ percent. On the other hand, when this tour operator builds up a list of travelers over the years, like Caravan, they might expect a much heavier response, since these people are familiar with the product and have already demonstrated a specific interest. Familiarity isn't the only factor, of course. The nature of the information, the value it represents, the timing, and the design of the package—all affect returns.

## Out-of-Home Media

As already indicated, the cost of billboards depends on things like size, location, and type. The larger billboards cost more; the prime locations (those with heaviest traffic) cost more; things like illumination, moving parts, extensions from the board, and other variations cost more. It is also more expensive to buy a painted board than a posted board, where a series of sheets of paper are pasted on the billboard surface.

You can't normally buy outdoor media for short periods, like a week. Most companies would like two months or longer. Obviously, if you take out a long-term contract for a year or more, you have a better chance of tying up a choice location.

It's dangerous to give ball-park figures for any costs in advertising, but here are some very general figures for billboard costs. To these should be added production costs.

In a modest-size city (like 500,000 population) you'd pay about $100 plus a month for the smallest size board, a junior board, in an average location, without painting or illumination. The larger boards (24 or 30 sheets—which indicates size, and not the number of sheets used in posting) would run from about several hundred dollars, with the top price for a painted-illuminated board coming in at something over a thousand.

## Radio

What radio and television sell is time.

As previously stated, the best radio times for AM radio are during the driving hours to and from work, mornings and evenings. For FM, the evening hours are most expensive and there are some valuable weekend slots.

You might be able to buy a 30-second radio spot on midday AM radio for under $25, even on a station with a decent audience. The top radio station in your area might want $50–$100 for that same spot. From then on, thinking only of AM radio in an average market, you could get into the $150–$400 range for the very best times.

If there are radio shows that bring in an unusually large audience, even outside drive time, you also pay a premium. Suppose that Notre Dame football was being broadcast exclusively over a South Bend station and picked up by one Chicago station. Assume, too, that the game was not being televised. A 30-second spot in that program would be very expensive.

You also pay a premium for special placement, like within the morning news or market reports, or adjacent to the evening weather.

The radio sales rep will show you what is available, tell you what type and size of audience the station has for each time frame (based on national research ratings), and give you the price for the time you choose.

## Television

Television also has its prime time—the evening hours that were mentioned earlier in this chapter. Of course, weekend afternoons are more expensive than weekday afternoons because they deliver larger audiences. If you check your local listings, you'll note that Saturday morning is programmed for children and Sunday morning revolves around religious services. Some travel programs find Sunday morning a good buy, since that type of show fits the quieter format and offers the viewer an alternative to a religious program.

Within those broad time frames, the price of a spot is determined by the size of the audience it plays to. Top rated shows, like *The Bill Cosby Show, Wheel of Fortune,* and *60 Minutes,* cost more than *Movie of the Week* or reruns of *W.K.R.P.,* because the former are watched by far more people. These positions change, of course, Not many years ago, *Laverne and Shirley* and *Mork and Mindy* occupied the leader board.

Specials, like *Amerika* or a Michael Jackson extravaganza or the football Super Bowl, call for special rate sheets. The Super Bowl is about as high as you go in buying national coverage, but the number of viewers are there.

Locally, you might be able to purchase a 30- to 60-second spot (and the minute spot doesn't cost twice as much as the half minute) for anything from around $100 to more than $500.

The media representative from your local station or stations will show you a series of pages on which are listed all the programs they offer. The audience totals will be given for each, plus the cost of time. Some will not be available to you because they have been sold in advance. You may scatter your buys through a week or month, buying commercial time on different days and at different times. or you can concentrate in a certain time period. A client interested only in women might want to focus on daytime soap operas, although these reach only housewives, not the growing female work force. One interested in men might buy into sports programming.

Remember that you also have to add on the production costs, which can be high on television. Whether you like it or not, you are competing with commercials that cost hundreds of thousands to produce and yours can't look amateurish by comparison. It must have a look of professionalism, even if it is inexpensively produced.

A few additional facts on buying space and time:

❏ Salespeople for the media have rate cards that give you the basic costs for their print and broadcast prices. There are also books (like Standard Rate & Data Service), which supply such figures, but the rate cards will be more current.

❏ When you buy in quantity, you save money. If you purchase 200 radio spots over a 6-month period, you'll earn a discount; this is true for television as well. In the print media, the discount goes by lines. After you use a certain number of lines (or inches) you are entitled to a discount. It's good to be aware of these since, if the cost-break point were 1,000 lines and you budgeted for 900, you could probably add the extra 100 lines and actually save money.

❏ There are other technical terms used to describe factors that some advertisers may desire—like reach or frequency. *Reach* defines the geographical impact of stations. *Frequency* looks at the impact in terms of the number of exposures of a single commercial.

❏ Discuss these and other cost factors in detail with the salespeople. Make certain you know what you are buying.

**AA—** Prime Time, Monday-Sunday 7:00-10:00 p.m.

| 1 | 2 | 3 | 4 | 5 | 6 | 7 | 8 | 9 | 10 |
|---|---|---|---|---|---|---|---|---|---|
| $500 | $460 | $420 | $380 | $340 | $300 | $260 | $220 | $180 | $140 |

**A—** M-F, 6:30-7 p.m.  M-Sun., 10-10:30 p.m.
Sun-6-6:30 p.m.  Sun., 9:30-10 p.m.  M-Sat., 6-6:30 p.m.
Sat., 6:30-7 p.m.

| 1 | 2 | 3 | 4 | 5 |
|---|---|---|---|---|
| $250 | $230 | $210 | $190 | $170 |

**B—** M-F, 12:30-1 p.m.  Sun., sign on
M-F, 2-3:30 p.m.  M-F, 3:30-
M-Sun., 10:30-conclusion

**TOTAL AUDIENCE PLANS**

| | 12 weekly | 18 weekly |
|---|---|---|
| Class AAA | 4 | 6 |
| Class AA | 4 | 3 |
| Class A | 2 | 3 |
| Class B | 2 | |
| Minutes | $486.00 | $711.00 |
| 30 Seconds | 390.00 | 576.00 |

Total Audience Plan announcement mus
uled equally over 7-day period and move
within time class. Combinable with wee
programs.

**5-MINUTE NEWS PROG**

| | AAA | |
|---|---|---|
| 1 time pwk | $73.00 | |
| 3 times pwk | 70.00 | |
| 6 times pwk | 68.00 | |

5-min program talent or ser
Rates on request for prc
or more.

**3-MINUTE FARM FEATURES**
12:00 N-1:00 p.m. and 6:00-7:00 a.m.
Monday thru Saturday

| 1 time pwk | $60.00 |
| 3 times pwk | 58.00 |
| 6 times pwk | 56.00 |

**SPECIAL CLASS A**
Participating
Annets. & 3-Min. Features
5-6 AM Farm Hour Monday thru Saturday

| Feature | Minutes | 30 Sec. |
|---|---|---|
| $48.00 | $44.00 | $38.00 |
| | 42.00 | 36.00 |
| | | 35.00 |

30 sec.
$44.00
43.00
41.00
40.00
39.00

aturday
$40.00
38.00
37.00
36.00
35.50

ru Saturday;
u Saturday;
unday
$35.50
34.50
34.00
33.00
32.50

14.00
43.00
42.00
41.00
40.00

SS B
Monday thru Sunday  $22.00
21.50

**4. GENERAL ADVERTISING RATES**
(Not less than 14 agate lines)  Line Rate Daily Sun.
a. Open rate, run of paper.............................. .94  .99

**WEEKLY INSERTION CONTRACT RATES**
Contract Required

| | | Consecutive Weeks | | | |
|---|---|---|---|---|---|
| Min. space per week | 10 Wks. | 20 Wks. | 30 Wks. | 40 Wks. | 50 Wks. |
| 100 lines, Daily | .84 | .83 | .82 | .81 | .80 |
| Sun. | .89 | .88 | .87 | .86 | .85 |
| 500 lines, Daily | .83 | .82 | .81 | .80 | .79 |
| Sun. | .88 | .87 | .86 | .85 | .84 |
| 1,000 lines, Daily | .82 | .81 | .80 | .79 | .78 |
| Sun. | .87 | .86 | .85 | .84 | .83 |

**YEARLY INSERTION CONTRACT RATES**
Contract Required

| | 10 TI. | 20 TI. | 30 TI. | 40 TI. | 50 TI. |
|---|---|---|---|---|---|
| 100 lines, Daily | .86 | .85 | .84 | .83 | .82 |
| Sun. | .91 | .90 | .89 | .88 | .87 |
| 500 lines, Daily | .85 | .84 | .83 | .82 | .81 |
| Sun. | .90 | .89 | .88 | .87 | .86 |
| 1,000 lines, Daily | .84 | .83 | .82 | .81 | .80 |
| Sun. | .89 | .88 | .87 | .86 | .85 |

**BULK SPACE CONTRACT RATES**
(Discounts given below apply to open rate)

| | Daily | Sun. |
|---|---|---|
| 1,000 lines during 12 mo. | .90 | .95 |
| 5,000 lines during 12 mo. | .86 | .91 |
| 10,000 lines during 12 mo. | .84 | .89 |
| 25,000 lines during 12 mo. | .82 | .87 |
| 50,000 lines during 12 mo. | .81 | .86 |
| 75,000 lines during 12 mo. | .80 | .85 |
| 100,000 lines during 12 mo. | .79 | .84 |

In the absence of contract, linage will be billed at the open rate
and rebated 12 months from the date of first insertion.

'VE WEEK
INT

ents and Programs

| | 5% |
| | 7% |
| | 9% |
| | 10% |

**Fig. 5–5  Every medium develops its own rate card and keeps it updated to reflect current audience and charges.**

❑ One category, called run of paper (ROP) or run of station (ROS), also saves money. This means they can fit your ad or commercial into any time or space slots they have available. A good paper or station will try to give you a decent blend of good and weaker positions. You can monitor newspaper placement yourself and the radio and television stations will give you a report on where the commercials aired. You may have to request this.

## COST PER THOUSAND

There's a formula, used primarily to compare magazine rates, called the CPM or cost per thousand formula. What it tries to determine is the cost of delivering one full-page, black-and-white, ad to 1,000 homes. Here's the formula:

$$\frac{R\ (\text{Cost of one page}) \times 1{,}000}{C\ (\text{Circulation})} = \text{Cost Per Thousand (CPM)}$$

If the rate (or cost) per page were $10,000 and the circulation 650,000 for magazine A, the CPM for magazine A would be $15.35.

Magazine B tells you that you can buy a full page in their magazine for a mere $6,000. Their circulation is 180,000 subscribers. Looks like a cheaper deal but, using the formula, you see that the cost per thousand in this case is $33.33—better than twice as high.

It's another way of looking at what you get for what you pay. Obviously, you should be comparing publications that have some similarity. It's not quite accurate to compare *Newsweek* with *Montana Farmer*; *Newsweek* versus *Time* or *U.S. News and World Report* would be a more realistic comparison.

This formula is also used on occasion to balance one newspaper against another (again assuming they are similar in scope), using the cost of delivering a 1,000 line ad to 1,000 homes or, in another form, the cost of delivering one line of advertising to a million homes. This latter formula is called a *milline rate*. In both instances the circulation is the divisor.

You can, of course, compare radio and television costs in the same way, figuring out how much it costs you to reach 1,000 viewers or listeners with a 30-second spot.

If rates are in line, the cost of space or time should rise with the audience reached, except where there are special reasons for charging a higher rate, such as the ability to reach an audience in a high income bracket.

## WORKING WITH MEDIA PEOPLE

Advertisers get to know the representatives of the various media. They listen to them, but make up their own minds. One should read and understand their rate cards, watch for special deals, and use as many media services as he or she can get for nothing.

If a person has a conflict with a certain media rep (and this can happen), they can request a different person. It's easier to switch, of course, when you're a big advertiser, but no medium really wants an unhappy client.

Anticipating needs allows plenty of time to make your media buys. This enables an advertiser to get a better selection and gives him ample time to thoroughly check copy and production. If you can schedule months ahead, at least in terms of space and time needs, that will be an asset to everyone.

Experienced travel marketers keep their own calendars of advertising buys and keep a careful record of everything purchased and scheduled. In a sometimes hectic business like the travel business, it's easy to forget deadlines. You don't want to be rushing to get an ad out at the eleventh hour. This is where mistakes are made and advertising dollars wasted.

Those in the travel industry who work with advertising agencies should still stay in touch with agency account reps and should provide some input on media buys, even though the decision making should be left, primarily, with the advertising experts. They have the tools and information and should be able to produce schedules that meet client requirements.

## CHAPTER HIGHLIGHTS

❏ All media have good and bad features.

❏ Newspapers are a preferred medium for travel advertising, especially for travel agencies, primarily because of frequency, flexibility, cost and the reference factor.

❏ For travel agencies, direct mail is a prime advertising source, and growing. The ability to personalize messages is the chief asset.

❏ While television is more the tool of larger travel accounts, it does offer many advantages, like the combination of sight and sound, which are compatible with travel advertising. Cost rules out its use for many in the industry.

❏ Radio, making a comeback, may be the "sleeper" in travel advertising, offering the unique opportunity to create a mood while controlling costs.

❏ With magazines, travel clients may enjoy some selection, good reproduction, and means of responding. Smaller accounts can take advantage of regional editions of national publications.

❑ Not much out-of-home advertising is done by agencies, but airlines and state tourism bureaus and hotels may have fairly extensive billboard plans, always keeping in mind the need for a brief message, a good location, and the short reading time.

❑ Other media, from the Yellow Pages to novelties, may range from essential to occasional advertising choices. Each meets certain needs and presents certain problems.

❑ The most sensible approach to travel advertising is to develop a media mix that fits the specific client requirements and budget.

❑ Media charge for time and space on the basis of the extent (and sometimes the nature) of the audience they deliver. The larger the readership, listenership or viewership, the higher the cost. There are various formulas for determining the cost of reaching a certain number of people—normally, a thousand—and careful planners employ this math to make certain they buy wisely.

❑ If an agency must do its own media buying, without the help of those in the advertising profession, those responsible for the planning should get to know the media reps and should learn from them, keeping in mind that they are, essentially, dealing with salespeople who have their own wares to sell.

■         ■         ■

## ❑ EXERCISES

1. Secure a rate card from one of the local media, bring it to class, and discuss costs. You may also want to interview a local media salesperson to see what he or she would recommend in terms of travel advertising.

2. From your library or a local advertising agency, get a copy of *Standard Rate and Data* to look at. Select a magazine and check the cost of a half-page black-and-white ad.

3. Figure out the cost per thousand for your daily or weekly newspaper or for your campus newspaper.

4. Assume you were advertising a long weekend (Friday noon through Sunday night) in Las Vegas, and you wanted to reach your target audience on radio and television in your area.

What radio stations and times (or shows) would you use (no more than 2 stations) and what television shows (no more than four) would you buy into? Explain your choices.

## ❏ *CASE PROBLEMS*

*1. Assume you want to advertise a new 600-acre dude ranch in Montana, one that has spectacular views of the Flathead Range and offers amenities like horseback riding, fishing, hiking, cookouts and other western fare. While the surroundings are unspoiled, the accommodations are first class. Price tags for a week's stay, including all meals and activities, is $1500. You've budgeted $40,000 for advertising in this initial year. Where do you think you might find your best prospects? What media would you choose to reach them, and in what relative proportions (or dollar amounts)? Why did you make these particular selections?*

*2. You have a budget large enough to permit you to buy six 30-sheet posters in your area to advertise a new French restaurant. Prices at this restaurant will be in the "high" range, according to your local standards. (Keep in mind, however, that price alone can be deceptive in trying to determine target audiences.) Assuming you had your choice of locations in your area, and that the boards would be up for two months, which locations would you select (be specific) and why?*

# 6

# CONSTRUCTING THE ADVERTISING MESSAGE

Once you know what you'd like to say, to whom you'd like to say it, and the manner in which you'll convey the message, you still have to know how to present the information in an interesting, even compelling, way. That's where creativity comes in.

Advertising agencies succeed and prosper when they have people who possess unusual creative skills. They are able to turn a phrase, to render a concept in a visual manner, to convince the individual to read, listen, or watch. These creative geniuses command high salaries and work on major accounts. Their connection with travel would be in the handling of large carriers or resorts or tour companies; they will not be available to the average-size travel agency.

There are still some very good creative services to be found in smaller advertising agencies. It definitely pays to use these when working with commissionable media, like radio and television. With print media, however, most travel agencies do their own work. To accomplish this, they try to identify someone within the company who has some creative flair.

How do you recognize this?

The creative mind is curious. It wants to know things, to learn things. It enjoys expanding on the possible solutions to a problem or the possible extensions of an idea.

The creative person may be a trifle insubordinate, may not take well to rigid rules, may require a long time to come up with an idea, and may be hard to budge once this idea arrives. That's why it's wise to set some guidelines for creative people to work within—not a straitjacket but some reasonable estimates of budget and deadlines.

We all know, too, that you may work on something an entire day without getting a single idea. Then, when watching television that night, a great idea hits you. The creative mind often works best when open and uncluttered, or when thinking of something entirely different.

The travel manager should look around the office. If you are blessed with several employees, then try to determine which one has a little style in writing, or who has a facility to describe travel experiences, or who possesses a little artistic skill. If no one emerges, or if you run a one- or two-person shop, you may have to tackle the advertising writing yourself.

One consolation. You don't always have to be clever. Some of the best ads are pretty simple. If you have something good to sell and the price is right, all you have to do is get this story into words and pictures. You don't need funny headlines or powerful photographs, just the facts, interestingly stated.

The person who has the responsibility for creating the advertising should be given enough time to do the job, and some relative quiet to complete it. Perhaps this may be a chore for after hours. In any event, it shouldn't be something a consultant does between phone calls and counter duty.

# RESEARCH PRECEDES WRITING

Any good writing requires research. Even in our novels, we expect the details to be authentic; we want the author to do his or her homework. In nonfiction, this is even more essential. That's why writers spend time in libraries, or interviewing or traveling. Before they can tell their readers something, they must first know it themselves.

When copywriters in advertising agencies set out to describe a new product or service, they try to live with that item. They want to know how it's made, and how much it costs, and how it compares to the competition, and how durable it is, and what it does for the consumer. They may need to know how it's shipped, what its drawback are, whether it appeals more to women or to men, how it can be identified, what age of purchaser dominates, whether occupational factors influence purchase, and any other facts that help them understand what they are selling.

When writing travel copy, that means you must have some idea of who the person is who will be reading your ad, or viewing it, or hearing it. You must also understand the specific package you are selling.

Suppose, for example, you are advertising an Alaskan cruise. If you've taken this cruise yourself, that's a great start. If you haven't, you can read about it in travel and other literature, or you can talk with someone who has taken the trip. In reading and interviewing be alert for key words or phrases that fire the imagination. These form the language of advertising.

You must also know how this Alaskan cruise is priced. Is it higher or lower than competition? If higher, then how do you justify the extra expense? If lower, you can concentrate on savings.

What you develop in your mind is a mental picture of a prospect in contact with your ad. Who is this person? What questions does he or she have in mind, and how can you answer them in your copy? Perhaps all you can do in a limited space is arouse interest and get prospects to phone, write, or drop in for more detailed information.

It's a good idea to list all of the good points on a sheet of paper before writing the ad. Pull out the key phrases, too, and set them down: "Sail beneath towering glaciers," or "Cruise the ice blue fjords," or "Experience a fantastic northern world," or whatever other phrases seem to sing a little.

Writing copy for state or local tourist attractions requires detailed knowledge of the territory. Visiting the sites is one solution, but there are also library sources, material from chambers of commerce, newspaper morgues, and personal interviews. Again, you are looking for the unique and effective items, things that have tourism appeal. Movie theaters and bowling alleys are fairly universal, but a reconstructed fort or a great fishing lake or a string of casinos are still singular. Find the attractions, gather the details, then find ways to bring them to life in print, on radio, or on television. Some refer to one aspect of this process as "positioning," deciding *how* you will talk about this particular product or service, and to *whom,* and *where.* Writing, research, creativity, and placement converge.

## FOCUS YOUR ATTENTION ON THE PROSPECT'S NEEDS AND WANTS

Sometimes a travel agency has a tour it knows is superior in every way, from hotels and meals to sightseeing and price. But, when it is written up, the language appeals to other agents, not to the consumer. There are things about the tour that may make you feel good, but what do they do for the prospect?

## Day-by-Day Itinerary

**Sunday, May 9—OMAHA - NEW YORK**

Depart from Omaha this morning this morning with UNITED AIRLINES, connection with the early evening AER LINGUS flight to SHANNON. You'll hear your first brogue and get your initial taste of Irish hospitality aboard this scenic flight.

**Monday, May 10—SHANNON**

Arrive in Shannon this morning where you are met and transferred to the FITZPATRICK'S SHANNON SHAMROCK INN with the balance of the day at leisure.

This evening—a special Irish banquet to welcome you to this enchanting land.

**Tuesday, May 11—SHANNON**

Exciting tour of Ireland's most musical country. Visit the spectacular Cliffs of Moher, the resort town of Lisdoonvarna—then slip into County Galway to see William Butler Yeats' hideway castle, Thor Ballylee, and the classic ruins of Coole Park. An evening trip along the lovely shores of Lough Derg and stop in the famed Merriman Tavern.

**Wednesday, May 12—KILLARNEY**

South to Ireland's most famous locale, the Lakes of Killarney. Stop at Adare, through to Rathkeale, Newcastle West, Castleisland and Tralee to Dingle. Tour Dingle with lunch in Dingle Town. Stops at Dunquin, at Tomasin's pub and scenic areas. Evening is at leisure, with overnight at the KILLARNEY TORC HOTEL.

**Thursday, May 13—RING OF KERRY**

You will thoroughly enjoy this swing around the Dingle Peninsula, one of Ireland's most scenic and historic spots. Lunch at the Derrynane Hotel. Balance of day free for shopping, jaunting car rides and activities on your own. Special evening of folk lore. Overnight at the KILLARNEY TORC HOTEL.

**Friday, May 14—BLARNEY**

Leave Killarney and drive over beautiful country. Pass Daniel O'Connell's birthplace and residence. Lovely Glengarriff, favorite vacation spot for De-Gaulle, to mystic Gougane Barra, source of the River Lee and seat of Saint Finbarr's monastic settlement. A fresh salmon lunch at Johnny Creedon's country hotel in Inchigeela, then to Blarney for a castle tour and a chance to kiss the fabled stone. Overnight at the HOTEL BLARNEY.

**Saturday, May 15—WATERFORD**

Depart for Cork City, for sightseeing and shopping. Leaving Cork, follow the coast to Waterford, with a stop enroute, if possible, at the Waterford Crystal Factory. An evening of traditional Irish Music. Overnight at the WATERFORD ARDREE HOTEL.

**Sunday, May 16—GALWAY**

Time for church this morning before departure from Waterford via Carrick-on-Suir, to Cashel for a tour of the Rock, historic site dating back to the Sixth Century. Travel along the lake coast road via Puckane to Portumna, then to Galway with its lyrical bay. Dinner and overnight at the GREAT SOUTHERN HOTEL.

**Monday, May 17—CONNEMARA - GALWAY**

Today—a tour of rugged Connemara, with its lakes and hills. Stops at Kylemore Abbey and Clifden. Stops will be made at Celtic Crystal and Connemara Marble factories enroute. Overnight in Galway with a special program arranged for you.

**Tuesday, May 18—GALWAY**

This is a free day. We suggest a day-long trip to the Aran Islands . . . or shopping, or perhaps a long walk around the Bay. See the Gladdagh, Spanish Arches, or the islands made famous by John Millington Synge. You may choose to relax and simply enjoy a day without activity for rest. Overnight in Galway.

**Wednesday, May 19—ROSSES POINT**

Leave Galway this morning for Tuam and Knock, with a stop for a visit in Knock. On to Sligo, with a tour around Lough Gill before continuing your trip to Rosses Point.

An evening on Yeats this evening in one of Ireland's loveliest settings. Overnight at the YEATS COUNTRY HOTEL.

**Thursday, May 20—SLIGO - DONEGAL**

A morning stop at Drumcliffe, then to Bundoran, Ballyshannon, with a possible stop at the Beleek Factory if available, Donegal town and on to Killybegs. Circle Mullaghmore with Lord Mountbatten's modern castle; dinner at the hotel, with an evening visit to ELLEN'S PUB for traditional Irish Music.

Overnight at the YEATS COUNTRY HOTEL.

**Friday, May 21—DUBLIN**

Leave Sligo, via Carrick-on-Shannon to Cavan, Kells, with a stop at Navan. Continue to Dublin with overnight at the ROYAL DUBLIN HOTEL. Dinner at the hotel with an evening at the ABBEY THEATRE.

**Saturday, May 22—DUBLIN**

This morning a comprehensive tour of the city of Dublin. The afternoon is free for shopping or touring on your own. Lunch and dinner are both on your own today. The evening is free. Overnight at the ROYAL DUBLIN HOTEL.

**Sunday, May 23—DUBLIN**

Time for church services this morning. An afternoon drive to Glendalough, Avoca with a stop at Avondale. Return to Dublin along the scenic coastal route.

Tonight will be the gala CABARET evening—an experience to treasure.

**Monday, May 24—DUBLIN - NEW YORK - HOME**

**Fig. 6–1   Even copy for brochure itinerary can be made to sound inviting.**

Perhaps you're proud because your office has some fancy new computers for ticketing. Great; but what the client wants to know is "what does the computer do for me?" Tell him or her. It makes processing faster and saves time. It enables us to find travel options quicker, making your flight plans more efficient and direct.

Perhaps you managed to get a very low tour rate to Las Vegas, even though occupying a first-class hotel. Be sure the client knows what a good deal this is, and why.

Talk, then, in terms of the client's interests, and not your own.

Hotels, for example, may feature quick check-in or convenient location, while family attractions announce reduced rates and airlines advertise extra leg room or expanded schedules. The secret to effective copy is thinking in the reader's terms.

## SOME COPY TIPS FROM A TOP AGENCY

Ogilvy & Mather, one of the nation's top advertising agencies, has placed more than 200 million dollars' worth of travel advertising. They've worked with Lufthansa, Air Canada, American Express, Cunard Line, the United States Travel Service, and others. A few years ago they took out a full-page ad in such publications as *The Wall Street Journal* and *The New York Times* to expound on what they had learned about writing "travel copy that sells."

Here are some of their suggestions:

1. *Spotlight the unique differences.* Let people know why they'll experience something different on this particular trip. This stems from doing a good job of research. Ogilvy & Mather mentions discovering that Europeans weren't really interested in mountains and beaches when touring America; they have their own. What they want to see are sights like San Francisco and Disneyland and the Grand Canyon and Indian reservations and New York City.

   For every tour description you write—or for any general description of your travel services—try to ferret out the reason this offering is different.

2. *Facts are better than generalities.* In this age of inflation, this is more true than ever. People want to know what they are getting for their money. Spell it out. Some ads go into great detail on what the trip includes; others even include such details as the exchange ratio for the American dollar. It's better to say, "As Low as $760" than to write "Reasonably Priced."

3. *Give your advertising a big idea.* This ties in with the first point. The Ogilvy & Mather ad points out the great number of ads competing for attention in some of the metropolitan travel sections and adds that "if your advertisement isn't based on an idea that stands out from the crowd," you won't have a chance.

4. *Don't shy away from long copy.* Most ad copy tends to be short. Sometimes, however, you have a message that needs

more time and space. Give it this time or space. If it's interesting, people will read it.

5. *Copy should allay anxiety about going to a strange place.* Travelers worry about the food and water, the political situation, about how they should dress, how much they should tip. If you have space and time, set their minds at ease. Or at least have them write for other materials that will do the job.

6. *Use research to test provocative new ideas.* David Ogilvy once advertised tours to France by doing headlines in French. Everyone thought this was a dumb idea—except David Ogilvy. He was right. Readership went up twenty-four percent.

7. *Give your product a first-class ticket.* Take a look at some of the local travel advertising. Does it demonstrate quality—or ineptness? You wouldn't do business with a firm whose correspondence was sloppy and unattractive. Ugly advertising also repels.

8. *"Newsbreak" advertising can make news of its own.* If you have some announcement that is really news, feature it. If yours is the first trip to the interior of China, or if reduced fares have just been approved, make that the focus of the ad. The energy crunch, for example, gave rise to a number of ads stressing the saving of gas and featured everything from home-state vacations to backpacking trips.

9. *Bargains are still irresistible.* Note the headlines in many travel ads: "LAS VEGAS $99"; "EUROPE FOR ONLY $2200"; "THE INCREDIBLE (BUT TRUE) MINIVACATION IN VAIL AT $44 PER COUPLE." Ogilvy & Mather once ran an ad for the QE2 which began: "Sail to Europe regular fare—Sail home free." A unique way to announce half fares. In just over a week, they had sold out two round-trip crossings.

10. *Make your coupon the hero.* This is an interesting idea. Instead of putting the coupon at the base of the ad, Ogilvy & Mather sometimes placed it elsewhere, including at the top. They claim it tripled business for one client, American Express. There are some mechanical problems with this, of course. It makes it easier for people to cut out coupons when they are on a bottom corner—if you have the corner of the page. Newspapers should also take care that they don't run coupons back to back on two sides of a newspaper page. What Ogilvy & Mather has to say, however, has merit because it is different, and therefore attention-getting.

11. *Make the coupon a miniature advertisement.* Since many people read only the coupon in an ad, why not put some sell into the coupon, rather than merely allowing space for the signing of a name and address? Even a line like this is helpful: "Please send me all the exciting details of the 36 Winter Cruises now available." On occasion, travel agencies have made the entire ad into a coupon format.

12. *Go the whole hog.* This top advertising agency recommends devoting the whole ad to a description of what is being offered. If you are advertising a new brochure on Great Britain, for example, you might say: "Page 9 includes pictures and values of all British currency" and "Page 10 give a capsule history of London."

13. *Don't scorn that grand old word—"free."* Even though it's used often, the word "free" still gets attention. So do old standbys like "new" and "save."

14. *Caption your photographs.* If you use a photo in an ad, a brochure, or a newsletter, give it a descriptive caption, telling what it represents. Twice as many people read captions as read the rest of the body copy.

Ogilvy & Mather have other tips, too, but these are the ones relevant to copywriting.

## WRITING COPY

This is no easy chore. Some of this nation's literary greats couldn't write a decent line of copy to sell a product or service. It's a different way of writing. The sentences are usually short. Sometimes incomplete. Advertising copy moves rapidly and packs a lot into a short space. The trick is to be conversational in tone, while including all the essential information, and to do both in an interesting and provocative manner.

It's easy to get corny. Some people think good advertising consists of selecting cute lines from other ads and adapting them to their own use. Wrong! Good advertising writing is that which grows out of the special qualities of your product or service. You know all you can about the thing you wish to sell; you decide what you want to say; and you learn to say it well.

It does help to read other ads. These stimulate thinking and give you a feel for the language. It also helps to have a decent vocabulary, one that can think of other ways to describe mountains besides "snow-capped."

It also takes practice. Like everything else, you learn by doing, and the writer who's willing to keep at it will certainly improve.

Here are some additional general tips on copywriting from people who do it for a living:

- ❏ Be honest.
- ❏ Be consistent. If you have good campaign going, stay with it.
- ❏ Be sure the reader, listener, and viewer remember the name of the company—not just your witty premise.
- ❏ Reason with the consumer; don't pound at him.
- ❏ Dramatize consumer benefits.
- ❏ Visualize the entire ad as you write the copy.
- ❏ Humanize the writing.
- ❏ Don't let your own ego get in the way of objectivity when critiquing an ad you've done.
- ❏ Get used to writing against deadlines.
- ❏ Remember that much of your copy may not be completely understood and much of the rest will be forgotten. So make it simple and memorable.

## CONSTRUCTING THE PRINT AD

There's a formula for writing ad copy that has been around a long time but which is still valid. It's called the AIDCA formula.

In this formula, the acronym stands for the following:

| | |
|---|---|
| *A* | Attention |
| *I* | Interest |
| *D* | Desire |
| *C* | Credibility |
| *A* | Action |

What the ad tries to do first is get you to look at it; second, to provoke enough interest to get you to continue to read; third, to create a desire for the product or service; fourth, to convince you that the offer is genuine and fairly priced; and, finally, to provide some means of acting on your impulses, such as a coupon, phone number, or address.

Actually, this schedule of items works for any kind of ad, not only print advertising. If you think through the ad you have assembled, you might check to see that all of these items are covered.

## ELEMENTS OF A PRINT AD

Most print ads contain four parts: headline, illustration, body copy, and signature.

There are ads, of course, that get along with less than all four elements. Sometimes, as in certain cigarette advertising, you may have only a large illustration and the brand or company name. Sometimes the ad may be all headline and copy, without an illustration. Leaving off the signature (the brand or company name) would be rare, but there are some ads—Sunkist, for example—that include the name in the illustration and see no need to repeat it.

We'll examine illustrations later, and not much needs to be said here about the signature or logo, except that it should be in evidence, and that it should work together with the rest of the ad. Let's concentrate on headlines and body copy.

### Headlines

There are many ways to write headlines. There is even a monthly service that ad agencies subscribe to that lists, by categories, a number of the best current headlines.

The aim of a headline is to get you to notice the ad. However, it must relate to the illustration and copy and can't merely be a trick to gain attention. Readers will resent being fooled by a headline that really had nothing to do with the subject advertised.

The headline is the attention-getter in a print ad, serving the same sort of function as an opening sound effect in a radio spot. While the headline should have some relationship to the ad's theme and content, it may take on a variety of guises, including some of the following:

☐ *News.* A headline may announce some legitimate news or merely couch the message in a news format. This could be the statement of a fare decrease, dates of sailing, or the creation of some special hotel amenities.

HERTZ PRICES PLUNGE IN FLORIDA.

OPENING WEST MAUI AGAIN.
(Hawaiian Airlines).

❏ *Benefit*. While all advertising appeals should be benefit-centered, some build the headline on the promise of some unique feature, like more leg room on a plane, star quality entertainment on a cruise, or king-size beds at a hotel. These should be recognizable as real benefits and not merely advertising jargon.

> HYATT INTRODUCES NON-STOP SERVICE AT DFW.
>
> CHAMPAGNE BREAKFAST AT NO EXTRA COST.

❏ *Challenge*. This format is designed to shake up the casual reader.

> AMERICA, YOU'VE BEEN PAYING TOO MUCH TO TRAVEL.
> (Vacations to Go)
>
> WHICH ONE OF THESE LANGUAGES WOULD YOU LIKE TO SPEAK?
> (Linguaphone)

❏ *Command*. The proposition is boldly stated, almost like an order.

> BEFORE YOU CHOOSE A PANAMA CANAL CRUISE, RAISE YOUR EXPECTATIONS.
> (Holland American Line)

❏ *Curiosity*. This headline technique prompts the reader to continue with the copy in order to satisfy a created interest.

> THE ONLY AIRLINE TO HAWAII WITH AN ACTIVE VOLCANO ON BOARD.
> (Western Airlines)
>
> FIVE VERY RELEVANT QUESTIONS ABOUT TRAILWAYS LEISURE TRAVEL.

❏ *Promise*. Similar to a benefit, this headline makes a statement about what the travel supplier will do for a client.

> OTHER STATES PROMISE A GREAT FALL VACATION.
> MINNESOTA DELIVERS IT.
>
> WE DON'T TAKE OFF UNTIL EVERYTHING'S KOSHER.
> (El Al)

❏ *Advice*. This headline looks almost like a friendly tip.

DON'T SETTLE FOR MERE HAWAII.

CHOOSE A CRUISE YOU'LL ALWAYS REMEMBER.

❏ *Single out a group*. This is a good strategy, but must be combined with a knowledge of the demographic or psychographic makeup of the readers of this particular publication. You must know your audience and can then single it out.

ATTENTION TRAVEL AGENTS!

FOR THOSE ACCUSTOMED TO SUPERIOR SERVICE.
(Marriott)

FOR LOVERS ONLY—A POCONOS HONEYMOON.

Besides these general categories of headlines, there are also ways to play with words, giving them a freshness and appeal that command attention. Remember that readers are normally arrested by language that appears out of the ordinary or that attracts through style or syntax. These are not easy headlines to write, can quickly become corny, and sometimes have little relationship to the product.

❏ *Take-offs*. These headlines may echo a popular book or saying or provide some variation of a familiar phrase.

THE SMILE THAT LAUNCHED 8000 ROOMS.
(Hensley Hotels/Harley Hotels)

BOOK AUSTRALIA WITHOUT BEATING AROUND THE BUSH.
(Jetabout)

❏ *Double meaning*. Like the double entendres that can be interpreted in more than one way.

ONLY ONE HOTEL IS REALLY SHIPSHAPE.
(Hotel Queen Mary)

WAIT REDUCTION.
(Midway Airlines, Inc.)

❏ *Double take*. In the manner of the classic movie reaction, these headlines cause you to look again since you can't believe what you just read.

MORE AND MORE AMERICAN CITIES AREN'T EVEN
AMERICAN.
(American Airlines)

EUROPE ISN'T WHAT IT USED TO BE.
(TWA)

❏ *Contrasting ideas*. Two seemingly dissimilar notions are combined to drag readers into the explanation.

INTRODUCING A BUSINESS HOTEL THAT FEELS LIKE A
FRENCH INN.
(Hotel Sofitel)

AFFORDABLE LUXURY.
(Snappy Car Rental)

❏ *Modern speech or concepts*. This category may employ puns, jargon, foreign phrases, and other contemporary motifs.

SUNTHING WONDERFUL.
(Indiana)

THE FLIGHTMARE IS OVER.
(Ladeco)

DESERT CHIC.
(Sheraton Scottsdale Resort)

## Writing the Body Copy

Even though their names are seldom known outside the advertising profession, the top copywriters are, as a class, the most highly paid writers in America. If they're good, they deserve their high salaries. Their words are often read by far more people than digest a runaway best seller.

Copywriters know they must get attention quickly, that they must retain it through colorful and convincing prose, that they must accomplish this in as few words as possible, and that the message must result in an acceptable number of sales. This isn't literature, it's marketing, but any writer could learn from the demands of the advertising scribe.

Advertising writing is different from other forms of prose, however. Sentences are normally short and often incomplete. Punctuation is for emphasis as much as for grammatical accuracy. Words become sentences. Paragraphs start with "and" or "but." The tone is more conversational, catchy, compelling. Except when seeking a

The decks are strung with lights that soar high above the sea, framing the deepening indigo of the night.

Far below you, on the water, the reflection of a tropical moon scatters into a thousand glowing bits.

When evening comes, on a Royal Caribbean cruise, you'll see that all the romantic stories you've heard about cruising are absolutely true.

You'll sip a vintage Bordeaux, savor a perfectly prepared leg of lamb, indulge yourself in Cherries Jubilee flamed right at your table.

You'll watch the silent passing of a freighter, far out on the horizon. And dance under more stars than you ever thought the sky could hold.

And you'll find that the warmth of the islands lingers in your mind, long after the sun goes down.

So talk to your travel agent about a Royal Caribbean cruise. For seven, eight, ten or fourteen days.

After all, some things are just too good to be left to your imagination.

ROYAL ⚓ CARIBBEAN
*Song of Norway, Song of America, Nordic Prince, Sun Viking Ships of Norwegian Registry*

**Fig. 6–2  Copy portion of a two-page ad spread for Royal Caribbean, showing the power of language to convey feeling.** (Courtesy of Royal Caribbean Cruise Line)

rare kind of effect, the structure is concise and the pace rapid. Even when describing something relaxing and langorous, the wording remains more clipped than a travel article on the same topic.

The body copy links elements of the ad together: the headline, illustration, and logo. It carries the reader from the initial moment of interest through an expansion of this idea, through a series of convincing arguments, ending with some sort of suggested command and information on the sponsoring agency. This prose must flow logically and should be easy to understand.

*The party's never over on The Dolphin! The Dolphin is the exciting new way to cruise to the Bahamas. And there's no other 3- or 4-night cruise like it.*

*Paquet chefs. A French, American and Continental menu. Free red and white dinner wines. Roomy, modern cabins with every comfort and convenience from private bath to wall-to-wall carpeting.*

*The gracious Barbizon Restaurant. The colorful Rendez-Vous Lounge. The spacious Cafe Miramar. The lively Cine-Disco.*

*And more.*

Notice the short and incomplete sentences, the use of colorful foreign names to cause excitement, and the inclusion of words like "spacious" and "lively" and even our old friend, "free."

Here's another example:

*Eurailpass is a single convenient rail ticket good for First Class travel in 15 countries. On trains that are fast, frequent, comfortable, often luxurious. Sleep on a train, gain extra daylight hours for sightseeing. Stop off, if you like, at some intriguing spot and continue later. You also get free or discount rates on many boats, ferries, buses, all over Europe. All this at an unbeatable bargain.*

Just count the bits of information contained in these 66 words. At least a dozen are conveyed in this short space.

And a final example:

*In Goa, watch the women, silhouetted against a bronze sky, take their bright fish to market.*

*In Udaipur, eat in a palace. In Kashmir, live on your own houseboat. In the Himalayas, breathe the thinnest air on earth. In Agra, walk through the most beautiful building ever built.*

*India is huge and varied. And magical. You will not be the same after you see it. Air-India would like to take you there. On one of our many tours.*

Some of the copy tricks mentioned before are also found in these examples, plus they use a colorful language that paints pictures for the prospective traveler. These tours are made to sound like adventures. You might quibble with a few lines. Will readers know that the beautiful building in Agra is the world famous Taj Mahal? The copywriter is gambling that the audience he or she wants to attract will have this information or look it up.

Here are some capsule tips about copy:

❏ *Be clear.* The copy must make sense. Not every writer may be clever, but all can achieve clarity. Read the copy over a number of times to make certain nothing is left out and that nothing is ambiguous. Even good copywriters sometimes neglect to include an important detail (like a date or a price) or they leave some confusing language unexplained (like eligibility for a special rate).

❏ *Be current.* Unless the writer is attempting to recreate a mood of the past, the copy must speak to the audience of today. Slang is quickly dated and a literate travel public will find tired phrasing uninteresting and unconvincing.

❏ *Avoid cliches.* Overused combinations of words like "lofty mountains" and "foaming billows" belong in a museum. Copywriters should strive for fresh images and concrete pictures. "Whitewashed sugar cube houses" provides a mental snapshot, as does "a canopy of aging poplars."

❏ *Use the active voice.* The passive voice—where the object initiates action—is less forceful than the active voice. Instead of writing, "Considerable savings may be experienced by the tourist," say, "The tourist will experience considerable savings."

❏ *Write tightly.* This is an advertising must. You have a limited amount of time or space. Messages must be terse. You can't afford to say, "Since everything must come to an end sooner or later, it's imperative that the person wishing to take advantage of this special offer must send in this coupon as soon as reasonably possible." You should say: "Offer ends March 30. Act Now!"

❏ *Use the language of the reader.* You don't write "viaggiatory" when you mean "traveling frequently," and you don't use "contemporaneous" when you could say "current."

❏ *Key words come at the end of sentences and paragraphs.* You don't hide important ideas; you employ them to punctuate an idea. Think of the punchline of a joke. Not:

> *As you may have read, prices on our Caribbean tours are the lowest ever because of some cost saving devices we were able to implement.*

This is better:

> *Because of some cost-saving devices we've implemented, prices on our Caribbean tours are the lowest ever.*

Sometimes, for emphasis or clarity, you may mention the key idea at the beginning of the sentence or paragraph and repeat it at the end.

❏ *Write for the individual.* Don't try to visualize a mass audience, like the entire circulation of a magazine. Concentrate on writing for one or two people you can picture and trust.

❏ *Rewrite.* It's a truism that "there is no great writing, only great rewriting." Work should be reviewed, checked, changed, polished. Everything can be improved. That's why you should allow yourself ample time for a first draft and several rewrites.

## The Close

Advertising copy must have a close—a windup. Just like a personal sale. Note how the insurance or car salesman tries to get you to sign before you separate. An ad must accomplish the same thing.

> See your travel agent for details.
> Mail this coupon to us today.
> Write for a free brochure.
> Call your travel agent. Or call us collect at _____.
> Use this 800-number to phone for rates.

You may devise more attractive ways to state this information, but don't get carried away. The important thing is giving the reader a reference for action.

# DIFFERENT STYLES FOR DIFFERENT MEDIA

Many things affect the way a smart copywriter puts an ad together. An ad in your Sunday newspaper would be written a bit differently than one in the symphony program—or it should be. An ad for a Mediterranean cruise would use different language than an invitation to the Calgary Stampede. You make the feel and look of the copy fit the message.

In addition, you write differently for radio and television than you do for print media. We'll look at some scripts later but here are some things to remember about writing for the broadcast media:

❑ Radio copy is written for the ear. This means many things. It means you should avoid words that are hard to distinguish (chief may sound like cheap); avoid words that give announcers trouble ("A tour treasure of unforgettable instances"); and choose language that evokes pictures.

❑ Radio commercials should have strong openings to attract attention and strong closes to reinforce the memory. Important words or phrases should be repeated.

❑ Don't try to crowd too many ideas into a short message. Concentrate on one or two ideas and get them across. Don't scream at the listener; use conversational tones.

Television also has its peculiar writing demands.

❑ You must know the technical possibilities of this medium before you can write. You must know what the camera can and can't do. You must develop a sense of how long the talent must hold up the brochure, for example.

❏ Take it easy on the viewer. Not too many scene changes. Don't make your spot like those amateur slide shows that hurry through the weaker visuals. Simplify the spots.

❏ Let the visual or video portion carry the weight. Avoid wall-to-wall words. If the screen can show it, you don't have to say it. Someone suggested that scriptwriters and TV ad writers should be charged $2 a word. That would force them to be terse.

❏ Keep the time in mind. If you have thirty seconds for your spot, don't write one that takes forty seconds to deliver, forcing you to rush. And don't write forty seconds of copy for a sixty-second spot and drag it out.

❏ Finally, never forget that a television commercial is an interruption. The viewer didn't turn on his or her set to see it. Therefore, you should make it as interesting and entertaining as possible.

Other media also have their own copy restrictions. For outdoor billboards the message must be short—perhaps five words or so. The same is true for messages on novelties. Direct mail, which we'll examine in more detail in chapter ten, must do a more complete job, anticipating and answering the prospect's questions.

So, know the medium, its assets and liabilities, and learn how to handle the different challenges.

## VARIED FORMATS

Take a look at your local travel page or section. Most ads look the same, right? You'd think there was only one way to write an ad: start with a headline, add some body copy, stick in a coupon. Perhaps you'll insert some clip art from a mat service; or get really daring and put in a headline extender, or subhead, beneath the main headline.

There's no need to be this rigid. There are many ways to look at copy, particularly if you have a little space to work with. A copywriter, in fact, should be able to handle everything from catalogue copy to poetry, from humor to "slice-of-life" conversation, from technical jargon to street talk. Consider these possibilities, for example:

1. An advertisement could tell a story.
   *Doug MacKenzie's grandfather used to tell him about climbing Goat Fell on the Isle of Arran, but he never appreciated the story until he tried the climb himself. Arran is just one of the stops on this 14-day Scottish Highlands and Islands Tour . . .*
2. A print ad could feature two characters talking to each other, using cartoons or photos, balloons or captions, or a combination of these. The comic strip effect is very popular.
3. Sometimes pictures and captions tell the story, and travel, in particular, lends itself to this approach.
4. You could come up with some gimmick: a bit of verse, humor, or pseudohistory.

Obviously, these suggestions won't fit every case. They may not fit most cases. The point is, you shouldn't be afraid to experiment a little, if you want the reader's attention. See what other agencies in other cities do and see if you can't learn something.

In fact, you should keep a swipe file of ads, articles, and brochures you admire. All creative people do this. There are very few totally original ideas; most of them are adaptations from something else. You'll discover you can derive inspiration from the work of others and that their ideas could provide a clue to your own needs.

## ADS BUILT AROUND A PERSONALITY

A number of travel-related firms use recognizable people as spokespersons in their advertising. Hertz employs O. J. Simpson and Arnold Palmer; British Airways featured Robert Morley; resorts may use tennis or golf stars. You needn't be famous to achieve this status. One New York hotel chain showcases the wife of the owner. The personality should, of course, fit the travel product. Morley is obviously right for British Airways, and Simpson and Palmer offer a combination of speed and ease. Madonna might not be the right image for a posh hotel but she could be perfect for a Hollywood tour package. Copy for these spokespersons must feel and sound right and must be comfortable for them. Arnold Palmer, for example, would not work as a hard-sell pitchman.

Considerable research and discussion go into the selection of a spokesperson, and the job can be a lucrative one for the star, often reaching seven figures.

The local use of personalities is widespread in the advertising of special tours. The personality may be a travel consultant who's built a following and whose name means something because the prospective traveler knows he or she will have fun and be expertly handled. Another type of local personality is the individual who has some special expertise in an area, either geographical or professional. A person who teaches a wine-tasting course might be a natural choice to lead a trip through the vineyards of France; a professor of Slavic mythology might be just right for the Transylvania tour; and the director of the community playhouse should attract attention with a New York theater week. Some persons are also associated with an area because of their own heritage or their ethnic associations. Tourists would enjoy traveling with them because they feel they know the territory.

A third group of local personalities could be those men and women who have no particular knowledge of travel, or the area, or a specialized profession, but who offer prestige to the tour. The mayor or governor, perhaps; or a local television personality; or someone prominent socially.

In selecting the tour personality, the travel agent assumes some natural following and figures others will sign on as the result of promotion and conversation. Don't be misled into thinking everyone knows these individuals. The copy needs to explain why they are such good choices. Perhaps a brief paragraph about their qualifications is in order, or, at least, a title and come-on line.

The personality should also be willing to promote the tour, by writing letters, making appearances, or cooperating in other ways. Advertising alone should not be expected to carry the full load.

Again, in the copy, try to capture the personality of the individual and don't merely stick a name or picture in the ad.

(Delmar Publishers' *Handbook of Professional Tour Management* covers the qualifications and duties of tour leaders in more detail.)

## COMBINING TOURS IN AD COPY

You can get an argument from many travel agents as to the relative merits of featuring each tour individually or buying a larger space and combining offerings. Using one ad for one tour certainly saves confusion and, if you purchase several smaller ads in one edition of the newspaper, it also adds repetitive value. On the other hand, with so many small space ads in travel sections, the larger ad has a chance to dominate. It may also indicate to the reader that you have a comprehensive agency with multiple choices.

If you do opt for the combination ad, there are some things to look out for. Most of them deal with layout and will be covered in the next chapter, but some pertain to copy. First, you need some headline that embraces all of the items included; second, you need individual copy that is different but consistent. Frequently, one trip or service will dominate, and the others cluster around it. Third, the copy should have a theme. Are you selling price? Or featuring diversity? Or talking about seasonal options?

If the combination ad fails to work together, either graphically or in copy, you end up with a mess. And messy advertising never helps.


## SELECTING A FEATURE

As we'll see when talking about layout, something must dominate in every ad. The same is true of copy. Occasionally, this decision is easy to make. You may have an exclusive tour, or a special personality, or a reduced price. This factor would then receive prominence.

When such features aren't obvious, you must do a little thinking. This is when knowledge of the prospects helps, and when it's good to be attuned to all of the outside elements that affect travel. There are tours that focus on an escape from winter, or saving energy, or attendance at an event like the Olympics. Then there are those tours you offer every year and you are strapped to think of something new to say. This is when you go back to the basics; read, listen, think.

Bone up on the travel area itself, and read the professional journals for travel trends. Often an idea will just pop out. "Dance a Hornpipe in Killarney" might be a good way to lead into an Irish tour that features tourist participation. "You've Seen the Exhibit; Now See the Original" would be an attention-getter for an Egyptian visit.

Copywriters should also be good listeners. What are your clients and your friends talking about? What ideas and concerns are uppermost in their minds? What sort of adventures are they looking for? In retail sales, the advertising department people always check with clerks who sell the merchandise to learn what customers are saying. Travel agents should do the same, particularly if charged with writing advertising copy.

After you've absorbed this information, take a little time to think. If you're always saying, "Is it Tuesday already? I've got to get that ad copy together before noon," you're just wasting money.

## COUPONS

Coupons are bigger than ever. Virtually every business uses them at one time or another. In travel, they are indispensable. You rarely have enough space to tell your whole story. You need to provoke sufficient interest to get prospects into your agency, or to move them to write for further information. You have to make this easy for them.

Coupon copy is fairly standard. You need room for name and address and, sometimes, a phone number. You may also need a lead-in line requesting a certain publication or even a check list if promoting more than one brochure. It's a good idea to put your own name and address on the coupon, too, since the reader may cut it out, separating it from the ad, and then be unable to remember where it should be sent.

Some maddening things are done by inept advertisers when it comes to coupons. They are so small that even the smallest type won't work effectively within the space given. They are located in the middle of a page and can't be readily extracted. Some advertisers, dominated by an unthinking artist, have produced coupons in reverse, white on black. You'd need a white pen to fill them out! Others, who are more aesthetic than rational, give coupons all sorts of shapes, from hearts to national outlines. These are the devil to cut out.

Keep in mind that the reason for the coupon is to make it easy for the individual to respond. Everything you do to diminish this ease just reduces returns. Think of this copy and layout feature as being very functional.

## TELL 'EM WHO YOU ARE

Those advertisers who produce white-on-black coupons have cousins who forget to tell the reader who sponsored the ad or how the reader can get in touch with them.

Every ad must have the name of the sponsoring firm, its address, its branch offices (if pertinent), and its phone number. You might also include office hours, logo or design that identifies the firm, and any slogan that is part of the agency's image.

Some companies use globes, ships, airplanes, kiosks, crowns, monograms, and other devices to identify themselves. Airlines often favor abstract designs connoting comfort and efficiency; resorts may incorporate floral symbolism; hotels are fond of clean logos and ornate lettering.

Slogans are often fairly ordinary. "We care for you," or "Ready when you are," or "We know the territory." Even so, slogans serve a purpose in terms of identity and may add to the institution's image. United Air Lines was the first to announce "the Friendly Skies," and, while that slogan may not stand detailed scrutiny, it serves its purpose and it belongs to United. Besides, constant repetition can make any slogan memorable.

Any form of writing takes practice, and copywriting is no exception. Reading the work of others also helps.

Still, there is no substitute for the combination of solid research into the unique features of a travel product and the creative mind of the experienced wordcrafter.

## CHAPTER HIGHLIGHTS

❑ The creative mind is relatively rare. If the skills aren't available at the organization, it pays to seek professional help.

❑ Before a word is set on paper, sufficient research should be gathered to discover and support the selling proposition.

❑ The key to good copywriting is to concentrate on consumer needs and wants and on ways of satisfying them.

❑ Ad experts at Ogilvy & Mather counsel copywriters to spotlight the unique difference; use facts rather than generalities; focus on a big idea; use long copy if required; allay anxiety; test ideas; give the ad a professional look; make news; headline bargains; feature coupons; tell the whole story; use proven language, like "free"; caption photos.

❑ Copywriters advise newcomers to be honest, consistent, reasonable, dramatic, human, and objective.

❑ Print ads conform to the AIDCA formula, which stands for Attention, Interest, Desire, Credibility, and Action.

❑ There are four elements of a print ad: headline, illustration, body copy, and signature.

❑ Headlines have various forms but all are designed to capture the attention of the busy reader. Among the kinds of headlines are those that convey news, benefit, challenge, command, curiosity, promise, advice, and those that specify an audience. Also effective are headlines that employ techniques like takeoffs, double-meaning language, double takes, contrasting ideas, and modern concepts.

❏ Body copy is terse, colorful, clear, fresh, personal, and conversational.

❏ Different media require different modes of writing. Radio copy is written for the ear; television copy combines the potential of sight and sound.

❏ Print copy not only offers a variety of graphic formats, it also admits many copy formats, like news, cartoons, photos and captions, or even a maverick approach, like verse or humor.

❏ Large corporations and small agencies may both use personalities in their ads to attract attention and to communicate some feature the client wants to get across.

❏ Among the miscellaneous aspects of advertising that deserve consideration are combining a number of tours in a single ad, the feature item as a focal point, and judicial use of the coupon.

❏ Logos and slogans identify travel entities.

■             ■             ■

## ❏ EXERCISES

1. Find the following:
   a. Two travel print ads with copy you admire, and two with copy you think fails. Comment on each.
   b. Two clever headlines in travel advertising.
   c. Four different styles of coupons, all in travel ads.
2. Respond to three different travel offers of brochures and information and compare and evaluate replies.
3. Select a specific tour or specific country and draft a research plan for getting information preparatory to developing an advertising campaign. Using some of these resources, type or write out a copy platform, spelling out what you are going to say.
4. List five tips for writing travel copy as outlined by Ogilvy & Mather and explain what each means. Bring in an example to support each point.

# ❏ *CASE PROBLEMS*

*1. Get a travel brochure from a local travel agency, or gather material from travel guides and other sources. With this information, write 150 words of copy and write a headline for this tour or trip. Imagine that this copy will be used in a 2-column by 8-inch print ad in the Sunday edition of the largest newspaper in your state. Indicate what the illustration will be and, if appropriate, indicate the logo. However, do not lay out the ad; this exercise asks only for the copy.*

*2. Find a print ad on a restaurant or hotel and, using the same copy points, turn this into a 30-second radio commercial or a 30-second television commercial. Remember the differences in the various media but also remember you are trying to address the same general target audiences with the same general approach.*

# 7

# THE DESIGN OF PRINT ADVERTISING

In addition to being able to write sparkling copy, the person who handles advertising for a travel agency must also be adept at visualizing the ad. This person must be able to see how the ad will look.

In fact, even as the writing is being done, there should be some concept of the physical structure of the ad. Both copy and layout work together to produce an appealing message.

## THE PRINCIPLES OF DESIGN

Some aspects of design are natural. The careful hostess arranges her table in a pleasing pattern. Pictures are arranged on a wall in a manner that looks right. We do many things unconsciously that are really the result of an impulse toward decent design.

In laying out an ad, we stick with the same principles. Layout means the attractive arrangement of all elements within a certain space. Those elements are the headline, illustration, body copy, and signature. All must work together.

This text can't make an artist out of you, but it can introduce you to some basics that can be employed in doing at least a rough copy of an ad that can be shown to an artist for finished work or given to the newspaper's art department to complete.

### Line

There are no lines in nature. The horizon, for example, is purely an illusion and distant objects that appear to be sharply defined by lines are really three dimensional.

In art—and in layout—the line is the first element. It's the basic tool. Horizontal lines are generally restful; vertical lines aspiring;

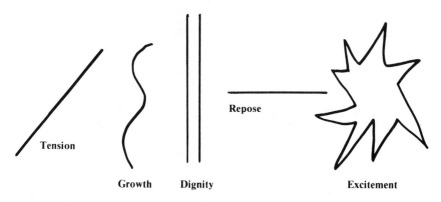

Fig. 7–1   The basic element in art is the line, which can convey a variety of moods.

wavy lines indicate growth or beauty; diagonals show stress or tension. A stack of lines of the same dimensions is boring; a stack of different length lines is more interesting. Lines, then, can do many things.

## Shapes

Three basic shapes are used in all design: the rectangle, circle, and triangle. These can become boxes, tubes, stars, elipses, TV-screen contours, pyramids, or any other shape you can think up, plane or solid.

Look at any work of fine art. In it you'll note that, although subtly rendered, the basic forms are the three mentioned above. These shapes are interwoven, overlapped, balanced, repeated, and they make up an artistically pleasing effect.

When layout artists begin their design, they often experiment with these shapes, placing them in different relationships, then flesh them out into the results they want. See Figure 7–2 for examples of travel ads in which you can see the trio of basic shapes.

## Harmony, Sequence, and Balance

The lines and shapes must still be arranged in a way to attract and delight the reader. This takes some talent and a lot of practice. If the designer fails to execute this task properly, the result looks cluttered, uneven, or disconnected.

**Fig. 7–2  The three geometric elements (circle, triangle, and rectangle) are seen in these two print ads.** (Courtesy of Japan Air Lines and Delta Queen)

This is where the artistic principles of harmony, sequence, and balance come in. They characterize music and literature, as well as oil paintings and sculpture. They also characterize good layout.

Harmony means a pleasing relationship among all the elements. We are used to this as a musical term, meaning that the various voices work together for a unified effect. In art (and layout) this term means that colors blend, typefaces work together, and everything looks as if it belongs in the same ad.

Sequence refers to the flow of an ad, the way our eye travels through the space. Generally speaking, our eye first lights on an area about a third of the way from the top of the ad. Notice how many good ads feature something in that spot. From here you might move through the copy to the coupon or logo.

If there is something exceptionally appealing in another part of the ad—a photo or a large price—we could go there first. Our eyes

The beauty of Sandestin is that we offer everything you need for a great vacation. A sugar-white beach, superb dining, 36 holes of golf, 16 tennis courts including grass and a 98-slip marina. Call your travel agent, or call 800-874-3950 toll free. In Florida call 904-267-8150. Before another day goes by.

**Sandestin Beach Resort**
Hwy. 98 East, Destin, Florida 32541

It's a beautiful day at Sandestin.

**Fig. 7–3 An example of informal balance, this Sandestin Beach Resort ad also demonstrates sequence (with the line of sight through the central figure to the copy) and harmony (the colors of the original are all warm tones). This also fits the "picture window" format.** (Courtesy of Sandestin Beach Resort)

would then follow a different route. But there should be some logical flow from one element to another.

The average person spends more time (60 percent) looking at the top of a page or the top of an ad than at the bottom (40 percent). The area with the longest attention span is the upper left quadrant. Obviously, if everyone laid out ads based on this principle, it would be a dull world. Ads succeed because they are different, but it's still wise to be familiar with reader's habits.

Balance is an element we're all familiar with. We look at pictures on a wall and see that they are out of balance. We align magazines on a coffee table.

Think of a teeter-totter in a park. If two persons of equal weight sit on each end, the teeter-totter is in perfect balance. However, this arrangement is not too interesting. More interesting would be a lighter person on one end, balanced by a heavier person close to the fulcrum.

We call the first situation formal or symmetrical balance; all elements on one side of a painting or layout nearly mirror those on the other. Informal or asymmetrical balance occurs when a heavier object on one side is balanced by an interesting item on the other, or by an area of vivid color, or some other device. Good design uses both kinds of balance, but the asymmetrical is preferred. See Figures 7–3 and 7–4 for examples.

## SOME LAYOUT PRINCIPLES

1. Don't forget that the copy if part of the layout. Squint at the copy block, seeing it as almost a solid. It should fit right into the ad in terms of harmony, sequence, and balance. Usually a rectangle, the copy could also be a triangle or circle.
2. Something must dominate in the ad. Perhaps it's the illustration, the headline, an oversized price tag, even the logo. If every element in the ad is given equal emphasis, nothing stands out and the ad is monotonous.
3. The rules of composition come with practice and with study of the work of others. If you can learn how to take good slides of your trips, you can learn to apply these same principles of composition to ads.
4. The rules of proportion also apply to layout. We talk about well-proportioned people and well-proportioned design. A 3″ x 3″ ad, for example, is blocky and dull. Better to do a 3″ x 5″.

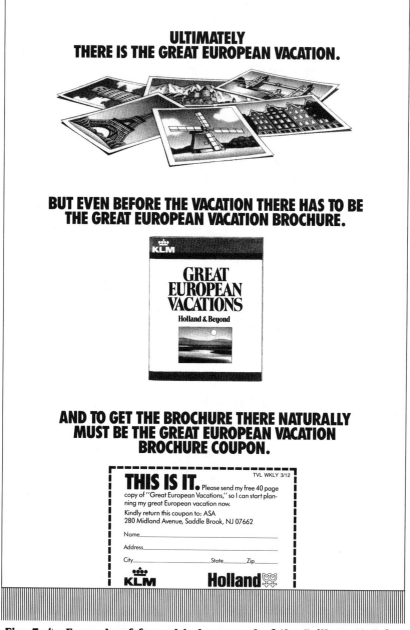

**Fig. 7–4 Example of formal balance and of the "silhouette" format.** (Courtesy of KLM and the Netherlands Board of Tourism)

The proportion is more pleasant. In fact, the ratio of 5 to 3 is supposed to be the most attractive relationship. Part of this, like other things in layout, comes from experience.

5. Remember that people read from left to right. That's how the comic strips are arranged. Ads usually read this way, too. If you have a person's face in the ad, for example, the eyes would be directed into the copy and not away from it. Heads would also be moving into the copy and not seeming to pull away from it.

6. Don't be afraid to leave a little white space—an area without any copy or illustration in it. That helps set off the other elements, and also gives the eyes a little rest.

7. Avoid the following:
   a. Visual cliches, like piggy banks for "save," and mortar board for "smart" and a policeman for "stop." These are corny and mark you as old-fashioned.
   b. Headlines that run vertically or diagonally are very hard to read. Don't fool around with these odd angles. The same is true of coupons that slant sharply.
   c. A cluttered look with too many items in too small a space.

## FROM ROUGH TO FINISHED AD

The professional layout person doesn't start by carefully drawing in every line in the ad or brochure. He or she does what is called a thumbnail, a quick, small sketch, just to see how the main elements in the ad might look. The artist will do dozens of these within a few minutes, to get a feel of what works and what doesn't.

Once the artist has something that looks promising, he or she will do a rough, a more finished sketch in which the elements are more well-defined. From here, the layout moves to the comprehensive or "comp" stage, which is a finished rough, a quality piece of art with the illustration clearly indicated, and the copy lines drawn in. This is ready to show to the client (see chapter eight).

If the client approves, the ad then moves from the comp to the final stage. Type is set, the photo taken or illustration drawn, and the whole thing pasted up, camera ready, to be shot and made into a printing plate.

Retail advertising may not be done this way. The large drug store and department store ads you see may be laid out full size, and various drawings and prices moved around and pasted down in what look like the appropriate spots.

You might do this with a travel ad, too. Suppose you were using the same general format week after week. There would be no real need for a rough. You'd just see what copy fit the design you had adopted.

The travel agent would not go to finished art, either—not like the professional layout person. If the travel consultant has any talent, he or she might get the ad to the rough stage, supply the copy and art or other elements, and turn the whole thing over to the newspaper ad department. They then do the finished ad, pull a proof for the client's approval, then make the finished plate for reproduction.

It's not wise to change an ad every week. There is great value in continuity and familiarity. At the same time, an ad that hangs around for a year or more begins to look old. Experiment with different formats and vary your ad from time to time.

## SOME AD FORMATS

There are any number of ad formats, but most fit into one of nine basic layout patterns. Not all of these work for travel agency advertising, primarily because of limited space, but aspects of them can be used on occasion, either in print media or direct mail by both small and large travel firms.

These nine designs are

❏ *Picture window* (Figure 7–3). This format features a large photo onto which copy or heads or logos are superimposed. Many beer and cigarette ads use this style. It is, in fact, the most common layout format for national advertisers.

 The nature of the picture determines where the type goes, and there is usually very little copy.

 When superimposing the type, don't put black type on a dark background or reverse (white) type on a light background. And don't put any type on a busy background, so that it can't be read.

❏ *Mondrian* (Figure 2–4). Named after the famous Dutch painter, this format follows Mondrian's technique of using different sizes of rectangular patterns in his art. More common in magazines than newspapers (but suitable to both), this format relies on good proportion.

The uneven blocks may contain illustrations, type, headlines, or mere color blocks. Sometimes the blocks abut each other; sometimes they are divided by light or heavy lines.

When setting something like this up, just pencil in the horizontal and vertical lines lightly until you get the effect you want.

The Mondrian layout can sometimes be useful in featuring a number of tours.

□ *Frame* (Figure 7–5). This is also a common format, particularly in newspapers, and is a favorite of travel agencies. It consists of the usual ad elements encompassed by some sort of border. While a handy design, the border does confine copy and limits the overall space.

□ *Typeface* (Figure 14–2). In this format, large headline type is the star. This is not too common for travel agencies because it leaves little room for details.

□ *Multipanel* (Figure 7–6). Unlike the Mondrian format, the panels in this ad are all the same size, much like most comic strips. These panels can be used to tell a story in sequence (with balloons or captions for copy) or can show different features of a product or tour. The panels usually run left to right, but can also run vertically.

The multipanel layout is also used to repeat elements of an ad, or even to repeat the ad itself. This has its own eye-catching effect.

Some advertisers have long favored the idea of running the same small ad throughout a publication, to gain the advantage of repetition. This format can attain some of this goal within a single ad.

□ *Copy heavy layout* (Figure 7–8). This is one in which the copy dominates. This may be because there is a lot to say, or because the message is complicated. Insurance companies and realtors use this format a great deal. So do many travel agencies.

While not particularly attractive, even a copy heavy ad can have style. Small illustrations may break up the copy or there may be subheads or other dividing devices.

The copy heavy ad may also stand out on a page where all the other ads are picture window or Mondrian layouts.

If the subject is of interest and the writing good, a prospect will read long copy.

❑ *Silhouette layout* (Figure 7–4). All of the elements form a silhouette. You may have to squint your eyes to see this. An irregular silhouette works better than one which is regular. The silhouette ad may be an actual silhouette or it may just resemble this shape when viewed overall.

Often, one of the edges of the silhouette will touch the side of the ad, just to keep the form from slipping away from the viewer, and from invading nearby white space. To gain the effect, imagine all of the areas blacked in, including the type.

❑ *Circus layout* (Figure 7–7). This never wins any advertising prizes, but it can sell goods and services. It's loud, brash, full of reverse blocks, starbursts, and other features. Price is often the focus. A grocery store ad is a prime example. There's a great deal of variety in a circus ad, but there still has to be some rationale to the design, and something has to dominate.

❑ *Rebus layout* (Figure 13–4). This gets its name from its similarity to those old puzzles where a picture substituted for a word. Of course, the ad can't be a puzzle; it has to communicate. So the text is sort of wrapped around the illustrations, which may be of varying size.

On occasion, you'll have only pictures and captions.

Many of these formats are used in combination. You'll see a picture window ad combined with a typeface ad, or a frame with a copy heavy ad. The nature of the message should have some influence on the choice of format. The space and the character of the surrounding ads will also affect your ad. It's fun to experiment with different ways to solve the layout problem, just as it's interesting to try various copy styles.

## WORKING IN SMALL SPACE

One of the difficulties with many courses in advertising is that students are invariably given large spaces to work in—full or half spaces. Upon entering the profession, they may have to confine their creativity to a few inches. This is a tough assignment.

After all, if budget were no problem and you could hire the finest photographers and select the most distinctive typefaces and pur-

**Fig. 7–5   Novotel uses a striking and simple "frame" format.** (Courtesy of Novotel/New York, A Division of Accor)

chase the largest available magazine or newspaper space, you should be able to come up with something that at least attracts attention. It' a challenge when you have to come up with a 2-column, 3-inch ad that contains all you want to say, and do it artistically.

Working in small space means that you have to minimize copy. You learn to condense. Your headlines must also be brief, and any illustrations must be small. You'll stay away from photographs because, even on magazine stock, they won't show up well. In the newspapers, they'll be blurred. You may not always have room for a coupon and must settle for an address and phone number.

You'll probably try to reach the public either through a clever headline or an unusual shape. You could also opt for some white space, cutting down on copy, but raising readability.

Notice the way the advertisers in Figure 7–9 have used a limited space.

**Fig. 7–6  Hertz employs a "multipanel" layout approach and features price, a key element in marketing rental cars.** (Courtesy of Hertz System, Inc.)

**Fig. 7–7   A good example of a "circus" layout. Again, price gets major emphasis. This is a 2-color ad, with the heads and firm name in red.** (Courtesy of Jetset Tours)

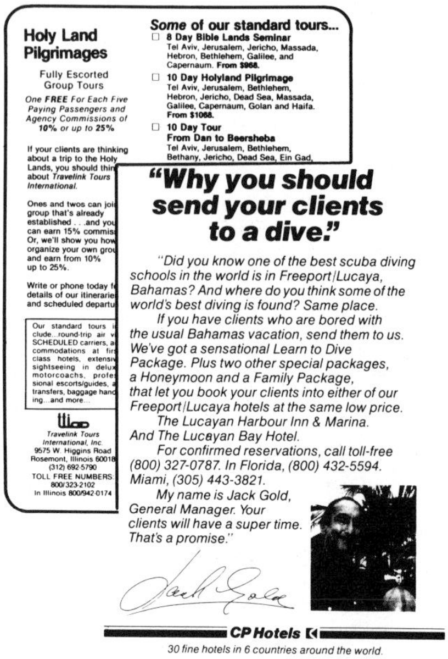

**Fig. 7–8  Example of a "copy heavy" format. For examples of other formats, see Fig. 2–4 (Mondrian), Fig. 13–4 (Rebus) and Fig. 14–2 (Typeface). (Courtesy of Travelink Tours and CP Hotels)**

# MAKE YOUR AD STAND OUT

Take a look at the travel pages of *The New York Sunday Times* or any other metropolitan newspaper. Or, for that matter, the travel pages of much smaller communities. What do you see? Ads crowded together, and dozens of small space advertisements competing for attention. Imagine one of these on the artist's drawing board, alone. It looks great, attractive, eye-catching. Then it disappears in that sea of similarity.

What can you do about this?

One of the old advertising truisms is that "if you're standing and everyone else is dancing, you're noticed." That means you don't have to be flashy, just different.

If the page you normally appear on is full of ads with reams of copy, try an ad with lots of white space and an open look. If the ads are all black on white, experiment with the reverse. How about using some unusual type or giving your ad a border that sets it apart? Or an illustration that forces the scanning eye to stop?

Notice what others are doing and imagine your ad placed among them. Then devise a way to render yours just a bit different. Like the motionless dancer, it will stand out.

**Fig. 7–9   The advertiser must always consider how the individual ad will look when sharing space with other ads, but this shows that small space ads can work.** (Courtesy of Black Mountain Ranch, Colony Club, Caribbean Club, Montego Bay Club, Half Moon, Far Horizons, Traveluxe, Pavilions and Pools, Estes Park, Hampshire House Hotel, Sitzmark Ski Lodge, Vail Reservations Inc. and Simson Bay Beach.)

## TYPOGRAPHY

As mentioned earlier, copy is not only informative, it can also be decorative. It's an essential part of the layout.

Copy is communicated via type, such as you are reading in this book. In the next chapter we'll talk about measuring and fitting type. In this chapter we look at the various styles of type available to you.

While there are hundreds of different designs of type and varieties of sizes for each design, type is generally divided into five broad categories:

❏ *Roman.* The basic typeface that has the small serifs or extensions at the end of the major strokes. These serifs make reading easier, particularly for longer articles. This is an example of a Roman typeface:

# abcdefghijklmnopqr stuvwx ABCDEFGH IJKLMNOPQR 1234

❏ *Block.* Sometimes called Gothic or sans-serif. The typeface has no serifs, making it harder to read over a long stretch, but giving copy a more modern look. Here's an example of the block letter:

# abcdefghijklmnopqrstuvwx yz ABCDEFGHIJKLM NOPQRSTU 12345678

❏ *Text.* This is the Old English effect seen on diplomas and some tea shops. Rarely effective for body copy but could be used in headlines.

abcdefghijklmno

JGHIJKLMN

123456

□ *Script.* This typeface resembles handwriting and gives an ad a more delicate or elegant look. It would be good, perhaps, for a honeymoon ad but less effective for a football excursion. You see this style used often in invitations. When the letters are not connected to each other, that form of script is called cursive. Here is an example of script:

abcdefghijklmnopq
rstuv ABCDEFGH
IJKLMNOP2RSTU

□ *Ornamental.* This category has the most variations. It could be anything from an Old West saloon look to the balloon lettering seen in displays. Here are some examples:

ABCDEFGHIJKLMNOP
abcdefghijklmnopqrstu
ABCDEFGHIJKLMN
abcdefghijklmn

There are more than a thousand different typefaces in use today and more are entering the market every day. This fact may not mean much to you unless you are in a major city where selection is vast. In most places, the variety will be limited. The travel advertiser should see what's available locally by requesting a type book or type specimen pages. If you absolutely need something else, you can try in larger nearby cities, or order type by mail. This, however, gets expensive. It's better to try to live with what you have, unless the choice is dismal.

As you'll note from the previous samples, and see even better by leafing through a magazine, each typeface has a different feel to it. This becomes quite important in travel advertising, since different countries also have a special feel to them. The type you'd choose for a headline for Mexico might be totally different than one for France. An American tour would look and feel different from an African safari. As much as possible, the type—particularly of the headline—should support this feeling.

Another caution is that the body copy should be compatible in type with the headline. This doesn't mean they must be the same, just compatible. You wouldn't normally use a Roman headline for a Block letter copy block, and you wouldn't use an Old English head for a Roman copy block. There are exceptions, of course, but this is the rule.

The advertiser should avoid mixing too many different typefaces. A couple of faces in one ad are usually enough. Five or six different faces stamp you as an amateur.

**Fig. 7–10  The type selected should look right for the subject of the ad.**

As with other things, keep samples of type that you like and see if they may be found in your hometown shops. After a while you'll get so you know what looks good and know what you can rely on. Typography, however, is a real science, and few people in advertising really master it. You don't have to get so good that you can immediately recognize size and family of type; all you really need to know is what looks right, and how it will fit your ad.

## ILLUSTRATIONS

If you have someone on your agency staff who can handle art—commercial art—that would be nice. Most agencies lean on newspaper art departments, art supplied by carriers and others, or on clip art. Clip art is furnished at a fee by an art service. These illustrations come in books assembled by categories like holidays, groups, sports, or travel. Virtually all of these are line art, meaning that they can be reproduced without "screening" like you'd screen a photo; they are simply made up of lines.

In such a travel clip art book you might find familiar symbols like the Eiffel Tower, the Pyramids, a cruise ship, couples running with suitcases, exotic foreigners, and other items. There would be several different books under the category of travel, and new ones are added periodically.

Even so, one of the detriments of clip art is that it begins to look familiar. Others can also buy and use it, so the originality is lost. However, it is cheap. You can buy a book full of illustrations for $5 or $10, which is far less than you would pay for a single illustration if you had it drawn at an art studio. When you come to something like a logo, which is going to be with you for a long time, it makes sense to use an art studio and not try to find something out of a book. Figure 7–11 is an example of line art from an instant art book.

You should also check to see what art is available from airlines and cruise ships and international tourist bureaus. They often have items you can adapt to your use. You'll also see travel agencies that lift sketches right out of magazine ads or brochures. You should not do this without written permission.

You'll also see references to mat services, which means that, instead of illustrations coming on regular coated paper, these will provide molds made of heavy paper (almost cardboard), rubber, or plastic. They are used just as any mold. Metal is poured into them at the newspaper or magazine and the resultant metal plate is used in

**Fig. 7–11   Instant art books provide ready-made illustrations and layouts for firms that have no art departments or ad agencies.** (Courtesy of Louis Mercurio Associates)

the printing process. The reason for using mats and not metal plates is because the mats are much lighter and more efficient to ship. The use of mats, however, has diminished, since most publications are printed by the offset method.

Illustrations should be appropriate to the theme of the ad. If you are promoting a light-hearted cruise, the graphic touch should also be light. Sometimes a cartoon works better than a heavy photo-like illustration. There are also trends in advertising art, with some techniques returning as part of our nostalgia craze.

You cannot, of course, just cut out an illustration and use it in your ad, unless you've paid for it or secured permission.

## PHOTOGRAPHY

The first word to be said here is that, if the photography isn't good, forget about it. Don't wait for the terrific slides from someone's brother-in-law and don't rely on an amateur to perform a critical photo assignment for you. Get a professional. It's cheaper in the long run.

Photography is used primarily in feature stories, magazine advertising and, rarely, in large newspaper advertising. Slides are also used in special presentations, television programs, and exhibits. Both slides and prints may be used in brochures or other printed materials.

You've seen company publications where black-and-white photos were out of focus, poorly composed, or inexpertly cropped. While this may look cute and please those who are featured, it leaves a negative impression on an external audience. Anything you use should be the best you can get.

In general, you want photos with high contrast, so that they'll reproduce. These pictures with grainy textures that sometimes win photo contests are no good for your purposes. Wherever possible, include people in the pictures. Ogilvy & Mather recommends "Photograph the natives, not the tourists." Normally, this is good advice. Readers would rather see Croats in colorful dance costumes than look at Americans watching Croats in colorful dance costumes. There could be exceptions to this. If you wanted to show the variety of things a tourist might participate in, of course you'd show the traveling American.

If used in an ad, the photo, like the headline, must tie into the general idea. If it needs explanation—and most do—give it a terse and interesting caption. Try to avoid the show-and-tell caption where you depict the Leaning Tower of Pisa and say below: "Begun in the 12th century, Italy's Leaning Tower of Pisa survived World War II virtually intact." Also, that line could be shorter.

When would you choose a photo over a piece of art? First, you'd have to have enough space and be sure the reproduction would look good in the medium you chose. Then you'd want to be certain that the photo did what you wanted it to do and was not merely decorative.

Photos have more immediacy than illustrations and are more believable. Seeing a photo of Victoria Falls is better than looking at a drawing of that landmark. You can also do tricks with photos that leave shock value, whereas the reader knows anything is possible with a drawing.

Most photographs you'll need will be available from suppliers. Some could also be in the newspaper or magazine morgue (file), and you may have compiled your own cache of pictures. In addition, just as with clip art, there are stock photo houses, where you can purchase photos in a variety of categories. These are not cheap, although they are cheaper than tackling most projects yourself. They also suffer from familiarity, a certain stiffness, and are often dated. Remember that things like dress and car styles change frequently, so the photos must mirror that change.

As with layout, try for something different in photos. Perhaps a different angle, or people doing different things (and not staring at the camera with a handful of souvenirs), or some exciting action. While the photo may also serve to illustrate or inform, its main purpose is to attract attention, like the headline.

## THE LOGO

This is your signature, or company motif, or emblem. It may merely be your company name in distinctive type, or it could be a piece of art that includes the company designation.

Whatever you choose should be pertinent, attractive, readable, and flexible. Consider how it will look in an ad, on a letterhead, on your window, on luggage, on television, on brochures, and even on novelties. If you intend to use color on occasion, reflect on how this logo will look in either color or black and white.

Try to be original and distinctive, and avoid being trite, imitative, or corny. Look at some of the travel agency logos. Some are good; most aren't. With a little thought you can stand out in this field.

If possible, an agency should employ an artist to design this symbol. Before you take this step, however, do a little thinking on your own. The more direction you can give the artist, the more economical the assignment. If the artist has to doodle around for days, coming up with samples you reject, the bills will mount. At $35-$75 an hour, it doesn't take long for a massive art bill to accrue. Explain what your company is and what it tries to do, suggest some concepts you'd like to see in the logo, and then let the artist do some roughs.

Some companies feel so strongly about their logos that they spend $25,000-$50,000 and more designing just the right item. This is beyond the reach of travel agencies but some expenditure is justified because of the long life and multiple use of this symbol.

## THE USE OF COLOR

For nearly all travel agencies, color is not a major consideration. Few advertisers would use it in newspapers and not many travel agencies employ magazines as a medium. In brochures, direct mail, outdoor advertising, and other media, some color might be used. This makes it worthwhile to consider a few aspects of color.

Like type, color has its own properties and its own abilities to affect the viewer. Note how major advertisers use color. Some cigarettes employ darker, redder, warmer tones, to emphasize the masculine image of the product. Many filter cigarettes are heavy on greens, suggesting a cool, cleaner smoke.

Obviously, when it can be used, color enhances the marketing of travel. The reader associates color with both beauty and excitement. A mountain sunset, an Alaskan cruise, or a night in Las Vegas all demand color to truly show them off.

Color also gives a little glamour to a headline, sets off a logo, or provides a tinted background on which copy or photos are displayed. When dealing with a photo, you have little choice of color; you normally try to capture the true colors. With other hues, however, you should try to select appropriate colors. Green has long denoted Ireland; cruises opt for blue or green. The color choice should fit the mood and subject.

There are three primary colors: red, blue, and yellow (or magenta, cyan, and yellow, in printing terms). These colors, mixed with each other and with black or white pigments, provide the full range of colors. These colors—or hues—may also vary in intensity or in lightness and darkness. The latter quality depends upon where they fall on the scale of values, a tone scale going from white to black.

As with other elements of a layout, colors should also be compatible. Any smart dresser knows this. Work with colors that complement one another, rather than clash with one another.

Also, avoid printing black lettering on a dark tint block. You can't read it. Neither can you read white lettering on a light tint block. Dark hues are also recommended for headlines rather than a light yellow or pink.

In printing, we talk about one-, two-, three-, and four-color work. Unless the printer has a four-color press, each time you add a color that means another pass through the press and, consequently, higher charges for press time. We'll see that in more detail in the next chapter.

## KNOW THE EFFECT OF PAPER

The weight, color, and finish of paper have an impact on the way an ad or brochure will look. You might also add "surface" and "grain" to that trio.

Paper, which is made from wood pulp, or, occasionally, from cotton or linen rags, comes in large sheets, for instance, 17" x 22". There are 500 sheets to a ream, and the weight of each sheet is expressed in the total weight of the ream. If you see a bond paper listed at 20# paper, that means the large sheets from which it was cut totaled 20 pounds to the ream.

Paper for the pages of books typically will be 60-, 70-, or 80-pound paper, and these weights are also used for brochures. For booklets, a heavier stock may be used for the cover—perhaps 90 pounds or above. Many national magazines use 60-pound paper, even 50-pound paper. One hundred and fifty-pound paper is about the limit and would seldom be used.

When deciding on the size of a brochure, it's wise to talk with your printer about the most economical way to make cuts in the large sheet. You may find, for example, that by tailoring your brochure measurements less than an inch, you could get another complete folder out of each sheet.

In fact, you should rely pretty much on your printer for advice on weight, color, texture, and availability. Paper has become difficult to obtain. You can't just find a sample of paper you like and go down and order it. It may not be in stock, and weeks could elapse before your order is filled. It's better to use paper that's on hand or that can be readily shipped.

Newsprint, which is used by newspapers, is made of groundwood pulp and serves well for a short period. Eventually, however, when light and air get to it, it turns brittle and yellow or tan.

Offset paper has a flat (non-shiny) finish and is very popular because of cost and versatility. Coated stock is more expensive but provides a better surface for photographs, and also impresses many people as designating quality. You can also buy papers with antique finishes, ripple finishes, or a variety of fancy weaves. These should be used sparingly, and only when the occasion demands something special.

Paper also comes in many different colors. When printing on these colors, keep in mind the way the type will reproduce. A dark paper would call for very dark or bold type. Even then it will be tough to read. A colored ink on colored stock also alters the look of both elements. Brown ink on green stock, for example, will look much different than brown ink on white or tan stock.

Printers have paper samples they can show you, along with swatches of available colors. Match these two items by putting the swatch next to the paper and see how they look. Even this test is not perfect, but it gives you some idea of the final result.

## THE TRAVEL PAGE OR SECTION

Some travel sections are full size (about 14½" wide x 22" high) and others are tabloid size (about 11½" wide by 14½" high). It takes a larger ad to dominate the larger page, but a full page in one is really not much different than a full page in the other—in terms of attention-getting, not cost.

Check the section your ad will appear in and recognize the problems and opportunities. You may want special placement, like the outside of the page, or near some well-read travel feature. The section may contain 20 pages and more than 200 individual ads, or it may be a single page with a handful of ads. The former situation is tougher to combat and more expensive to buy.

A really unusual ad will gain readership, even in a relatively small size, but when you are looking at bulk alone, it takes about a third of a page to dominate the other ads.

# MISCELLANEOUS DESIGN PROBLEMS

The design possibilities are endless, so a list of things you should do is impossible to compile. If the design works, it works, and that's the best test.

There are, however, things you shouldn't do. Many of these have been mentioned already, like ignoring the ad's balance or harmony, letting elements float around loosely, forgetting to have something dominate, printing so that people can't read the copy, mixing too many typefaces in a single ad, failing to tie headline, copy, and illustration together, and so on. Here are a few tips:

- ❏ Don't harden your thumbnail sketches. Let them be loose at first, then firm up the lines.
- ❏ Repeat some elements in an ad occasionally. This adds to the idea of simplicity and also keeps the reader's attention.
- ❏ When you run your ad across two pages, learn how to deal with the gutter—the space between pages. Running a headline across ties the ad together; or repeating an element on both sides; or carrying a tint block across; or matching large type on either side. There are many devices. Check several magazines and note how they handle this.
- ❏ Get all the information you can from printing and paper salespeople, newspaper and magazine salespeople, and other professionals.
- ❏ Save ads you like, type you find attractive, paper you'd like to try.
- ❏ Come to terms with your own art ability, or that of anyone in the office, and realize what you can and cannot do. If there is limited talent, your only hope lies in clip art, imitation, an art studio, or the newspaper's art department.

# NEW TECHNIQUES

A word should be added here about the innovations in design made possible by new tools, especially computers. Computer graphics, popular as a way to create electronic effects on television, now have increased use in preparing art for printed materials. Logos, in particular, are the frequent subject of computer experimentation. Computers also allow designers to play around with layout, moving elements within the space, substituting other elements, blowing up or reducing certain items. Once the layout is complete, the touch of a button can move the design to the metal plate stage, just prior to printing.

It is also possible to print on different surfaces, from metal to cloth, which previously would not accept ink.

## CHAPTER HIGHLIGHTS

❏ Many aspects of design are natural and are as applicable in advertising as in ordinary life.

❏ The basic elements of design are line, rectangle, triangle, and circle. These serve as the basis for all layout and illustration.

❏ Just as in art, harmony, sequence, and balance characterize layout.

❏ Important layout tips include remembering that copy is part of the layout; that some element must dominate; that composition and proportion improve with practice; that white space is valuable; that type should be ordered so that it is easily read.

❏ The nine most common layout designs include: picture window, Mondrian, frame, typeface, multipanel, copy heavy, silhouette, circus, and rebus.

❏ A high percentage of travel advertising utilizes small space, so the ability to convey a message within a limited area is important.

❏ The five most common categories of type are Roman, block, text, script, and ornamental.

❏ Both illustrations and photography should be appropriate, professional looking, and compatible.

❏ Effective use of color and intelligent selection of paper are also critical to good design.

■        ■              ■

## ❏ *EXERCISES*

1. Using travel sections of newspapers and magazines, find an ad in each of the nine format categories covered in this chapter.
2. Bring in three print advertisements for travel and isolate the basic design elements in each.

3. Working with larger travel ads, trace only the circles, rectangles, and triangles in three ads. Use a ruler, pencil, and tracing paper for this.
4. Bring in two print ads, one showing formal and one showing informal balance.

## ❏ CASE STUDIES

*1. Using the same brochure you used for the case problem in chapter six, turn this into an ad that measures 3 columns wide x 8" high (or deep). Make this as attractive as you can, assuming you are going to show it to a client. Draw in the headline; indicate the copy by lines (but type the copy on a separate sheet); use an illustration or photo, either drawing it in or pasting something on your layout; and invent a travel agency name and logo to identify the ad. You can decide on format, on the use of coupon or not, and on other factors. This ad will appear in the Sunday edition of your newspaper, on the travel page or travel section.*

*2. Take a legal size sheet of paper and experiment with it in terms of one and two folds, then do a rough layout of the brochure (a rough dummy), using as subject matter a local hotel or tourist attraction. Indicate copy, but don't write any copy (except for headlines) and also indicate photos or illustrations.*

# 8

# THE MECHANICS OF PRINT PRODUCTION

Like so many other aspects of advertising, production of both print and broadcast material is a specialty. It's not necessary that the practitioner or the agency manager know how to produce the ads, but it is helpful to understand how they are produced and what steps can be taken in advance to make production better and more economical. Again, there is no substitute for talking with the experts and visiting the print shops or recording or television studios to see exactly what the process entails.

To appreciate what transpires from concept to finished product in print advertising, let's follow a newspaper ad from the time it is merely an idea until it appears in the Sunday travel edition.

## WHAT HAPPENS TO AN AD

First comes the need. Let's say you want to advertise cruises to the Bahamas. Here's the way this might go:

1. You'd collect all the information you can get, tie down the details, settle on dates, costs, and other items.
2. You'd consider the budget and determine how much money you can afford to spend on advertising and still make a profit. This would affect the size of the ad and the number of insertions. (You might, of course, lay out an ad first and then see what it would cost, but this is a more sensible routine.)
3. You'd come up with a central idea and devise a copy platform for all the advertising.
4. You would do a number of thumbnail sketches to get an idea of what design might work, or you might incorporate the new information into a previous ad format.

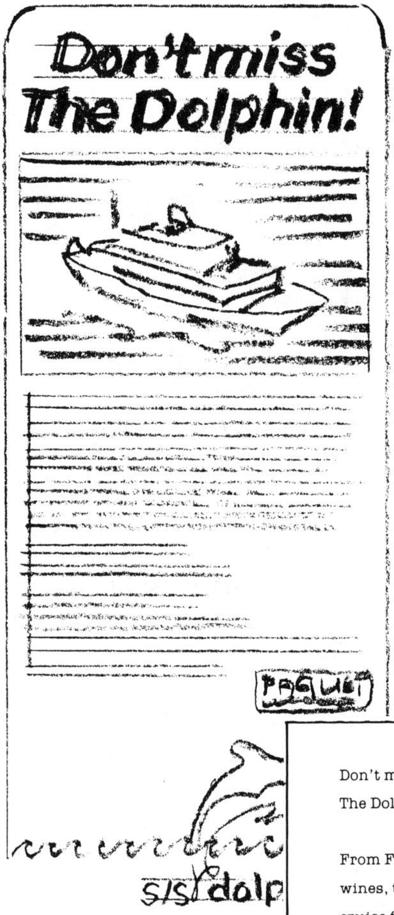

**Fig. 8–1  Rough of proposed print ad, without copy.** (Courtesy of Paquet Cruises, Inc.)

**Fig. 8–2  Copy should be typed on separate sheet, keyed for position in ad, and marked for type sizes.** (Courtesy of Paquet Cruises, Inc.)

Don't miss

The Dolphin!

From French chefs to free dinner wines, this is the exciting new way to cruise from Miami to the Bahamas. 3-night cruises to Nassau any Friday from $170 to $370. 4-night cruises to Nassau and Freeport any Monday from $215 to $450.

Ask your Travel Agent.

Paquet Cruises, Inc.
1001 North American Way
Miami, Florida 33132 • 305-374-8100
Registered in Panama

(Paquet logo and S.S. Dolphin art to be furnished)

HEADLINE:
20/20 Helvetica Bld. Ital.
2 lines centered

TEXT:
8/9 Helvetica
Light
X 11½ picas
Rag. Rt.

5. Once the copy and layout are approved, you would provide the art department of the newspaper (or your own artist) with your rough idea and the typed copy. Copy for ads is always typed on separate sheets and the ad layout merely indicates, by use of lines, where the copy will go (Figure 8–1). The typed sheet might look like Figure 8–2.

   The pencil markings indicate the type families chosen— Helvetica Bold Italic and Helvetica Light and the size of each.

   Now, the average travel agent would not be familiar with typefaces or sizes. For that matter, neither would many advertising agency personnel. Their layout would indicate the approximate size they wanted the letters and might include a sample of the type wanted for each spot, and the art studio production person or, more likely, the newspaper art department, would spec (specify) this type, indicating style and size.

6. Once the type has been marked up (as in the example), it goes to the typesetter. Newspapers have their own composing rooms, but there are also typesetters and printers who set type. The type is set to match and fit your layout and instructions, and a copy of this type, suitable for reproduction, is sent along to the art department.

7. Meanwhile, since you have decided you want to run a photo of the ship in your ad, you will need this photo. It's likely that one may be furnished, or you may have to have the picture shot. A glossy print is supplied to the paper and marked up to fit your layout (as we'll see later). At this time you would also furnish the distinctive signature copy and logo.

8. The art department or studio then pastes down all the elements on heavy paper stock, positioning the illustration and the typeset copy, then drawing in or setting in the border. This is the time to be certain all corrections have been made.

9. A proof is pulled from this pasteup (which is said to be camera ready) and a proof is run off. This is the first copy but looks just like the ad should look in the paper. The proof is for your approval. If you catch any errors, you indicate the changes. You might also correct sizes or alter anything else that doesn't look right, but as stated above, it's wiser and cheaper to make changes earlier.

10. After you've approved the proof, the ad department gives the go ahead to the printing department. Your ad is given a spot on the appropriate page and run as part of the entire paper. The result looks like Figure 8–3.

**Fig. 8–3**   (Courtesy of Paquet Cruises, Inc.)

# MEASURING TYPE

Let's retrace a few steps in the previous list of steps involved in the production of an ad, and examine them more closely.

Type, for example, has the artistic and psychological function we looked at in the previous chapter, but it also has mechanical properties.

The height of the type is expressed in points. There are 72 points to an inch. That means that 72-point type is roughly one inch high, from the top of the tallest character to the bottom of the lowest character below the baseline. Thirty-six point type, then, would be half an inch. Eighteen-point type will approximate one-fourth of an inch. All of these sizes would be used in headlines. The normal body type would be 10–12 point, and this is the size type you'll find in newspapers and magazines. Here are some examples:

**10 POINT MEDIUM**
What is type for? Obviously to read, and to read with as little discomfort on the part of the reader as possible. But reading at

**12 POINT MEDIUM**
What is type for? Obviously to read, and to read with as little discomfort on the part of the reader as possible.

If you want type to have a more open look, you may add a small amount of space between lines. Taking a cue from the days when this space consisted of a small strip of metal inserted between lines, this process is called leading (pronounced ledding).

Type is measured by picas when measuring lateral distance. We say that a line is so many picas long, or a copy block so many picas wide. Why picas? Because they are easier to work with than fractions of an inch. There are six picas to the inch.

The human eye will only span so much space comfortably. That's why most columns in magazines and newspapers are about 12–13 picas wide (2–2¼ inches). The copy shown is 10-point type with an extra two points of leading, making it 10 on 12 (shown as 10/12) and measures approximately 13 picas wide.

> bold or decorative or flourished
> letter, the very qualities which
> are successful

Estimating type by eye is risky. Few people (if any) can spot the difference between 9-and 10-point type, or one or two points of leading, or even between headlines of 36 and 42 points.

You specify the type you want and, if it looks too small, you move up a size. If it's too large, you back down a size, or cut copy.

## COPY FITTING

Another technique that is good to know is how to copy fit type. This works two ways—when you have something already written and are wondering how much space it will take, and when you have the space and wonder how many words you can write.

There are a number of ways of estimating this. The easiest way is by using charts that tell you the space required for certain sizes of type. Another way is to draw a square inch around the type and count the number of words in that square inch and then multiply by the number of square inches in the allotted space.

Both of these methods get a little complicated for the person who is doing this only periodically. A simpler (though longer) way is to just paste a piece of copy—any copy—that has the type size you want in the space you have to fill. Then count the words.

When you start with typed copy, count the words (or characters, with each typed letter and each space representing a character) and then determine how many lines you will need in the type size and block you have chosen.

In the previous type example, there are approximately five words to a line and approximately thirty characters to the line. "Approximately" is used here because the copy block is really too short to estimate words and the spacing in these lines is irregular. However, assuming these figures worked, it would be a simple job to set your typewriter for thirty characters and then all you would have to do is count the typed lines to see how much space you require.

When you are doing something regularly, like a quarterly brochure, you'll find it simple to use columns of type from back issues to paste on the dummy (which we'll explain later) to stand for copy in the upcoming issue. Here's the step-by-step way to do this:

1. Count the number of characters per line in the previous issue.
2. Set your typewriter for this number and type your copy.
3. Count the number of typed lines.
4. Count the same number of lines on previously printed copy, cut out this block and paste it in your dummy. If you've done everything right, this piece of old copy should be very close to the copy for the next issue.

You can, of course, do the same thing for an ad, particularly when you are using an identical format but new copy.

## A FEW FINAL WORDS ON TYPE

In the last chapter we looked at the four general categories of type but mentioned that there were more than a thousand variations, called typefaces or families, that can be selected. You see names like Garamond or Caslon or Stymie or Bodoni, and these denote type specimens that have different looks, sometimes obvious, sometimes subtle. You pick the style that seems to suit your message—but don't get too cute. Remember, it still must be read.

You'll also see the terms series and font used when referring to type. Series means all sizes within a single design, like everything from 6-point to 48-point in Helvetica, including caps, italics, and boldface (heavier or darker letters) and lightface (regular printing). A font is limited to a single size within that series—like 6-point Helvetica, again including all variations, like caps and lowercase, boldface and lightface, and italics, in that single size.

In addition to indicating spacing between lines, some designs also require spacing between letters or words, or they require that lines be tightened up. The first method is called letter spacing where you have a very open look; the second method is called condensing, and there are special condensed typefaces. When you condense, of course, this means you get more letters in the same space required for normal spacing. This should be taken into consideration when copy fitting.

## HOT AND COLD TYPE

All type used to be set via the use of hot metal. Machines, called monotype or linotype machines, served as small foundries, casting into metal the letters or lines that a typographer typed on the machine. This is called hot metal type or hot type. It is still in use today.

Cold type is normally the product of a photographic process. The characters are typed onto film or paper by exposing a negative to light, much as you would in developing any film. You have different faces to choose from and you can vary the size of type by changing the focal length of the camera. This is usually done automatically.

There are also typewriters that type your copy on a clean sheet that can then be pasted up and photographed. This is also cold type.

With the development of computers and their attendant printers, a whole new form of cold type arrived. Some firms have even gone to "desktop publishing" for things like newsletters, setting up the type in the machines, even to proper spacing, sizing, and layout, and then printing "hard copies" for their readers. Besides the "dot matrix" type (which has a computerized look), there are the more popular "letter quality" typefaces that resemble other forms of typesetting.

When the type is set—either reproduced on a page or, as metal, locked into a frame—it is made part of the ad or brochure by being pasted onto the layout, or included in the larger frame that contains all elements of the item to be printed. This is what the printer works from.

# LETTERPRESS AND OFFSET

While there are four ways to print, including silk screen, gravure, offset, and letterpress, only the latter two methods have much use for the travel agency. Silk screening is used for posters and outdoor work, while gravure is employed for the printing of special color sections of newspapers or certain books. The choice is usually between letterpress and offset for ads and brochures.

Letterpress is the older method. In this form of printing, raised type is used, much like the rubber stamp printing sets youngsters enjoy. The raised portion is inked and it prints on the paper, which is pressed against it. Both hot and cold type can be used in this process, although hot metal characterized the first use of such a system.

Offset lithography is based on the principle that oil and water don't mix. Once the camera ready copy has been pasted down, a picture is taken and this is transferred, electrically or chemically, to a thin metal plate. The letters aren't raised as in letterpress printing, although all the images do stand above the plate an imperceptible distance. After being treated with oil, the plate is washed, removing oil from all but the image areas. These areas then accept ink, while the plain areas reject it. The plate is wrapped around a cylinder which transfers the printing to a second cylinder, which then prints it on paper.

Offset lithography has become the more popular method because it is usually (though not always) cheaper, and because it is a more flexible system to work with.

Newspapers use both letterpress and offset techniques, with the latter dominating. No matter what process is used, the result will be only as good as the material supplied. A poor layout will remain a poor layout, and a dull photograph will remain a dull photograph. The only problem is that this ineptness is now made public. That's why it pays to supply the printer with decent copy and visuals.

# PHOTOGRAPHS

This is a subject in itself and has spawned many books. Here we need only look at a few mechanical items.

The photograph you have chosen may not be the right size for your ad or brochure, or its composition may suggest the elimination of certain extraneous items. This means reducing or enlarging or cropping.

Normally, you'll be working with an 8″ × 10″ photo, although you could also have in hand a 4″ × 5″ print. Let's suppose you have ad space that allows for a photo that is two inches deep. You'll want to know the width. This involves setting up a simple ratio, thus:

$$\frac{4}{2} = \frac{5}{x} \qquad x = 2\frac{1}{2}'' \text{ (the width of the photo)}$$

Actually, it is unnecessary to go through all this arithmetic, since a slide rule will provide the answer immediately. Many people who work with layout keep a circular slide rule handy, set up the ratio above, and just read over to the appropriate number. Some calculators also provide this function.

Only you have determined your new dimensions, you should write these instructions on the back of the photo, using a grease pencil or felt tip pen: (Never use a pencil or ball point pen, since this could show through the other side.)

Reduce to 2½″ wide × 2″ deep

*or*

Blow up (enlarge) to 7½″ wide × 6″ deep

Sometimes you may want to crop certain portions of the photo to produce a more pleasing shot, to get rid of distracting background, or to bring one of the dimensions into harmony with another when you reduce or enlarge.

In the latter context, suppose you had a photo that was 8″ × 10″ and you wanted it to be 3″ × 3″. There is no way to get that proportion without trimming a couple of inches off the width of the photo, or by making adjustments to both width and depth.

Sometimes a figure in the background will be out of place, or a sign will give away a locale, or a car will date the picture. You could remove the offending item in a variety of ways. For example, using an air brush, which sprays a fine coat of paint over the object,

**Fig. 8—4   Photos should be cropped on the margins, not on the picture surface.**

concealing it, and creating a background that blends with the rest of the picture, or you could mask out the item with acetate. The easiest way, however, is to crop the picture.

You decide what portion of the photo you want (keeping in mind the final dimensions you need) and then place the crop marks, using a grease pencil, in the appropriate places on the margin of the photo (Figure 8—4).

This instruction would be written on the back of the photo, with grease pencil or felt tip, like this:

Crop to 3½″ wide × 5″ deep

If you intended to reduce or enlarge after you had cropped the picture, you'd state the cropping information first, and then the instructions about reducing or enlarging.

Be sure to double check all your figures before committing them to writing. It gets expensive when you have to redo photos and plates.

When there's a long caption for the photo, it's probably wiser to type this on a small piece of paper and attach it (using rubber cement or scotch tape) to the back of the picture. If you are identifying people in the photo, start left to right and say: "L to R: Mary Smith, John Jones, etc." If the picture needs a credit line for the photographer or supplier, put that here. Also include any instructions about returning the photo and to whom it should be mailed.

You could, then, have a photo with all these details on the reverse side or on a separate typed sheet of paper:

Crop to 3½" wide × 5" deep
Reduce to 2¼" wide × 3¼" deep
Caption:
Please Credit:
Return To:
   (Address)

Drawings and paintings can also be marked up in similar fashion, including instructions about cropping and reducing. When cropping a work of art, however, it's wise to get a living artist's permission. He may conclude that you ruined his proportions merely to accommodate your mechanical requirements. This artwork should also be credited.

## SCREENING PHOTOS

The average travel agency manager is not going to have to worry about screening photos, but it should be mentioned briefly that photographs, if reproduced directly from prints, would look like dark smudges. To preserve the gray values in these photos, a copying camera equipped with a set of screens is used to reshoot the original photo. These screens break the photo into a picture made up of a series of dots, called a halftone.

The screens are designated according to the number of dots they produce per linear inch. For newspaper, for example, a 65–85 line screen is used, producing fewer dots further apart. This is because newsprint tends to blot and a finer screen would run together. For smoother paper, such as found in magazines, you use screens varying from 100–150 lines. Obviously, you can achieve more sensitive reproduction on the finer papers.

To see this, take a magnifying glass to any halftone in a newspaper or magazine and the dot structure becomes apparent.

The light and dark values in halftones are made possible because, in the photographing process, large dots are photographed on the negative where the light is strong and small ones where the light is weak. When ink touches these dots on the plate more adheres to the larger surfaces and this creates the illusion of tonal graduation.

As mentioned elsewhere, in small space ads photos do not work as well as line drawings because the definition is difficult to achieve, especially in newspapers.

## THE BROCHURE

If ads start with thumbnails, then brochures begin with folding paper. You try to decide what size brochure you want and how you want it to fold. Figure 8–5 shows a few of the options.

The size of the brochure is going to be determined by how much you have to say and how much you want to spend. You could end up with a twelve-page booklet, composed of three single-fold pages, or you might be satisfied with a single sheet, printed on both sides, and not folded at all.

Keep in mind that, when you go to larger booklets or brochures, you move by fours. You can't really decide to have 9 pages. You go from eight to twelve, unless you want to do something fancy, like a gatefold, which is an extra two pages that swing out as an extension

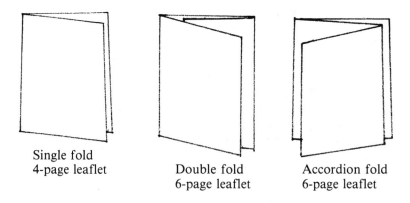

Single fold
4-page leaflet

Double fold
6-page leaflet

Accordion fold
6-page leaflet

**Fig. 8–5**

of another page. Even then, you're at ten, and not nine. Better, however, to stick with multiples of four.

When a brochure is printed, the pages are not printed one at a time. They are probably printed eight pages at a time, maybe sixteen pages, sometimes four pages. These pages are assembled in a certain rotation that makes for proper final order after folding, and printed in one pass through the press. Ask your printer about this when you give him a job and he'll tell you how the pages lay out.

Why is this important? Well, if you intend to use color on part of the booklet and not the other, it would be advantageous to know which pages worked together so that you could specify one without the other.

Another thing to discuss with your printer, especially when you are considering doing an off-size brochure, is the question of the most economical use of paper. Remember that paper comes in large sheets, like $35'' \times 45''$, or $25'' \times 38''$, or $17'' \times 22''$. Consider the number of pages of the size you want that will cut out of the large sheet, without leaving a lot of waste paper. If your page size were $8\frac{1}{2}'' \times 11''$, for example, you could get four sheets out of the $17'' \times 22''$ sheet, but if you increased your page size to $9'' \times 12''$, you would get only two pages out of the same sheet, and leave a lot of waste paper.

## THE DUMMY

The layout for a brochure (or folder, leaflet, or booklet) is called a dummy. The dummy is prepared so that you can experiment with different designs, and so that the printer will have a guide when he prints your piece.

Again, you might doodle on some small pages first, just to see what you might want to put into the brochure. Then, if you know what you're doing, you would get a piece of the same paper you intend to print on, and do your sketching on that. If the dummy is for a small leaflet, fold the paper first, and then indicate illustrations and type. If a larger booklet will be the result, go page by page.

Anyone who begins working with dummies eventually devises some shortcuts. For those not gifted with artistic talent, for example, there is always tracing paper, which can be used to trace art or photos, or to serve as a guide for tracing typed lines. This traced page can then be photocopied, giving you a firmer paper to work with. Do this for every page, pasting succeeding pages back to back, and joining other pages with transparent tape.

For example, in a sixteen-page booklet, you'd paste the cover (page 1) to page 2, and page 15 to the back cover (page 16). Then you could join these two dual pages by scotch tape. Do the same for pages 3–4 and 13–14, and lay these on top. Piece by piece you build the book. If you wish, you can staple the entire booklet at the crease. This isn't the way an artist would do it, but it works well for an amateur.

You can also paste on to the dummy any regular items you have on hand, like your logo, or a piece of art, or some standing type that can be used again. This, too, is the place to show samples of type or color.

The copy for the brochure, like the copy for an ad, goes on separate sheets, which are keyed to the proper dummy page. Artwork and photos are similarly keyed so that they can be properly positioned.

The important thing to remember is that the dummy is a guide. You're not going to print from it. The printer will provide you with a proof of the brochure before he prints it so that you can see if it resembles what you had in mind.

After the printer has the dummy, copy, and illustrations, he follows the same routine as in ad production—setting type, pasting up, showing a proof, making a plate, running the job. He also has to handle the illustrations and work within any color restrictions or paper requests that you submitted.

Final reminder: The more you can do and the clearer you can make your wishes known (by clean and accurate copy, a workable dummy, and specific color and paper specifications), the less risk of disappointment.

## USING BROCHURE SHELLS

Tourist offices, carriers, and certain resorts may supply the travel agency with a brochure shell, a folder with some photos or artwork already on some of the pages, but with space for the agency to add its own information or illustrations.

Let's say you planned a Rhine cruise. From one of the ship companies or from the German tourist board, you might be able to get shells that had color photos of Rhine scenes and, perhaps, even an attractive headline. You would then add your specifics, like dates, and day-by-day sightseeing, and conditions, and, perhaps, information on the tour leader.

You could, of course, receive a shell that had nearly everything in it, including the itinerary. You might then add only very little copy.

The advantage of using a prepared shell is that you save on paper, illustrations, and gain the advantage of color while adding only one color for your copy.

## CREATING THE BROCHURE

Brochures should invite reading. Take a look at the racks of brochures in any travel agency. The good ones snap right out. That's a start, but the inside must maintain this same level of interest.

The cover of any brochure is something like a billboard advertisement, featuring a minimum of copy and a strong illustration. Its purpose is to arouse curiosity and get you to continue reading.

The initial inside page sets the theme, perhaps in summary fashion, or gets the story going. After that the details are communicated in logical and colorful fashion, using a lot of subheads or illustrations to break up the pages. You may proceed page by page or treat the entire inside as a single sheet and carry the copy completely across it. The prose must be terse, informative, and compelling. Just as a good salesman intrigues a prospect with product benefits before spelling out the cost, so a good brochure emphasizes the delights of any tour before adding such mundane items as price, baggage requirements, and passport information.

Again, like the sales pitch, there should be an unmistakable close, and a means of responding. A coupon could be enclosed, or a return envelope supplied, or at least a phone number and address featured.

Collect a handful of brochures that appeal to you and analyze them. What makes them special? Is it the attractive graphics, or the crisp copy, or the manner in which the entire booklet flows? Figure out how they accomplished this effect and try it yourself.

## COLOR REPRODUCTION

You need not be expert in rendering color or producing color, but you must be able to recognize the difference between good and bad color work. Notice, for example, how important color is in depicting food. A steak on the grill can't look too light or too dark; it must have just

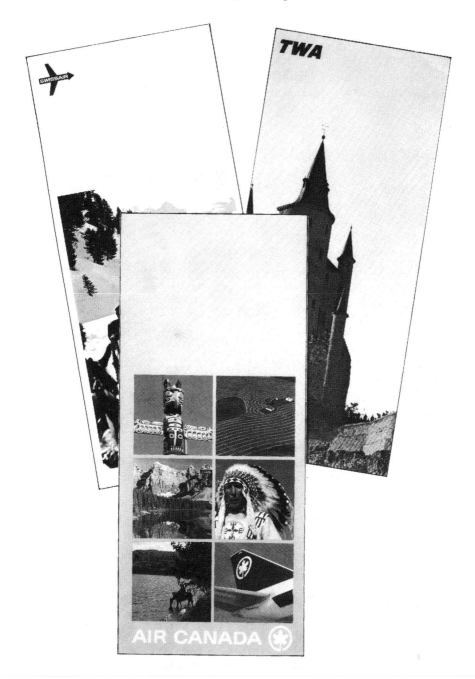

**Fig. 8–6 Some examples of the many shells available from airlines.**
(Courtesy of Swissair, TWA, and Air Canada)

the right shades of red and dark brown. A washed-out photo of a Mexican fiesta also loses its charm. And a brochure printed on a sickly green or deep purple stock is a certain loser.

Admittedly, color work is not a major concern of the individual travel agency. Few of their ads are in color and even the company newsletters tend to be just black on white. The color brochures are generally supplied, and their colored billboards rarely use more than a few basic colors. Still, it helps to have some idea of the way in which color is printed, and that's the reason for this brief section.

In reproducing a color photo, you start first with a good picture. If the slide or color print or color transparency is weak, regardless of darkroom magic, the result will also be weak.

Assuming the original print is good, here are the steps that go into reproducing this in a color ad or brochure.

First, the picture must be separated into the three primary colors (magenta, cyan, yellow) plus black. This is because each color will be printed separately, using a separate plate, for a total of four plates.

You separate out the magenta or red by shooting the color transparency with a camera that has a green filter over the lens. Why green? Because it is a combination of blue (cyan) and yellow, so it filters out these two colors and allows only the red to seep through. The blue is achieved by using an orange filter; and the yellow by using a purple or lavender filter. The black plate is composed largely of highlights to achieve definition.

New developments in color separation, including laser beams, are becoming more common today.

On a regular press, then, the yellow is usually run first, the paper dried, then the red press run occurs, another drying period, then the blue run, drying, and finally the black. It's obviously important that, during all these press runs, the register be perfect, meaning that each plate fits perfectly with the previous one. Otherwise, you would get a shaky-looking result with garbled colors.

As mentioned earlier, there are also four-color presses that can accomplish all of the above with one pass through the press. And there are fast-drying agents to speed the drying process.

If properly done and printed on high-quality paper, the end result should mirror the beginning photo.

The above explanation refers to four-color work. For two-color work—like black and red—you do two passes through the press, specifying the areas you want red, and those you want black. For example, you might set a headline in red, or a piece of art in red, and keep the type black.

You could also specify a duotone, a combination of black and one other color to give your halftone a different look.

Keep in mind that color is a sensitive medium. It may seem like an artistic idea to put one of your halftones in black and green but imagine how the faces of people in the photo are going to look. Also keep in mind that type must be read. If you put it in green or light blue, it may be difficult to read. Red could be hard on the eyes.

Tint blocks—a light color screen behind type and/or illustrations—may sometimes be very effective. For example, many companies, in producing their annual reports, find that a light screen behind some of the columns of figures helps to set them off and also relieves the monotony. Again, however, you must be certain you can read the copy. A screen that is too dark or type that is too light, or the use of two colors that disappear into one another destroy readership. You can specify how dark you want the screen by asking for anything from a 10 percent screen (very light) to a 90 percent screen, which is the next thing to a solid color or solid black.

You can buy colored stock (paper) in many shades, or you may also print the shade you want on the paper, producing the same general effect. You can then add other colors to this colored stock, using the same good judgment you would use in papering your home. Lavender on tan is not very appealing, but dark brown on tan could be. Bright reds and greens are always going to look like Christmas so, unless that's the effect you want, better try something else. Collect pieces you admire and check with your printer about duplicating these color combinations.

Caution is the watchword. A poor color job is worse than a poor black-and-white job and much more expensive.

## NEWSPAPER AND MAGAZINE REPRODUCTION

As stated earlier, magazines normally use a paper that has a much smoother or glossier finish than newspapers. This makes your ad look sharper and your color look richer. It will also keep your ad around longer. After a certain number of uses in the newspaper, you'll see letters start to fill in or break down or look muddy. At that time, you should get a new cut, or plate, and furnish it to the paper.

Although newspapers have come a long way in the past decade in the use of color, they are still very limited. Again, the porous paper is the reason. They must stick with primary colors and fundamental combinations. Even then, four-color work is risky. Two-color work, however, often looks quite good, and is worth trying.

Some advertisers print their own ads on glossy stock and then supply them to the paper for inserting. This ensures better quality color, but you have to have enough pages in your insert to make it worthwhile, and you still have to pay a fee for inserting. You'll notice that, in the past decade, the use of inserts in newspapers had increased significantly. There has been very little published research on this subject but some advertisers—like discount chains, nationwide department chains, film companies, and others—evidently find these very effective. Few travel agencies have tried this method, because of expense, but it might be worth experimenting with on an annual basis.

When considering reproduction in either newspapers or magazines, be certain you read their mechanical requirements for insertion. This information may be found on their rate cards or in *Standard Rate & Data Service* publications. You'll learn what sizes they want, how the publication is printed (letterpress or offset), what they need from you (plate, cut, velox proof, camera-ready copy), what their deadlines are, and similar data.

## SOME FINAL PRINT PRODUCTION TIPS

1.  Develop your skills as a proofreader. If possible, catch errors in the initial typed copy. The further along you get in the production process, the more expensive it is to make changes. Read the printer's proof carefully. It's easy to miss words with transposed letters, words that read properly but are not the right words, and words that appear in headlines (which are often ignored). It's a good idea to have someone read the original copy as you check the proof. A "typo," which hides as you search for it, inevitably looms large when it's printed.
2.  Be certain you allow sufficient time for the printer to do your work. If you ask him to work nights and weekends in order to meet your deadline, your costs escalate.
3.  Be certain that everyone who has to approve the project does so in the beginning stages.
4.  Be curious around production people. Ask questions; watch. See how they do things, what shortcuts they take, how they save money.
5.  Realize you cannot attain the impossible triad of price, speed, and quality. If you want speed and quality, the price goes up. If you want speed and economy, the quality suffers.

6. Remember that new methods are constantly coming on the scene and that innovations like computer graphics may replace some of the earlier illustrative and reproductive methods discussed here.

## CHAPTER HIGHLIGHTS

❏ Every print ad starts with research, budget, a central idea, a method of presentation, and the various mechanical steps from concept to publication.

❏ Those designing their own ads should be familiar with measurement and copy fitting of type. The height of type is measured in points, with 72 points to the inch, and width is measured in picas, with 6 picas to the inch. There are several methods of copy fitting, ranging from the use of typebook charts to working from past copy and setting the typewriter (or computer) for the appropriate line length.

❏ The two most common forms of printing are letterpress (which uses hot metal) and offset lithography (which uses a variety of "cold" type methods).

❏ Besides learning how to take decent photographs, agency personnel responsible for printing should know how to crop and reduce and caption pictures.

❏ Producing the brochure starts with folding paper and involves the creation of a dummy, which serves as the model for the printer.

❏ Although the travel agent need not be an expert in color or in the effects of paper on reproduction, it helps to know the pitfalls and the possibilities, especially those that save money.

■          ■          ■

## ❏ *EXERCISES*

1. If you were instructing a person new to print production, list five things you would tell this person to watch for in keeping costs under control.

2. Using a large photo in a magazine or brochure, indicate how you would crop this to produce a different effect. Also show how you would reduce or enlarge this to fit a new format.

3. Put together a rough dummy of a brochure featuring a tour of your choice. Indicate pictures and copy.
4. Find a photo in a magazine that lends itself to the promotion of some particular tour. Crop it if you wish. Build an ad around it, merely indicating the copy.

## ❑ *CASE STUDIES*

*1. The travel agency you work for has just received permission to organize some special tours to Russia, tours which will focus on the villages and the people. A drawback to interest among prospects has been the concern that Russia may be drab and dull. Just concentrating on production items, like type, paper, color, and general appearance, do you have any ideas for counteracting this image?*

*2. A new 300-room hotel plans to open soon in your town. It's in the class of Hyatt and Hilton and you are hired to help design some of the print materials they will require. They want your ideas on three items. One is a program to hand out to guests at the "topping off" ceremony when they hoist the last beam in place to complete the hotel. Another is an invitation to 1,000 prominent citizens to attend a special inauguration dinner in the hotel ballroom. The third piece is a menu for a picnic, featuring German cuisine, which will be held in the hotel parking lot (decorated as a Beer Garden for the event), and open to the general public at a cost of $10 per person. A German band will play for guests and imported beers and wines will be served. This latter event, to be held soon after the inaugural dinner, is to introduce the hotel to the general public. What are your ideas on type, paper, and general style for each of the printed pieces?*

# 9

# PRODUCING RADIO AND TV SPOTS

Radio and television are two media that are not used enough by travel agencies and, when they are used, the commercials are often poorly produced and fail to take full advantage of the medium.

The assumption in this chapter is that the particular agency does not have a large production budget, so whatever it produces must be done economically. Obviously, if money is no object, you can hire the talent, create your own special music, and even shoot on location in some exotic tourist haven.

For most travel agencies, however, the production of broadcast and telecast materials has to be spartan, unlike carriers and hotel chains where budgets are larger. There *are* ways to produce acceptable radio and television spots without spending a ton of money.

## THE IDEA

First you need a good idea—a good idea that fits with radio or television. It's not enough to merely translate print copy to these media and feel you have created another good advertisement. Each medium is different, and each requires its own kind of idea.

From this basic idea, you write the script, keeping in mind the sound qualities of radio and the visual qualities of television.

## RADIO

Radio is written for the ear and that can sometimes be a blessing. Bagpipes, for example, instantly suggest Scotland. You don't have to show Edinburgh Castle or the Trossachs. The listener creates his or her own images. Think of all the sounds that work for travel adver-

**179**

tising: surf, a ship's whistle, the sound of a plane taking off, roulette wheels, laughter, glasses tinkling, animal sounds, the San Francisco trolley bell, sports crowds, the sizzle of a steak, and thousands of musical items.

You can create pictures with sounds—and with words.

*When the mists have lifted and the castle ruins fade, it's memory of green that remains—the colors of early apples, ripe olives or aging moss, all interlaced like tweed, with errant rock wall seams.*

*Natives trap these wild guinea hens, slit their plump legs and seal in berries and herbs before slowly roasting them over a reed fire.*

Language creates an atmosphere, draws a picture, and you sneak up on readers and listeners with information.

## Radio Formats

Because radio is so versatile, there are many ways to conceive a commercial. Here are a few of the more common formats:

❏ *The straight sell.* This is a spot where an announcer merely delivers the copy without any special effects or dramatization. With the right announcer for the right product, this can be effective, especially when some feature surpasses the norm. You've heard many of these.

  *Starting on June 1st, Allied Air Lines will launch the first direct flight to New York—at the low, low price of $139.*

❏ *The testimonial.* Many advertisers find this to be a most successful method, although few travel agencies employ it. Obviously, the better known the person delivering the testimony, the more impact it will have. There are also testimonial format spots where the copy sounds like a testimonial, but the speaker is anonymous. These may also be believable.

  *When I thought about touring Canada, I figured it would be just like driving across the United States. Was I wrong! On only the second day, my wife and I thought we'd been transported to Europe.*

❏ *The dramatization.* This format sets up a story premise. It may be a travel agent talking to someone on the phone, two friends discussing a trip, or a wife talking over vacation plans with her husband.

> HUSBAND: *I don't feel like driving another thousand miles, but . . .*
> WIFE: *But you'd like to have a car when we get there?*
> HUSBAND: *Yeah, you know, to get places.*
> WIFE: *Here, look at Acme's fly-drive package . . .*

❏ *The musical.* Sometimes the whole spot may be music, like a 30-second jingle, perhaps supplemented by an announcer giving information, like an address or phone number.

❏ *The promotional (or institutional) spot.* This is the sort of spot that talks generally about the travel business, or why you should use a travel agent, or what is happening to fares, without pitching a specific tour or other offering. It is supposed to garner good will, and help with name identification.

❏ *The humorous spot.* Humor is tough to write, but very effective. People like to repeat jokes, right? They also repeat funny commercials, and that's a big plus. The problem is that few people can write humor. Some ads are meant to be funny, but they're not. They age fast. Others are genuinely comic, and you turn up your radio when they come on. Stan Freberg, Bob and Ray, Stiller and Meara—there are the big names. You remember those Blue Nun commercials, or the Lanier Dictating Machine spots? Great Stiller and Meara routines.

You have to be careful when writing funny things about travel. There are ample opportunities for humor in travel but some aspects won't stand for much kidding. Stan Freberg produced a rare dud when he began a commercial for a West Coast airline with the line: "Hey, you there with the sweaty palms?" You may joke about your fears with friends, but you don't like to be reminded of them in connection with an appeal for flying.

There are all sorts of combinations of these spots, and there is also what is called the integrated spot, which consists of an advertising plug within a program. Some local disc jockeys make what seem like spontaneous comments about a product or service. If the personality involved has a following, this isn't a bad way to go.

## Some Tips for Radio Writing

1. *The opening and closing statements must be strong.* You want to grasp the casual listener's attention. Imagine yourself in your car, with the radio on, or working at night with the FM

tuned in. Because radio is a "background" medium, you may be completely unconscious of exactly what is being played or said. Consequently, you have to get the listener to pay attention. Some sound effects of music may do it, or some statement that produces an instant alert.

*Concerned about travel safety?*

The closing statement must also have something memorable about it. What do you want this listener to take away from this commercial? A name, an address, a phone number, a date? This will probably be a repeat of some earlier information, given here to reinforce the message in the mind of the audience.

*So, don't delay. Send today for your free European booklet. Just write: Travel Management Inc., 300 North Arapaho, Kingston, North Carolina. That's . . .*

2. *Keep your sales points to a minimum.* Radio messages can't be complicated. Ask yourself what the basic information is that the listener must have. Be sure this gets across, and don't clutter the spot with too many details. Citing a long list of cruise options, cabin assignments, and prices is hopeless on radio. Sell the scenic and recreational aspects, and have them write or call for specifics.
3. *Keep a conversational tone.* You're not selling a potato peeler or circus tickets. Travel ads should normally sound relaxed, unhurried. The delivery should be personal, warm, and intimate, not frantic and hard sell. Talk to the individuals; don't shout at the mob.

   One of the problems here has to do with timing. Don't write forty seconds of copy for a thirty-second commercial. This forces the talent to read rapidly. Write a little under, and give the announcer a chance for a more conversational presentation.

   When timing a spot, read it aloud to a stopwatch. And ask one or two others to read it aloud. This way you'll be sure it works before taking it to the sound studio or radio station, and you'll avoid having to cut or pad while paying for studio and talent time.

   Remember that your aim is persuasion, and you rarely persuade people by screaming at them, or pushing a string of words in their direction.

4. *Avoid cliches and superlatives.* Descriptions like "fun in the sun on the sandy beaches," and claims like "the greatest tour ever assembled" won't convince many listeners. Be believable.

5. *Create pictures with words.* This was mentioned earlier, and it's a tough discipline, trying to be picturesque without being trite, corny, or too ornate. Foreign words sometimes add color, and so do specific names instead of general names. It's better to say "motor beneath an arch of linden and aspen" than it is to say "drive underneath arching trees." Help the listener to see what you're talking about.

6. *Repeat important words.* One of the values of radio as a medium is its ability to install memorable phrases or jingles. Don't be afraid of saying something more than once. Perhaps it's a deadline date for signing up, or a one-time price, or a phone number. Give it to them at least a couple of times. You'd be amazed at how many times you can mention a company name in a thirty-second spot without being obnoxious.

7. *Be careful of tough things to read.* Certain words are hard to read, particularly in combination with other words. Saying "underneath the arching aspen" might be a bit tricky for most announcers. Try this one: ". . . welcoming in the winter wonderland." Or this: ". . . a memorable journey aboard this spotless twin-screw cruiser." Adverbs with *ly* in them can be difficult, like *extraordinarily,* and so can words with *un* in them, like *unenviable* or *unavoidable.* Some good words are rough in themselves (*applicable*), or look like other words (*ingenuous*), or sound like other words (*health* for *help*). Some words hiss, like *sensational,* or they pop, like *power-packed performance.* Try your commercial aloud and get a substitute for those words that sound bad on the air.

8. *Use shorts words and sentence fragments.* Not always, of course, but sentence fragments usually work. Use short, terse statements and short words. It's better to say a "great tour" than a "stupendous tour."

9. *Indicate punctuation to your talent.* When you have words that are particularly important, and that need to be stressed, underline them. When you want to indicate a pause use a double hyphen:

> . . . *but three days on Maui--now that's something* special.

Be certain that the person who will read the copy understands what it means and the way you want it to sound.

10. *Dialogue must be credible.* If you have two or more people conversing, their speech must sound something like normal speech. You can't put hard sell in the mouths of ordinary folk, and you can't make the exchange too obvious.

> RALPH:   *Where are you going on vacation this year, Gladys?*
> GLADYS:  *Reputable tours has an all-inclusive package featur-
> ing comfortable twin-bedded rooms in Europe's most
> prestigious luxury class hotels, complete with in-room
> television and digital wake-up alarm systems.*

Even when the premise is absurd or humorous, there must be some logic to the conversation. It shouldn't sound like "advertisingese."

## Some Other Attention-Getters

Listen to some radio commercials yourself and note the different methods they have of forcing you to listen. Kids' voices, for example, unusual accents, sound effects (like the Alka Seltzer fizz), a familiar star's voice, a tie-in with current events, a real-life interview, or some different musical effects capture a listener's attention.

You can also slow down or speed up the voices; you can set a familiar tune to a different tempo; you can be funny; you can hitch-hike on a station feature. One travel agency has a standing order with a local radio station to broadcast a Hawaii commercial every time the temperature gets below 20 degrees or there's a snowstorm.

## Producing the Radio Commercial

Once you have the script in hand, you should determine what music or sound effects you want, and what kind of talent you want for the reader(s). If you can bring all of this with you to the recording session, so much the better. The more you have set, the shorter the recording time should be.

Sound recording studios and radio stations also have talent pools and music and sound-effect libraries. You can call and ask if they have something that will work for you. The radio station announcer may also serve as your announcer. The problem with this latter idea, of course, is that it doesn't permit contrast, and the voice may be too familiar.

You bring enough scripts to give one to the talent and one to the sound engineer, at least. You'll also want your copy to check as the spot is being recorded. In the simplest of setups, the announcer may be in one booth, and the engineer (with the music and sound effects on record or cassette) in an adjoining booth. The engineer cues the music and the announcer, and puts the spot together, timing it and adding the appropriate sound levels. When it's finished, it's played back for you. If you're not satisfied, you say what you don't like, and try again. After you approve, as many dubs of the commercial will be made as you need to supply all the stations you will be using.

If you have enough money, of course, you get even fancier. You might have your own special jingle written. There are companies that specialize in this work, charging anywhere from $1,500 for a jingle based on a tune already in stock, to $7,500 and up for an original tune to fit your specific lyrics.

You could also have a live orchestra or combo at your recording session, for which you would pay the musicians' hourly rate, and probably double for the leader. You would also pay for rehearsal time.

The normal routine would be to bring the script, use the station or studio music and effects, and pay for an announcer and for the extra dubs. While the radio station may provide studio and engineering services free (if you are advertising on that station), the recording studio will bill you for studio time. The recording studio, however, normally gives you a superior product.

## The Script

Script copy is double spaced, with the name of the character (or announcer) on the left and capitalized. Sound effects (sometimes written SFX) and music cues are also capitalized.

If you understand the technical jargon (like FADE UNDER when you want the music to go below the announcer's voice) that's helpful. However, if you can just describe the effect you want, the engineer will provide it.

Figure 9–1 is a sample radio script, intended for a thirty-second spot. This script is fairly tight, so you see that you can't get a lot said in thirty seconds. If you have a longer message, buy a sixty-second spot.

In this rather uncomplicated spot, the firm name is repeated three times and the phone number twice, without overdoing it. Had there been any words in the spot that were difficult to pronounce,

EXCURSIONS INC.                JOB#: 191

(Address and Phone)           DATE: 11/13/87

DESCRIPTION: 30 SEC "CALIFORNIA"
  (Radio)                   TALENT: Ivan Nossen

---

SOUND:    "CALIFORNIA DREAMING" UP AND UNDER

NOSSEN:  (UP TEMPO DELIVERY)  Stop dreaming about California. Excursions Inc. invites you to live your dream. Excursion Inc.'s ten day California Highlights Tour takes you through the hills of San Francisco and the seafood delights of Fisherman's Wharf; through Hollywood's studios and the homes of stars; to the San Diego zoo; and for a breathtaking drive along Monterey Peninsula and around the fabulous Hearst Estate. Write or call for details. Excursions Inc. at the Harvard Mall, 677-2208. That's 677-2208. Make your dreams come true.

SOUND:    "CALIFORNIA DREAMING" UP AND OUT

**Fig. 9–1**

these would have been followed by the proper phonetic spelling (IN PARENTHESIS AND IN CAPS). Keep in mind that numbers take as long to read as words.
    Finally:

❑  Be careful of slang or cute language. It dates rapidly.
❑  Clever music and sound effects don't replace good writing.
❑  You may sometimes get a radio tape from a carrier, tourist office, or resort, with room left at the end for your identification or tag. This can be recorded as above, or left to the booth

announcer at the radio station to add each time the spot is played. You have to notify each station of this in writing, as accompaniment to the tape.

# TELEVISION

It should be unnecessary to remind scriptwriters that television is a visual medium, and not merely radio with pictures. You think in terms of pictures; you visualize the commercial. In fact, whenever you can let a picture do the work of words, let it!

Keep in mind that the average over-18 viewer sees about 3½ hours of television daily. A lot of commercials pass in front of his or her eyes. Many of them aren't even seen, not only because they've taken this opportunity to leave the room, but because they simply don't register, even when the person is watching the set.

Very little of most television commercials is retained. Half the time the viewers can't recall the sponsors of a commercial they admired. A fourth of the time they credit a favorite spot to the wrong sponsor.

What you have to say, then, must be interesting, compelling, and memorable. You also have to realize that you have interrupted the program the viewer was watching, so your commercial should be somehow rewarding and worth the intrusion.

## Television Formats

❏ *Straight announcer.* While this may be okay on radio, it is usually dull on television. They refer to this as "talking heads" and there is little excitement in this approach. As with any statement, however, there are exceptions. And sometimes a straight announcer may provide a contrast with flashier commercials.

❏ *The testimonial.* This is probably more effective on television than on radio. Now you can see the person giving the testimonial, and this has added credibility. To liven up such a spot, you can place the person giving the testimonial in some interesting setting.

❏ *The demonstration.* One of the major advantages of television is that it can show as well as tell. If you were doing a spot on how fast your computers can process a ticket request, why not show the computer in action? Or, instead of talking about

cruise accommodations, show the viewer an animated chart.
Contac shows the tiny capsules, and some antacids let you
watch their product dissolving stomach problems. Travel has
many things (and more appetizing things) to display.

❏ *The "slice-of-life" commercial.* This kind of spot features people
talking about a product or service, like housewives discussing
coffee or laundry—or an agent and a customer talking about
travel options?

❏ *The story.* Some commercials tell a story. Some of the award
winners from companies like Coca Cola and Kodak unfold a
complete tale in thirty or sixty seconds, with very few words.
Other stories take the form of a crisis (like stale sandwiches or
spotted glasses), which is solved by a product (often presented
by a company symbol, like Mr. Clean). Travel agencies can
also use this approach to convince the viewer of the convenience of using a travel agent, or the ease of getting a car
rental.

❏ *The musical.* This is generally expensive and wouldn't be used
much by the travel agency, although it could be effective for
the cruise line or airline. In this commercial, the music is the
star, and there may be a chorus line, a pop singer, or some other talent. It's like thirty seconds from a Broadway musical.

❏ *The special effects spot.* Here the star is the camera. You drop a
man into a speeding car, or make a travel brochure appear
suddenly in the hands of a would-be tourist, or freeze the character in midair. You've seen this often in commercials that feature expanding washing machines, tiny announcers walking
inside car engines, or the Jolly Green Giant patting a cartoon
child on the head.

Some of these are difficult and expensive; others are simple
enough to be handled by your local TV studio. If you have something
like this in mind, visit with the producer-director of the TV station,
explain the effect you want, and let him or her suggest ways to
accomplish it.

## Some Tips for TV Writing

❏ Understand the way the camera operates, knowing what it can
do and can't do. In fact, be conversant with the entire production technique.

❏ Don't include too many shots or scenes. The viewer can't handle multiple changes within the brief framework of a TV commercial.

❏ Consider color, and the way things will look in color.

❏ Favor close-ups over long shots. Remember that virtually all television sets are relatively small. If the picture shows a distant figure, this makes it harder to catch expressions and even harder to understand. Use both types of shots, of course, but the close-up should dominate.

❏ Remember that you can superimpose type over the screen. Type can be used to identify people speaking, to caption a scene, to highlight a price, and, certainly, to feature a firm name, address, and phone. It doesn't hurt if the audio also repeats this information as it's being shown.

❏ Match sound to the pictures (or audio to video) but let the pictures carry the weight of the message. What is being said must tie in with what is being seen, but there is no need to explain something that is perfectly clear to viewers watching the tube.

❏ Stay in touch with the latest equipment, including the lightweight portable cameras that are handy for location shots, and the expanded control boards that multiply the available special effects. Character generators, computer graphics, and other tools may also be handy.

## The Storyboard

After the script is written, there is often another intermediary step before production. It's called the storyboard. This is a visual depiction of the commercial, much like you'd see in a comic strip. It enables the producer-director to better understand what you have in mind.

Sometimes the picture panels in the storyboard are drawings and sometimes they are photos. Polaroids, for example, work quite well. The storyboard may be rough or finished, depending on time, money, and who needs to see it.

You can buy special sheets that have a space for the picture and for copy under the picture. This makes the whole process simpler, since you can type the attendant copy into the space beneath the appropriate illustration.

# VACATION AMERICA IS ON TV...JOIN US NOW AND SHARE OUR TRAVEL CLOUT!

We're going on television in a big way...with hundreds of spots to acquaint millions of people with the Vacation America concept and to bring them into Vacation America travel agencies for all their travel needs. We'll be on the most popular shows like: Merv Griffin; NBC News; Today Show; etc.—with a major campaign that will benefit Vacation America agencies. If you join us now you could have that Travel Clout, too. Call Michael Brent today, Toll Free (800) 223-1735 for all the interesting—and profitable—details.

**Man:** I need a vacation!

**Woman:** It's so late . . . hope we can get reservations!

**Michael Brent:** Relax! With Vacation America you have Travel Clout! You see we're a network of travel agencies.

Travel professionals who can get you where you want to go, when you want to go, at the lowest price available.

**Woman:** We're on our way!

**Man:** Thanks Vacation America! You gave us Travel Clout!

Check the travel section of your local newspaper for the Vacation America Agency nearest you.

**VACATION AMERICA INC.,**
521 FIFTH AVENUE, NEW YORK, N.Y. 10017
(212) 867-8530 or (800) 223-1735

PARTNERS IN TRAVEL WITH AMERICA'S AGENTS.

**Fig. 9–2    Vacation America, Inc. uses a storyboard as the basis of a print ad.** (Courtesy of Vacation America Inc.)

## The Television Camera

In a sense, the lens of the television camera does what the eyes do—only more. It can move up and down, the way the eye would examine a person from head to toe. This called a tilt and instructions would be to "Tilt up" or "Tilt down." It can move from side to side (a pan) and you can write into the script: "Pan left to right" or "Pan right to left." You also have a follow pan where the camera follows a moving object, with the background blurred; or a whip pan, where the camera whips across the scene, causing a blur. This latter technique is sometimes used to show change of time or locale.

The TV camera also has a zoom lens which can move toward or away from a scene or person, either slowly or rapidly. This really replaces the dolly shot, where the whole camera was pushed forward or pulled back, but there could be occasions when you would also want to dolly.

A truck shot is one where the camera moves laterally on wheels, either following some action or covering a wide panorama. And a crane shot is one where the camera is overhead, on a crane or cherry picker, in order to shoot down on the subject.

## The Shots

A number of different terms are used to describe the size of the subject you are viewing on your screen.

Beginning with the extreme long shot (ELS), which would encompass a whole panorama, like a chase scene in a western, the script can call for any of the intervening shots, such as: long shot (LS); medium long shot (MLS); medium shot (MS)—which would take in a person's whole body or most of the body; medium close-up (MCU)—a torso shot or closer; close-up (CU)—tight on head and shoulders; extreme or tight close-up (XCU, ECU, TCU)—face only, or even a portion of the face.

Directors also talk about full-length shots and reverse shots (showing you what the actor is seeing, at 180 degrees from him), and "package two shots," which mean an actor and a package (or brochure), and many other variations.

Again, the travel agent needn't be familiar with all this technology, nor does he or she have to write these directions into the script. As long as the script explains what is required, the director can call for the appropriate shot.

## The Editing Possibilities

When the director sits in the booth helping you to put together your commercial, he or she can speak directly into the earphones of two or three (or more) cameramen who are on the studio floor. The director can also see what each camera is seeing. These images are shown on a bank of monitors in the booth. Transitions from image to image can be handled in a number of ways. The technical term for these transitions is optical effects.

❑ *Fade in and fade out.* The director can start from black and then bring in a scene, or go from a scene to black, before introducing the next scene.

❑ *Dissolve.* Instead of going to black, one scene merges momentarily with another. The blending may be rapid or slow, depending on the mood and pace you desire.

You sometimes have a match dissolve where the object in one shot nearly matches the shape in the next. A globe, for example, may turn into a rotating tire.

❑ *Wipe.* There are dozens of variety of wipes. A new picture can come down like a curtain, across like a sliding door, explode from the center, sneak in diagonally, and so on. Some of these may be artistic; some are merely cute.

❑ *Miscellaneous.* You may use fast motion or slow motion; you can split the screen so that you see both ends of a phone conversation; you can have multiple images, like the reflections of a score of mirrors; you can use the chromakey; or you can superimpose type or other objects over the scene.

## Sound

Although the visual aspect of television is the more important, sound remains a key element. You indicate this on the script just as you do with radio. The two most often used terms are "direct sound" or "voice over." Direct sound or lip sync means that the person being shown is doing the talking, with his speech synchronized to his lip movements. The sound is usually recorded at the same time the film is shot. Your normal TV drama uses this technique. Voice over means that an off-camera voice is doing the narrating, such as you experience when watching many documentaries—or, for that matter, most travel films. This is added later.

You'll hear people say that something is "out of sync" when the lip movements don't match the sound exactly. And the expression

**Fig. 9–3   Film technique is sometimes used to produce TV documentaries or travel shows.**

"wild sound" refers to just leaving the mike on to catch things like traffic or cocktail party noises or jungle birds. These may be used later as background for other sounds.

## Ways to Produce TV Shows

In the early days both television shows and TV commercials were done live. There was a certain spontaneity to this that was exciting, but there was also the possibility of error. Easy-to-open doors stuck; ice cream melted in the dish; actors missed cues.

Today, with rare exceptions like the occasional spot on the *Tonight Show,* all commercials are taped. Most shows are also taped, except for fast-breaking news and live sports.

When you tape a commercial, you can play it back immediately, to see how you like it. You can then make changes, running the tape back, and rerecording on it. Or you may just cut a second tape and compare the two spots.

Besides live television and the nearly universal videotape, you also have film. Some commercials are filmed and then transferred to tape, because film is a bit more versatile and a bit sharper. Tape is improving every year, however, causing more and more shows and commercials to be made this way.

Film can be run on a separate projector and just integrated into whatever spot you are producing. Slides, too, are placed on a special slide chain that can also be made part of the tape during the production process. Before this was possible, the cameras would use photos that were placed on tote boards and illuminated, so that the TV camera could take a picture of it and transmit it live.

## How Commercials Are Produced

As mentioned above, you could film an entire commercial and put it together in a film studio, using film editing equipment, just as they do to produce Hollywood films. Or you could take some film to the TV studio and have it transferred to tape. Or you could tape the whole show in the studio, using live performers, and integrate appropriate films, slides, art, or music.

For most travel agencies, the routine will be more like this:

❏   A script is produced.
❏   Talent, props, and music are obtained.
❏   A time and date are set for recording at a local TV studio.
❏   The director takes your script, rehearses the talent, cues the appropriate music and visuals, and puts the tape together.
❏   If you approve of the results, he can make you videotape dubs, just as the sound studio produced sound tapes.

If you use an advertising agency for your radio and television, it would perform all of these chores for you, from script to seeing that the right videotapes arrived at the right TV stations. You could go along to watch production if you wished, but the agency would handle the details.

## The Script

While the script is the first thing that is done, it seemed appropriate here to discuss it last, since a knowledge of production must come before any sensible writing can be accomplished.

There are some variations on the way a television script might be written—particularly if film is involved—but the usual format is to place the video (or visual) instructions on the left of the script sheet, and the audio portion on the right:

| VIDEO | AUDIO |
|---|---|
| MCU BROCHURE | ANNCR: Write today for this new brochure describing the week-long Nile voyage. |

Sound cues are also indicated under audio, are printed in capital letters, and underlined (at least this is one good method to use).

Figure 9–4 shows one way the previous radio script in Figure 9–1 might look on television.

## A Few Added TV Tips

❑ If you are supervising production of the television spot, make certain everything is ready to go—*and* rehearsed—before you go to the TV studio. Television studio time is expensive.

❑ When the producing is being done, the director is in charge. You don't stand over his or her shoulder making suggestions. When the spot is taped (and before it's taped), you can make your suggestions.

❑ You have to develop a sense of time. For example, how long do you want the theme music to stay up? If the talent is holding up a brochure, how long does he have to hold it in order to have it register with the audience?

❑ You also have to develop a sense of timing. When you get experienced at writing a spot, you can get pretty close to the right time for a 30- or 60-second spot, without having to do a lot of cutting or padding.

There are some guidelines. You can figure about two words a second, straight talk. But there are so many variables. You may use a character voice that requires a slower delivery. Or you may want to leave a picture up with only music behind it. It may take only a few words, for example, to describe a film sequence that takes 10 minutes on the screen. If you write 60 words for a 30-second spot and 120 words for a 60-second spot, you'll be close—but *full*.

❑ Remember that TV screens have rounded edges, so don't put important things like a phone number or address in the corners.

❑ Any visuals you use must fit the dimensions of the TV screen, meaning that they must have a ratio of 4:3. So the artwork could be 12″ wide × 9″ deep, for example.

EXCURSIONS, INC.                              JOB#: 192

(Address and Phone)                          DATE: 12/4/87

DESCRIPTION: 30 SEC "CALIFORNIA"
   (Television)                              TALENT: Rick Francis

---

| VIDEO | AUDIO |
|---|---|
| | SOUND:  "CALIFORNIA DREAMING" UP |
| AERIAL SHOTS |           AND UNDER |
| OF CALIFORNIA | RICK:  Stop dreaming about |
| COASTLINE |        California. Excursions Inc. invites you to live your dream. |
| MONTAGE OF | SOUND:  MUSIC UP THEN |
| CALIFORNIA |           UNDER |
| SCENES | RICK:  Excursion Inc.'s ten day Cali- |
| SAN FRANCISCO |        fornia Highlights Tour takes you through the hills of San Francisco and the seafood delights of Fisherman's |
| OVERHEAD VIEW OF |        Wharf; through Hollywood's |
| PARAMOUNT STUDIO |        studios and the homes of the |
| LION PACING IN CAGE |        stars; to the San Diego Zoo; |
| SEASCAPE WITH SURF |        and for a breathtaking drive along the Monterey Peninsula. |
| SUPER ADDRESS AND |        Write or call for details. |
| PHONE NUMBER |        Excursions Inc. at the Harvard Mall, 678-2208. That's |
| COUPLE ON BEACH |        678-2208. Make your dreams come true. |
| SUPER LOGO | SOUND:  MUSIC UP AND OUT |

**Fig. 9—4**

Another consideration when using slides is that slides on the horizontal axis work best. Those that are taller than they are wide either get cropped at top and bottom, or they have empty space on either side.

❏ The commercials you see for national products cost anywhere from $15,000 to $150,000 to produce; sometimes more, rarely less. While the travel agency can't compete with these types of expenditures, it still must produce something that doesn't look like poor quality by comparison.

❏ Don't forget to figure production costs in your budget.

❏ Test your commercial before an audience before it airs. Take them to the studio to see it. Pick average prospects, not your own employees. See if they understand it, if they remember it, and if they regard it favorably.

## RADIO AND TELEVISION TRAVEL SHOWS

There are few travel shows on radio, but that doesn't mean the package isn't adaptable to radio. With a little thought, a good radio show could be developed, built around interviews, traditional music, and straight information. This might not sustain for thirty minutes but a series of five-minute programs works well, and would not be difficult or expensive to produce.

The advantage of a show over a commercial is not only length, but, if done properly, a greater amount of interest and credibility.

Travel programs on television are fairly common. Some of them are expertly done; some of them are hardly more interesting than your neighbor's vacation slides. The secret is to minimize the individual or group conversation, and to show visuals that have impact. Coming up with an interesting topic is also a plus. The alert agent will tie the program into current news events, or into seasonal travel, or into a topic that has a high degree of appeal.

Many films are available, of course, but these should be screened in advance for their appropriateness. Slides can be used effectively, and it helps to bring lively people on the set for interviews. Generally speaking, it's wise to center each program on a specific topic (like shopping in Europe) or on a particular geographical area. This keeps the show tight and logical.

Some travel show sponsors have films and slides they've shot, or they use film and slides shot by friends and associates. These visuals must be good. You can excuse some poor photography when you are explaining your efforts to friends in your home, but this program is being televised to thousands (well, you hope there'll be thousands) of strangers.

The same principle applies to the question of who should host the show. If you're good at it—and some travel managers are—then you can run the program yourself. If not, get a professional announcer. Think of the terrible work done by many used car dealers.

If you use a professional announcer, you or someone from your staff should also be highly visible on the show. Perhaps you are interviewed at the beginning and end, or you help out with interviews of guests. The trained announcer then carries the show but the viewers get to see what you look and sound like.

A typical travel show on television could go this way:

1. Opening segment of introductions and setting of the stage for this specific program.
2. A film or slide sequence.
3. An interview.
4. More film or slides.
5. Closing segment and wrap-up.

You must be certain you get strong agency identification. This can be accomplished by designing a set that features your company name and logo as background, by occasional supers (type superimposed over an image) on the screen giving your name and title, and by periodic reminders by the announcer.

Most travel shows occur at hours when the audience potential is smallest—in nonprime time. This could be on Saturday or Sunday mornings, perhaps, or on early weekend afternoons. This is less expensive for the agency and the local station may also be quite happy to have this show aired if its quality is acceptable.

You can help build an audience by doing some direct mail to your list of clients and prospects, informing them, perhaps monthly, of upcoming programs.

The show will likely be taped a few days in advance. As with commercials, the more you can do in advance to ensure a professional look, the better off you'll be. Sloppy performances connote a sloppy business.

## MISCELLANEOUS

Keep in mind that there could be variations of the radio and television formats covered in this chapter. Sometimes a TV segment on travel may be part of a general news or entertainment feature. Or travel experts could be invited to participate in an interview show, or requested to comment on radio or television on some current travel event.

Because most travel agents do not have large advertising budgets, it's smart to think of other ways that an impact may be made on these media.

## CHAPTER HIGHLIGHTS

❏ Every successful radio or television spot starts with a good memorable idea.

❏ Radio is written for the ear and, with a little imagination, can quickly create a mood or atmosphere.

❏ There are numerous radio formats, including the straight sell, the testimonial, the dramatization, the musical, the promotional spot, and the humorous spot.

❏ Radio commercials should be credible, conversational, fresh, uncluttered, and written to be read and heard.

❏ Scriptwriting, while a special skill, may be learned by the creative agency person, with a little practice.

❏ Television is a visual medium and also has a variety of formats, including the straight announcer, the testimonial, the demonstration, the "slice-of-life," the story, the musical, and the special effects spot.

❏ Scriptwriters should be familiar with the technical possibilities of the TV cameras and editing board, and should also know the shorthand for different types of camera shots and angles.

❏ The television script is often augmented by a storyboard which, using drawings or still photos, serves as a plan for the spot.

❏ Besides using television as a medium for advertising, travel agencies may also host travel shows or make guest appearances.

■          ■          ■

## ❏ *EXERCISES*

1. Identify national or local radio spots that fit each of the formats mentioned in this chapter.

2. Observe a television commercial (for any product) that appears regularly in your viewing area and list the visual effects and variety of shots.

3. How do commercials for airlines on television differ from those you have seen for the same airlines in print? Give a specific example.

4. Check with a local radio station or sound studio to see what sort of sound effects library it has. Make a note of the different sound effects under a single category, like crowds, trains, or whatever.

## ❏ *CASE PROBLEMS*

*1. Find a print ad in a newspaper or magazine. Select one that has sufficient copy to support a radio or television script. Also make your selection based on your appraisal of the radio or television potential of this material. Using this copy platform, and adding as you see fit, write a 30-second radio or TV script, indicating sound effects, music, type of talent, and, for television, both video and audio.*

*2. Develop a 30-second television commercial to attract visitors to your area from a distance of no further than 8 hours by car. Write the script for this, indicating the features you will present and the copy you will use to present your area. Also indicate what audience you have in mind.*

# 10

# THE OTHER ADVERTISING MEDIA

Provided you have the money, there are dozens of other ways to advertise besides the regular print and broadcast media. Some of these—like direct mail—could prove the best approach in a specific advertising campaign.

## OUT-OF-HOME MEDIA

This category sums up all of the poster-type advertising, from illuminated billboards to taxi-top cards. Virtually all of these (with the exception of ads inside subway cars or on bus benches) share the problem of allowing little time for reflective reading. That's why all of these considerations must go into the creation of such posters:

1. *The background should be simple.* A background that is too busy, having a lot of conflicting elements, will cause problems for the reader. He or she will find it difficult to focus attention on the ad and difficult to make sense out of the copy.
2. *Copy must be short.* Use as few words as possible. Many designers recommend keeping the number of words under five. In any event, this is no place for a long message.
3. *Use short words.* An occasional long word may be an attention-getter, but it's wiser to use crisp Anglo-Saxon prose, rather than long Latinized terms.
4. *Make the illustrations large.* Tiny, subtle illustrations won't work. You need SIZE! If you're advertising a flight to Hawaii, you want a plane that covers most of the board, or a huge palm tree, or a larger-than-life King Kamehameha. A few coconuts hidden in a corner will be lost to motorists or pedestrians.

5. *Make your colors bold.* There are exceptions to this, but pastels look washed out, and they fade quickly. Stick with the bright, vibrant hues.
6. *Employ readable type.* The few words you use must be in a typeface that is large enough to read and in a design that is easy to make out. An elaborate script, or an Old English type, might be impossible to interpret when you're driving by.
7. *Be sure your agency is identified.* Small logos and indistinct type are bad news. In fact, the two things that should emerge from any poster are your name, and the reason to patronize you.

## PRODUCING THE POSTER

Although this may not be accurate for every type of poster, billboard, or bus card, you'll find that a preliminary sketch with a ratio of 1 to 2¼ will suffice. A workable size for such a sketch, for example, might be 4″ high × 9″ wide. When you come down to creating the artwork that will be used to make the poster, however, you'll want to be certain what dimensions are more exact. Check this with your sign company.

To produce the large billboards you see on your highways, the original artwork is put into a projector that blows it up to the exact size needed, projecting it against the paper, wood, or metal surface on which it is to be painted. For painted boards, the painting can be done right on the surface which will be used. For paper posters, the drawing is used to make stencils, and the individual panels for the finished billboard are silk-screened, meaning that paint is squeezed through the stenciled areas, much as you might stencil an article at home.

If a large number of boards will be used, it is usually cheaper to lithograph them, rather than using the silk-screen process.

When the individual panels are finished, they are brought to the site and posted. Each panel is glued on, overlapping its neighbor, to give the appearance of one solid advertisement. The names of billboards are somewhat confusing, since a 30-sheet poster, for example, contains not 30 panels, but only about 12.

**The Poster**

The standardized poster panel is usually 24 feet, 6 inches long and 12 feet high and can accommodate 3 different sizes of poster: the 24-sheet, the 30-sheet and the bleed. All 3 sizes involve a proportion of 2¼ to 1.

**24-Sheet Poster**
Many years ago when printing presses were smaller a poster panel required 24 sheets of paper. Today with larger presses, fewer sheets are needed, but the original term remains. Above right is a typical paper pattern for a 24-sheet poster, which measures 19 feet, 6 inches by 8 feet, 8 inches. The area between the design and the frame is covered with white blanking paper.

**30-Sheet Poster**
The 30-sheet poster, measuring 21 feet, 7 inches by 9 feet, 7 inches, provides about 25% more space for the design than does the 24-sheet poster. The additional space is taken from the blanking area. Middle right is a typical paper pattern for the 30-sheet poster. Through careful planning of the pattern, 4-color printing can be limited to a minimum number of sheets for lower production costs.

**Bleed Poster**
In the bleed poster—40% larger than the 24-sheet—the design is carried all the way to the frame. This is done by printing the minor variations in the overall size of poster panels, essential elements of the design—such as copy or logo—should be positioned at least 6 inches from the edges. This will ensure their appearance on the smallest panels.

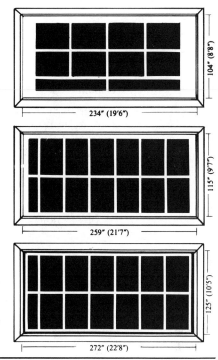

**Fig. 10–1** (Courtesy of Gannett Foundation)

# A FEW REMINDERS

☐ At a distance of 100 yards, a 24-sheet poster (9' high × 20' wide) appears about as large as a postage stamp.

☐ Severe changes in weather affect outdoor posters, washing out colors and, on metal boards, popping out the paint.

☐ Be conscious of the placement of colors, since a little thought while laying out the poster may save several extra press runs.

❏  If a large photo is used in an outdoor advertisement, the local sign company may not be able to handle it. This may require the work of an out-of-town specialty shop, with a large enough camera to tackle this assignment.

❏  Perhaps even more than any other medium, the outdoor field demands early and close consultation with the ultimate supplier.

# TRANSIT POSTERS

Posters in subway stations, and cards ranged above subway car windows, have been staple advertising items for many years. Those inside the cars have the advantage of a captive audience who may have little else to do but read those signs. Those in subway stations get through traffic as well as local pedestrian traffic but need to be larger.

Cards on the top or rear of taxis and on the side, back, front, and interiors of buses all have value, particularly as name recognition tools. Frequency of use is a major factor in creating a lasting image.

# DISPLAYS AND EXHIBITS

There are occasions when a travel agency may be called upon to locate an exhibit or display in a convention hall or shopping mall. The primary need for display materials, however, is likely to be within the agency itself.

Many agencies have a cluttered look. There are a hundred different items, from wall posters to ship models, all scattered about with no apparent sense of proportion or organization. The trick is to look exciting without appearing messy. This takes someone with as much courage at removing items as in adding them. Frequent changes are healthy and attractive.

The rules for organizing exhibits are little different than those for good layout. You want harmony, sequence, and balance. You want the proper proportions, an appealing mixture of colors and themes, but without any sense of confusion. The travel office should seem a warm, interesting, and efficient place to visit.

When exhibiting your wares elsewhere, keep in mind that a static exhibit is the least likely to attract a crowd. Something should be going on. Perhaps it's a continuous slide show, or travel films, or a

**Fig. 10–2   Even a homemade sign may serve an advertising purpose.**

contest in which passersby can participate, or some live entertainment. A display of pictures may attract an audience on a slow day, but not when there are other more exciting choices. Since production, transportation, and space rental may be expensive, travel firms have to weigh carefully the prospective value of trade shows and exhibits.

## NOVELTIES

Many firms specialize in the production of novelty items, from pens to shoehorns, and from emery boards to golf tees. There are literally thousands of items to choose from, and one of the desirable skills to have is the ability to select something appropriate.

You always want something that is useful, so that it will enjoy a long life, and something that allows for decent name identification. You may also have to consider things like cost and distribution.

Matchbooks are one of the more popular novelty items and certain match companies can produce a variety of containers, from the standard folder to cylinders (for products like Campbell Soup and Babo) to boxes shaped like trucks or buildings. Not much copy can be placed on these items, but, again, a strong agency identification is paramount.

Before ordering any novelties, the agency should also consider how it is going to distribute them. Will they be sent through the mail to regular customers? Handed out over the counter? Given away at an open house?

Failure to plan wisely can result in a large and useless inventory. Many politicians, for example, have invested in thousands of bumper stickers, only to discover that they can't get them circulated or used.

## DIRECTORIES

Directory advertising isn't usually too imaginative and perhaps it doesn't have to be. After all, when you use a directory, you're already looking for certain information. You've by-passed the attention and interest and desire factors, and are looking now for credibility and action factors.

You would tailor your ad somewhat to the directory. If you were advertising your agency in a Chamber of Commerce directory, you might want to stress commercial accounts more. In a telephone directory or city directory, you're appealing to a general audience and will include more general information. The ad should still be attractive, and it should anticipate the usual questions an information seeker has in mind. Obviously, it should also include a striking agency identification.

Check your ad and copy periodically. Advertisers have a tendency to repeat their directory ads year in and year out. This can result in stale promotional efforts. Keep the ad looking fresh.

# DIRECT MAIL

There's no question that this advertising medium has considerable potential for travel agencies, but they must know how to use it properly. The secret of direct mail is to pinpoint just the right audience, tailor a message that's perfect for them, and give them a means of responding.

Direct mail advertising isn't the same as mail order advertising. The latter term is used to define ads that sell goods through the mail and appear in newspapers and magazines, usually including a coupon. Those late-night record album offers on television are also mail order ads.

Neither is direct mail advertising synonymous with direct advertising. Direct advertising encompasses direct mail, but also includes merchandising across the counter, door-to-door giveaways, street vendors who distribute samples, and other forms of reaching the consumer directly.

Direct mail refers to advertising that reaches the consumer through the mails, instead of appearing in the mass media, like newspapers or television.

Since 1928, direct mail advertising (*if* it meets the postal requirements) is entitled to a bulk rate. Generally, either first- or third-class mail is used.

Over 30 billion pieces of direct mail are sent to people in the United States each year, which means that every man, woman, and child receives more than 140 individual pieces annually. Some days 5 or 6 pieces may be in the same mail. That emphasizes the need for a package that stands out.

## Mailing Lists

The first consideration in the use of direct mail is the development of a workable list of recipients. You want a list of the best prospects, those most likely to be interested in that particular mailing piece. If you could do this with scientific precision, no other advertising medium could touch direct mail. You would be able to talk only to those potential consumers who had the desire and the means to respond to the offer. Such precision, however, is rarely possible, although experts in this field obviously do better than amateurs.

These lists are cleaned regularly, meaning that they are checked for changes of address, deaths, and the like. For a number of these lists, the sender is required to supply a sample of the mailing package.

## The Travel Agency List

If you are setting up a direct mail list for a travel agency, where would you begin?

For commercial accounts, you'd certainly want a list of the major business firms, preferably one that listed the chief executive, his or her secretary, or the purchasing agent. If there were a purchasing agents' group in town (and if they typically bought travel packages), you might work from that list.

But how would you go about securing regular clientele?

You might be able to get a list of those who traveled anywhere during the past two years. Or you could get a list of subscribers to travel magazines. Or you might work on occupational lists containing people (like secretaries and teachers) who generally travel. Or you could build up a "Gold Coast" list of the city's wealthiest individuals.

If you were trying to sell a special tour—say, a two-week tour to Ireland—you could direct your mail campaign at ethnic groups, like the Ancient Order of Hibernians, or Friendly Sons and Daughters of Saint Patrick, or members of the Irish-American Cultural Institute. You might even do a telephone check of those with obviously Irish names.

For a tour of Europe's Catholic shrines, you might try to locate lists of the congregations in all the Catholic parishes. A trip to Israel would seem to indicate a list of synagogue memberships, plus members of the Jewish community center and B'nai B'rith.

Most of the larger communities have direct mail houses, and these firms both broker lists and perform all the mailing mechanics (addressing, stuffing, mailing). You can also buy lists from national firms, if they meet your need. Lists are sold for so much a thousand names (usually anywhere from $25 a thousand to $50 a thousand), and are available on magnetic tape or labels, or in some other form.

If the list is large, it's wise to buy a few thousand and experiment with them, before committing to larger numbers.

Let's say you have available, in a large city, a list of 50,000 persons who have purchased air tickets over the past two years. You should buy 5,000. If it remains good, then buy the list.

What do we mean buy good? Well, this will vary. On a cold national mailing for a charitable cause, sponsors might be happy with a

1.5% return; 2% would be very good. With a local mailing, returns could be higher, depending on what you were selling. This argues again for selectivity. If you could isolate the best prospects among the 50,000 above, that would be the thing to do.

## The Direct Mail Package

Typically, a direct mail package would include a letter, a brochure, and some method of responding: either a return postcard, or a blank and a return envelope. These will be enclosed in a mailing envelope.

The mailing envelope should be attractive enough to encourage opening. Sometimes a window envelope is used, with an address or part of a message showing through; sometimes a provocative statement is printed on the outside envelope. The sender's first step is to get you to open the envelope. As more and more direct mail advertisers use up the bag of possible tricks, it gets increasingly difficult to be different. Many readers can quickly spot insurance plans or retirement plans or swatches from cloth coats, and they may discard the package without peeking inside.

Travel has a lot of romance and interest going for it—naturally. So the travel manager should not be too hard pressed to come up with a gimmick line or illustration that arouses curiosity.

IS A BARGAIN TOUR REALLY A BARGAIN?

TIM KIELTY HELPED SAVE THE HAY IN TIPPERARY.

IF YOU MUST HAVE A HOT DOG ON THE VIA VENUTO . . .

The letter may not have as many readers as the brochure but, if the prospect really gets interested, he or she will take time to read everything.

The trick to writing decent letters is to write to one person. After all, only one person gets each one. It must sound personal and human. Machines are available today that also make the letter look personal and individualized. So, have a typical prospect in mind and sell him or her, using the language that will excite and interest, and remembering to answer all his or her potential questions—or almost all of them.

Using a narrative hook to start a direct mail letter is a good technique. After all, addressing a stranger as "Dear Friend" is a little awkward, and "Dear Sir" is too formal, and often inaccurate. Many letters begin with some quote or statement to entice the reader to read on. For example:

> *I'd never use a travel agent because they cost extra.*
> *WRONG!*

or

> *If you thought the only Roman ruins were in Italy, you're in for a surprise.*

The first paragraph in these letters is usually short, as are most paragraphs, but they should be varied for length. You don't want the letter to look like a child's primer, nor do you want any huge paragraphs that scare the casual reader. Break up the bulky paragraphs and use frequent subheads to separate the page(s) of copy. The idea is to make perusal seem simple and pleasant.

Sometimes you may center some of the information, like this:

> *Here are three reasons to visit Russia NOW!*
> *Fares are low.*
> *The weather is perfect.*
> *It's the festival season.*

Like radio, direct mail features strong opening and closing paragraphs. Don't just wander into the reader's consciousness, and don't hang around after you've said everything. You must be truthful and factual, avoiding "advertisingese" and obvious exaggeration.

You must also keep the prospect's interests in mind. What are his or her possible motives for making this journey, or for using your other travel services? Speak to these. Emphasize the benefits. This helps build credibility along with desire.

Remember to convince the reader about the differences involved in doing business with you. There are always alternatives. Even if you are the only agency in town, there is the choice of going directly to the carrier. You must show the prospect why your route is better.

Generally, you don't tell the prospect the entire story. You want to save something for the office visit or the follow-up brochure. Cramming every bit of information into the direct mail piece could turn off the prospect. Perhaps he or she thinks February is a bad month for a vacation, or reacts against a visit to the Berlin Opera, or fails to understand one of the expenditure items. You should not be devious, but you should leave some unanswered questions. A face-to-face conversation can alter many presumed biases.

The exception to this rule is when direct mail is used as mail order direct mail, meaning that it must do the whole job and get the order. This would be rare in travel advertising, since the prospect does have many things he or she wants to know, and because the cost of a trip is usually significant.

The format of the letter can take any form, just like an ad. It can be chatty and conversational; it can tell a story; it can be a testimonial; it can be humorous; flat-out factual; or very soft-sell. You select the method that seems best for this particular story.

Finally, there are mechanical ways to get attention as well. Some letters are typed using different colored ribbons for emphasis, they include the prospect's name (inserted manually or automatically), or they employ gadgets.

Gadgets are items that are stuck on the letterhead or somehow made part of the package. Many are corny, like a toothpick and the accompanying admonition to "Pick One of Our Sensational Tours"; or a tiny shoe with an adjacent statement reading: "You'll get a boot out of our low prices." You've seen swatches of cloth, paper clips, pennies, and other items. If you go the gadget route, here are some cautions.

- ❏ You can't send unlit matches or sharp objects through the mail.
- ❏ Be sure the gadget is appropriate to your message and not just an unrelated gimmick.
- ❏ Be sure it isn't offensive to anyone.
- ❏ Be sure it sticks or stays in place.
- ❏ Make certain it doesn't overpower the message.
- ❏ If possible, make it something useful.

If there is a brochure as part of the package, it should complement the letter, but also have its own appeal. Remember, when printing, that the brochure, letter, and other inserts must fit whatever size external envelope you've chosen. Usually this will be a #10 envelope, the long envelope that measures approximately 9½" long × 4⅛" high. You also have to be conscious of weight, if mailing first class.

Brochures are sometimes mailed by themselves—as self-mailers—with the back page blank for the address of the recipient.

The return card or envelope needs to be convenient and comprehensive. The convenience is for the prospect; the comprehensive aspect for you. You try to make it as simple as possible for the individual to reply. A prepaid envelope is the usual choice. The respondent needs to put no stamp on the envelope; you pay the

**Fig. 10–3  Using a multipanel layout design, Fodor's showcases some of its many colorful brochures.** (Courtesy of Fodor's Travel Publications)

postman for each returned envelope. While this is more expensive than a regular stamp, don't forget that you pay only for those that are returned.

The regular stamp on the return envelope, while more expensive and wasteful, might be better in some instances—such as with a small and tested mailing list. The stamp somehow seems more urgent than the prepaid statement.

You can also request that the post office notify you of changes of address, in order that you make the appropriate change in your mailing list. For this service you pay a charge. This may seem like a waste of money but it's not when you consider what it costs to get a new and untried name. Most mailers would not make this request each time they mailed, but would confine the change-of-address request to one or two times a year.

The return card should have sufficient information on it to allow you to properly handle any further business. The name and address, certainly, along with the zip code, should be included, but you may also have a place to check for certain brochures the prospect would like, or tour dates he or she would prefer. On some occasions, you may request a phone number, and you could solicit other information as well.

Obviously, you must have an efficient system for processing all of the direct mail responses. If someone replies right away and then waits for weeks or months before getting the brochure or a call, you've probably lost that prospect.

There are many, many other facets to this complicated but effective medium of direct mail. Here are merely a few last minute reminders:

❑ Plan your printing well ahead, making sure that all pieces of the package fit together and arrive together. If you are hung up waiting for one element, that's just as bad as having nothing ready.

❑ All of the principles we applied earlier to advertising and to good printing also apply here.

❑ Stay abreast of postal regulations, which change fairly often.

❑ You can build your own lists from directories, club membership lists, trade publications, distributors' lists, government files, trade show registrants, and from many other sources, including your own mail responses. Or you can go to mailing houses, to list brokers, or even secure a list of lists from *Standard Rate & Data Service.*

❑ When examining a list for potential use, you want to know how it was compiled; how old it is; how often it's updated; how

it's maintained; what selectivity you have; and how well it did for others.
- ❏ Certain trends, like more working wives, the move to suburbia, a larger senior citizen population, and rising income and educational levels all enhance the value of direct mail.
- ❏ Your lists must be zip coded.
- ❏ You'll need a system for keeping the names, either a computer with punched cards, metal plates, or 3″ × 5″ cards.
- ❏ First class has prestige, speed, and a better track record for results. But it's expensive and might be impractical.
- ❏ Make direct mail part of your total advertising campaign, and not something separate. Each medium should reinforce the other.
- ❏ Remain attuned to timing requirements, attempting to have your direct mail hit when the prospect is in the most receptive mood, and when the other direct mail competition is lightest.
- ❏ Don't try to get too many items into a single mailing. You're usually better off if you concentrate on selling one major item or on promoting one travel area.
- ❏ Take advantage of appropriate flyers and stuffers that are supplied by tour operators, carriers, and other suppliers. You may need to add only your name, address, and phone number. These serve well as interim mailings.

## CHAPTER HIGHLIGHTS

- ❏ Various other advertising media are available to the travel agencies, including special directories, novelties, and displays.
- ❏ Outdoor advertising is good for name recognition but doesn't allow for long messages. Location of the boards is a key factor.
- ❏ Direct mail, if properly handled, can be very efficient. Time should be spent on developing the most efficient list, and on producing a message that gets attention and garners results. An easy method of response helps secure a higher return.

■          ■          ■

## ❏  *EXERCISES*

1. Pick a section of your town and drive or walk through it, mentally selecting appropriate places for outdoor boards.

2. Bring to class three pieces of direct mail, along with your comments as to the likely audience, the attractiveness of the package, the effectiveness of the copy, and the other aspects that may or may not enhance results.

3. Do a rough design of a display that could be used to promote travel to any country (you pick the country) and that will be used as part of an international fair on your campus. You are limited to an expenditure of $500 for the materials and construction of the display. Describe the contents, the staffing, any giveaways, and other pertinent information.

4. Select your favorite restaurant, which is convenient to the main business area of your community. Write a letter to the businesses nearby to try to build up luncheon business for this restaurant. Also describe how you would go about building up your mailing list.

## ❏ CASE PROBLEMS

*1.  Assume that the* Art Treasures of China *is being exhibited in a large city about 400 miles from you. This is the closest this exhibit will come to your community. Your travel agency plans to conduct a 3-day tour to this exhibit city, building other events around the exhibit itself. You have been asked to draft a direct mail piece to prospects. What groups do you think might belong on your list? Write down the general theme of your mailing, plus the opening and closing paragraphs of the letter or brochure.*

*2.  Design and write the copy for a billboard on a cruise through the Greek Islands. In your particular area, what two locations do you think would be best for this board?*

# 11

# PUBLIC RELATIONS AND PROMOTION

While advertising and direct sales may be the more common promotional tools in the marketing of travel, the various opportunities presented by effective public relations techniques should not be ignored. Public relations (PR) is always a strong adjunct to advertising and sales and may sometimes have more impact than either of these tools. Frequently, it is the least expensive way to go.

Each industry employs public relations a little differently. Corporations have PR staffs which are professionally trained and experienced. They must augment the efforts of these internal personnel by the addition of outside counsel, professionals who handle numerous PR clients. Public relations specialists are also found in government, education, entertainment, health care, the military, nonprofit enterprises, and elsewhere.

In the travel industry, public relations staffs are likely to be found only in the larger companies: cruise lines, hotel chains, and the like. However, everyone in this industry has public relations problems and opportunities, so a knowledge of the principles of public relations is essential.

There are myriad definitions of public relations, beginning with short ones like "doing good and getting credit for it" to the longer versions adopted by professional associations that stress the management, research, communication and evaluation aspects of the discipline. In both instances, long or short, there is a consideration of the necessity for public relations to first accomplish positive results and then to publicize them. Calling media attention to something that is inadequate or incomplete is counterproductive.

Public relations differs from advertising in several ways. You pay to place an ad in the paper or on television, but you don't pay the media to print or broadcast news releases (although you probably pay people to write them). You have more control over advertising,

**217**

too. Once the ad is accepted, it runs as you submitted it. Not so with publicity. Your release can be edited, severely cut, even dropped in the wastebasket.

Publicity—which is only one tool of public relations—is much more economical than advertising, has more credibility, and has the added advantage of possible placement anywhere in the paper, including page one.

Most practitioners of public relations would view their profession, however, not as a publicity generator, but as a management function, with all the facets this concept entails.

Looked at in its complete form, public relations involves detailed research, elaborate planning, a thorough knowledge of communication, and a precise evaluation. Just as the advertising campaign has its many levels and phases, so does the public relations campaign. The PR person studies the background of every problem, analyzing its causes, and searching out the experience of others; discusses possible alternatives before settling on a course of action; then initiates the action, either through publicity, or special events, or some other form of communication. Then the planners go over the strengths and weaknesses of what ultimately evolved.

Few travel agencies seem to take full advantage of the benefits of public relations, confining their programs to an occasional party, some participation in local clubs, and a few news releases. Airlines, on the other hand, issue in-flight magazines, sponsor open houses, inaugurate charter flights, publicize their activities in the trade and consumer media, participate in community events, provide funds for worthy causes, and are involved in other similar programs. Cruise lines and hotels follow suit. State and local tourism bureaus find public relations an excellent forum for extending their limited budgets, flying in travel writers, providing special events calendars to consumers, maintaining an entertainment hot line and staffing other functions.

## HUMAN RELATIONS

The basis of good public relations is good human relations. While it is true that public relations is organized and planned—even calculated—the psychology on which PR programs are predicated is a determination of the motives and responses of individuals and groups.

This begins with an attitude. If the travel consultant feels hurried and frustrated, this state of mind will be communicated to the clients. Each contact in an agency is a one-to-one contact. The client, consciously or unconsciously, is judging the entire operation on the behavior of the one consultant he meets. Therefore, this relationship should radiate warmth, interest, and efficiency.

In addition to personal contact, the travel industry conducts a lot of business by telephone. This is a trouble spot. One of the problems is volume. There are many incoming calls, plus clients at the counter, and, perhaps, representatives from tour operators and carriers on the premises. It's tough to field all of the incoming calls with dispatch and amiability—but that's what must be done. Curtness, long periods of waiting, cutoffs, confusion, lack of attention, lack of knowledge, failure to follow through are all errors that must be avoided. You can't score every time, of course, but it's just as easy to be pleasant as it is to be brusque. Your telephone voice should tell the other party you're glad he or she called and that you'll attend to his or her needs completely and accurately.

If you're going to succeed at human relations, you have to have some idea of what makes people tick. A course in psychology wouldn't be a bad start. Look back at chapter three. The things said there about individual motivation apply as well to human relations and public relations. The more you understand why people do things, the better you'll be able to deal with others.

## RESEARCH AND PLANNING

A commitment to good human relations attitudes is necessary, but it isn't enough just to be nice to succeed in public relations. The individual must know what he or she is doing, and this means research and planning.

People in the travel industry must understand human nature and perceive trends and should be aware of available data on matters affecting the industry and their role in it. Assumptions aren't enough; the effective employee works from a basis of facts. These facts support planning, allowing the travel professional to decide on a course of action from among several alternative options. Planning, in fact, distinguishes public relations from other positive events, like the two weeks of sunshine that produce a delighted tour group.

One of the best-known acronyms in public relations is R.A.C.E., which stands for Research, Action-Planning, Communication, and Evaluation. Every PR program involves these steps to some degree.

You gather information, plot a course, implement and communicate the plan, and—always—you evaluate the program and the results.

# COMMUNICATION

Although communication seems simple enough, it is actually a complicated process. Getting an idea from one head to another is tough enough, but when you attempt to translate this idea for a mass audience, the problems multiply. There are audience predispositions to contend with, the proliferation of messages, the ineptness of the communicator, the improper use of language or channel of communication, poor choice of timing, and a host of other roadblocks.

The able communicator tries to eliminate as many roadblocks as possible. Above all, the communicator makes sure that what is said or written has in it something of value for the receiver. Without such a benefit, most Americans will simply turn off the message.

It may make a motor coach company feel good to announce that this is the company's fiftieth year in business, but that means little to the potential consumer. When the carrier adds that this anniversary means $50 in savings for every passenger, it gets attention. Running through all advertising and PR messages is the notion of some consumer benefit.

# COMMUNITY RELATIONS

As with advertising, the goals of public relations involve the identification of certain publics to whom communications must be sent. Present clients form one obvious public; the media form another. Among the remaining publics, the community at large rates a major effort. After all, this is the place where you live and work. You're expected to be a good and a concerned citizen. This means some participation in the activities of the community, including club memberships, attendance at business and social functions, contribution to community causes, purchasing supplies locally, and general support for the aims of the community.

People are bound to have some impression about your company. Either they like it, dislike it, or known nothing about it. The last two conditions are bad. You want to impart a positive feeling. You do that, not by one big campaign, but by consistent attention to playing the role of good neighbor.

This sort of reputation not only brings the routine customer to you, it also paves the way for easier access to larger accounts.

One final caution: All of the socializing is for naught, of course, unless the company is well run, and has earned a name for congenial and effective operation and competitive pricing.

# PUBLICITY

Getting stories printed or aired is merely one of the tools of public relations, even though it may be the most familiar activity of this profession. Publicity is available to the smallest travel agency and to the largest airline, assuming both have something newsworthy to submit.

Publicity refers to news stories that originate outside the normal reportorial channels, and which are placed in the media by groups and individuals who have an interest in seeing this news promulgated. There is nothing wrong with this practice. In fact, a majority of news stories on the local scene stem from news releases submitted by persons not employed by the media. There simply aren't enough reporters to go around to cover all the possible events.

This doesn't mean that editors and news directors are sitting around waiting for news to arrive, or that they will be joyously noncritical about every news release that appears. They will try to impose the same professional standards they expect of their own staffs, with some few allowances for occasional amateur standing.

First, the person issuing a news release must be able to recognize news. Anyone can appreciate the fact that a big fire is news, or a major crime, but there are thousands of other things that also make news. For example:

❏ *Important names make news.* The Kennedys and Madonnas and Burt Reynolds of this world generate publicity, even when they do fairly minor things. Fame is relative, of course, and people who would make no national splash may succeed in getting local coverage. A state senator attending the opening of an agency branch office may be worth a few lines in the paper or seconds on the news. So might the departure of some sports hero on your cruise ship, with a couple of honeymoon tickets in his hand.

❏ *Unusual things make news.* A couple celebrating their fiftieth anniversary sign up for the "Swinging London" tour. That's news! You'd have to secure the couple's permission, of course, before releasing anything. Whole families touring Europe make news, and so do veterans returning to the site of their combat years, and individuals who opt for an individualized excursion to some off-beat area.

❏ *Current events make news.* Consider all the possibilities in this area. Readers and viewers are anxious to know about safe travel in world trouble spots; or concerned about the effect of devaluation of the dollar on their travel plans; or want to know about gasoline shortages and prices; or wonder if there are still seats available for the Olympics; or want to find out when an airline strike will be settled; or would like some estimates on crowded holiday schedules; or are curious about some of the charter bargains. The travel agent has a host of chances to say things that interest the public.

❏ *Ingenuity makes news.* There are possible news stories all around you; it just takes a little imagination to see them. Suppose you did a survey of client needs and desires for future travel—this would make a news story. Whenever a little-known country makes the news, it's possible you have some staff member who's visited there and can be quoted. There are all sorts of possible ties with national and international stories.

❏ *Some regular events make news.* Whenever you have an open house, a special film showing, a change in personnel, an annual report that's published, a new service—all of these have news potential. All this takes is a little work and a little know-how, and it's well worth the effort.

## THE NEWS RELEASE

A news release doesn't have to be a creative work of art; in fact, it shouldn't be. What it must be is accurate, complete, and professional. This is not an advertisement, so you can't use any puffery. Neither is it a chatty letter, so you can't use cute phrases or homey expressions. Remember that it's supposed to be news. You must include all the details and you must have the correct information. Supplying a wrong date or place, or a misspelled name, will make all your future stories suspect. Before any release is sent out it should be checked thoroughly for error, for statements that may be confusing, and for details that may be ambiguous.

## The News Release Format

There is a standard way to write a news release, and sticking to this
format is a definite plus. At least the news desk will give the story a
look, figuring the person that wrote it probably also has news judgment and style.

Here are the elements of a news release:

1. In the upper left hand corner of the sheet, you should type
   your name, address, and phone number. This identifies the
   person who prepared the release and gives the editor or news
   director a contact if he or she wishes more information. If the
   letterhead already gives the address, the name and phone
   number will be enough. Sometimes PR people also list their
   home phone numbers. This is a nice gesture, and lets the media people know you will go out of your way to be helpful.
2. Beneath this identification, you supply the details about when
   the story should be released. This line is usually capitalized
   and underlined, although there are various ways to handle it.
   For most stories, you'd use FOR IMMEDIATE RELEASE,
   meaning that the news director or editor is free to air or print
   the story right away. If there is a certain time designated for
   this particular release, you would use that terminology. For
   example: FOR RELEASE FRIDAY P.M., AUGUST 14. This
   sort of restriction should be used sparingly.
3. Leave about two inches between the release information and
   the body of the story. This is so the editor can write his headline when the story is printed.
4. Even though you are writing about something purely local, it's
   a good idea to get in the habit of using a dateline. This means
   that the story should begin with the place of origin and the
   date it was written. Like this:

   ST. LOUIS, MO. (JULY 22, 1987)—

The place of origin may not always be the same as the place on
the letterhead. A New York public relations firm, for example,
may represent a St. Louis firm, so the story on their letterhead
might still bear the Missouri dateline.

The date is important, too. Suppose a story reads FOR IM-
MEDIATE RELEASE but the person to whom it's directed is
out of the city for a few days. Later, that person has no idea
how long the story has been around unless it's dated. Sometimes, incidentally, a story may be dated in the upper right
hand corner and, occasionally, at the bottom of the story.

5.  The news story should be typed, not handwritten. It should be an original or a photocopy, never a carbon. A carbon tells the recipient he or she is second; a photocopy indicates he was treated the same as others.

    Margins should be wide (1½"), copy double-spaced, and at least 1½ inches left at the bottom of the page. This is so the editor can edit.

    The paragraphs should be indented about seven spaces, and the pages should look clean, and be free of strikeovers and messy erasures.

6.  News stories themselves are structured in what journalists refer to as the inverted pyramid, meaning that the important facts are all up front, in the first paragraph of the story. This is not a short story with a surprise ending.

    The first paragraph answers the questions of who, what, where, when, and why (the five W's) and, sometimes, how. The remaining paragraphs in the story spell out other details in logical fashion. Sentences and paragraphs should be short and punchy. You must avoid flowery language, lines that read like advertising, and copy that works hard to make a dull topic sound like news.

7.  If possible, confine the news release to a single page. If you go to extra pages, be certain you don't carry part of a paragraph over to the next page. Splitting paragraphs or sentences is not a good idea. At the bottom of this page, write "-more-" to indicate that additional pages are to come. On the upper left of the next page, identify the story in a word or two, and write the page number like this: 2-2-2-2.

    When you reach the final page and come to the end of the copy you indicate this by:

-END-

*or*

###

*or*

-30-

    The designation -30- is the most common form. It's an old typographical and journalistic way to note a conclusion.

8.  Before you let the story out of your hands, check it again for accuracy, spelling, grammar, completeness, and tightness.

Robert Hunter

AMX Travel Agency

2536 The Mall

St. Louis, MO.  65282

(314) 572-9054 (O)

(314) 544-2592 (H)

FOR IMMEDIATE RELEASE

ST. LOUIS, MO., (JULY 22, 1987) -- A new film on the ten most popular ski areas in the United States will be shown Saturday evening (July 25) at the Travel Fair held in the Laclede Landing Auditorium. The 30-minute film, titled "Win, Place and Snow," will be shown on the hour beginning at 10:00 a.m. and running until 8:00 p.m. There is no admission charge.

"This is our fourth year hosting the Fair," said AMX president Lucy Forrester, "and we hope the one day event will attract at least 5 thousand visitors."

-30-

For radio and television, it's a good idea to write a different and shorter release, keeping in mind that these news releases must be written so that they can be verbally delivered, rather than printed. As we saw earlier, writing for the ear is somewhat different. Since time is a more restrictive factor than space, you must keep releases for radio and TV brief. For television, you would also try to come up with some visuals, such as a color slide of the new facility, or an architect's drawing of the addition. Better yet would be some video-tape footage, if you can talk the local stations into shooting some or if you're large enough to have your own in-house video equipment.

Here are some additional tips for dealing with the news media:

❑ Treat all media equally. Don't play favorites in giving out information.

❑ Respect deadlines of the various media. Don't deliver stories to the media when it is too late to get into that day's paper (if that is your intent) or to make that evening's newscast.

❑ Don't try to get your material used through pressure or pleading. News should sell on its own merits.

❑ You may be able to get marginal news stories, which would not be used regionally, into a local paper. This is because the local angle makes it news. A new branch opening in Des Moines, Iowa, isn't news in Pittsburgh, Pennsylvania, but it is in Des Moines. National airlines, of course, provoke wider interest, especially in those cities they serve. Hotels, on the other hand, may suffer some of the same limitations as local travel agencies, unless they are part of a chain.

❑ Be cooperative with the media, offering help when they request it, and passing along news tips you may have, even when they have no connection with your business. Don't try to bury an unpleasant story; just get the complete truth out quickly.

❑ Don't use colored stock for news release letterheads—at least not shocking pink, or some other flashy color. Also avoid too much ornamentation in the letterhead design.

❑ If your release includes photos, note this on the release, usually at the bottom, thus:
ENCLOSED: Photo of new Ariel cruise ship.
You may also include a caption.

❑ Keep your mailing lists up to date. Sending a news release to the attention of a person who hasn't been with the TV station for five years marks you as an amateur. Be sure you know the proper name of the travel editor on your local paper.

❏ Newspaper photos should be 8″ × 10″ glossy prints, in good focus, and with strong contrast for better reproduction. TV stations prefer slides and film. In both cases, strive for interesting subject matter.

❏ Don't neglect the trade journals, which may not have a direct impact on consumers but which do help establish prestige.

## EVENTS FOR THE MEDIA

Don't assume that the news media are anxiously awaiting a chance to attend a news conference; they're not. Only call a news conference when you can't disseminate the information any other way, when the story will be enhanced by on-the-spot photo coverage, or when a newsmaker is passing through your city and will be available only for a brief time.

Some firms have periodic press parties for the media. Large travel agencies might want to try this but it makes little sense for small- or medium-sized agencies. These parties are merely good will gestures, without a news reason. They can be expensive and they are not always that well attended. Perhaps an occasional luncheon with those who write travel pieces would be much better.

Media events make more sense for other areas of the travel field. Local and state tourism bureaus, for example, often mount get-

**Fig. 11–1  Promotional kits inform and impress corporate clients.**
(Courtesy of Travel & Transport)

togethers for the media, to introduce some new campaign or to wine and dine visiting reporters. Inaugural flights and voyages may also be occasions to involve this media, and hotel openings customarily add local (sometimes national) media to the invitation list.

## THE MEDIA KIT

If the company does conduct a news conference—let's say for the announcement of a grand opening—consideration must be given to a place (probably the agency or company office itself), a time (a couple of hours before the deadline of the major daily is a good rule), and an invitation list (usually all those who write travel news, plus, in this case, business reporters or general assignment reporters).

You'd also want some kind of media kit. These kits contain such items as a news release, fact sheet, photos, and other information that will help the news person write a good story.

## THE TRAVEL ARTICLE

A majority of travel articles, in all media, are staff written. Travel articles from syndicated sources would make a distant second. The remainder come from free-lance writers and from those people who perform a public relations function.

In an article titled "Gatekeeper Research: How to Research the Travel Editor," (*Public Relations Journal,* August 1978) Elaine Goldman and Barrie L. Jones list a dozen of types of stories preferred by travel editors. In order of preference, from first to twelfth, these were:

1. Budget trips
2. Regional pieces
3. Family travel
4. One-day destinations
5. Price information
6. How-tos
7. Seasonal
8. Convenience/service
9. International
10. Package tours
11. History/nostalgia
12. Luxury vacations

The travel article (and book) has a long and distinguished history. People like Boswell and Dickens wrote travel articles; Ernest Hemingway was a first-rate writer of travel pieces. There are fine articles on travel being written today, in a much different style than the early chroniclers—more crisp, and more journalistic rather than literary.

When writing travel articles, there are some general and some specific points that need to be made.

1. You should visit the place you write about. This seems like an obvious fact, but a number of authors try to write about areas with which they have no personal familiarity. It usually shows. You should also spend sufficient time in an area to get a decent impression of things. Otherwise, your writing is liable to be shallow.

2. While gathering material for an article, be cautious about the information source that deliberately misleads, or "puts you on." Check every fact.

3. Do your homework in advance, so that you can ask intelligent questions and save both time and unnecessary writing.

4. Develop the requisite writing skills. Good writing is good writing; the only thing different about good travel writing is the subject. Good writing means such things as:

   ❑ Having something to say.

   ❑ Understanding the nuances of the language. This is particularly necessary in travel, where so much depends on the writer's ability to recreate the scene.

   ❑ Avoiding cliches—a dangerous temptation in travel writing. Nothing will destroy interest faster.

   ❑ Arranging your ideas in some logical sequence, giving the reader a sense of purpose and progression. This may mean an outline before you start writing, and it may also mean considerable rewriting.

   ❑ Becoming adept at providing bridges between ideas and between paragraphs. This gives a feeling of easy continuity.

   ❑ Learning how to heighten interest. You achieve this through dealing with topics that promise a benefit to the reader; by including meaningful quotes; through a good sense of humor; through the arousal of curiosity; and through the knack of putting yourself in the reader's place.

❏ Writing clearly, using active verbs, trimming out unnecessary jargon, and preferring the simple to the complex. Writing should be like conversation, not like instruction.
❏ Being willing to rewrite and to cut with judgment and courage.

To do the best job as a feature writer, travel personnel must always keep the reader in mind, considering what he or she knows or would like to know. The writer tries to respond to questions readers might ask if they had a chance. Travel writing is informative, even providing prices and addresses, and it's colorful, attempting to re-create for the reader the sense of being there.

## Leads

Like any good article, the travel piece begins with a strong lead sentence, something that will reach out and pull in the casual reader. This lead may take many forms. Here are a few:

❏ *Question.* Why is Aruba one of the most popular destinations for young Americans?
❏ *Challenge.* Walking tours of the Lake District aren't for everyone; you have to be in shape.
❏ *Quotation.* "Like a lot of my friends," recalls Jack Lausterer of Mineral Wells, Texas, "I figured I'd be bored on a cruise."
❏ *Description.* At night the surf breaks close to your door, lulling you to sleep, and, in the distance, you can hear the faint clinking of a ship's bell.
❏ *Narrative.* Frances Meynell drove her rented Audi onto the deck of the Ardrossan ferry.
❏ *First person.* I'd never spent any time in Mississippi, not since World War II.

There are many others—teaser leads, contrast leads, humorous leads, poetry, flat statements, foreign phrases and dozens of similar ways to attract a reader's interest.

After that the story proceeds logically, creating pictures with words, and building in information the reader might like to have.

*Following the sunrise tour of the seven hills, the visitor might settle for a cup of richly brewed coffee and a sweet wheat roll at Antonio's ($4.00) before heading for the local museum (Open 8:00 a.m. to 4:00 p.m., except Sunday), which has an unusual collection of Belgian china.*

Travel agency personnel don't often write articles, but there is no reason they shouldn't. All of them travel frequently, know the business, have a grasp of what should be of interest to the reader, and should have imbibed considerable local flavor.

It can't hurt to query the local travel editor about doing a piece for his travel section. The article could not, of course, be self-serving, but name identification alone would be worth it. You can always get mileage out of such articles, too, by reprinting them and including them in mailings to your client list.

Writing talent would be more common in other areas of the travel industry, like the hospitality or carrier companies, or in the offices of tourism bureaus. Features may be a regular part of staff duties, both for company publications and the external media.

## THE NEWSLETTER

Hotel chains have their own newsletters, primarily for personnel and shareholders, and so do airlines and cruise lines. Most of these are less selling tools than they are means of communication with "family" members. External selling pieces have a different character to them. Tour operators also issue periodic brochures that may have the character of a newsletter but generally stress specific tour options.

Many travel agencies find that their own newsletters, published quarterly, bimonthly, or even monthly, are one of their best recruitment tools for travel. As with everything else you do in the travel business, this newsletter should have a professional look. It should be clean, informative, interesting, and attractive. Some of the material used will be purely local: new staff, new branch offices, local travel groups, local package tours, and so on, while other items may have a national flavor.

Laurence Stevens, writing in *The Travel Agent,* suggests keeping a newsletter file into which you drop clips from trade magazines, travel sections of newspapers, and other sources. He further suggests the use of art and photos, avoiding the staged shot of a group around an airplane, and the inclusion of client comments and stories (always, of course, clearing this with them before printing).

Keep in mind that the newsletter is a selling tool, but that doesn't mean hard sell. The first requirement is that people read it. You have to give them something worth reading, and you work your message into that kind of copy. After all, even if you didn't plug upcoming tours but wrote a genuinely appealing newsletter, with plenty of company identification, you'd have a successful mailing piece. In choosing articles, try to stay current, anticipating reader interest, and, when you can, presenting something truly unique.

Companies that have sufficient funds have the type set and the newsletters printed by outside firms. Budget may not be a major consideration. For the smaller travel agency, however, with fiscal restraints, it's possible the newsletter might be produced on an electric typewriter or some other more sophisticated typesetting machine. These may then be sent to a quick print shop or some reasonable job printer. If neatly done, these may suffice, although they won't match the more expensively produced work. As one soon discovers, it takes only a little more effort and a little more money to do an acceptable job rather than a sloppy one. A poorly designed, written, and produced newsletter is worse than no newsletter at all, and should be avoided.

## SPECIAL EVENTS

Special events are part of the stock-in-trade of the travel industry. These planned affairs may range from a film showing for a small group of potential tour members to the launching of a new cruise ship or the grand opening of a hotel or the staging of an elaborate travel exhibit. Whatever the occasion, the proposed event must always be evaluated in advance in terms of its merits and effects compared with cost and effort. Special events take time and they may also eat into a tight budget. Those who produce these events must be certain the return is commensurate.

The watchword in special events is *details*. Every need must be anticipated and every problem prepared for. Before and during the events, constant checking goes on, and, after the event, evaluation is essential. How did it go? How did you do? How did your staff members perform? Did you reach your goals? Did you stay within the budget?

It makes good sense to jot down a check list for special events and go over each item until you're certain it has been accomplished. This means that sufficient time must be given to planning. You can't crank up a decent client party in one week. That doesn't even allow time to print invitations. For just about any event, a minimum of six weeks is desirable, with more complicated events demanding longer lead times.

When you contemplate staging a special program, you begin by clearing the date, making sure it is one you and your staff can live with, and one that offers a minimum of conflict for the expected guests. Next you tie down a facility, such as a meeting room or restaurant, making certain it can handle the anticipated audience. Then you firm up the program, arranging for films or speakers, and deciding on the way the function will go.

Now it's time to issue invitations and/or disseminate publicity. The invitation list must be prepared in advance, and you'll want to give the printer a week to ten days to print the invitations and your staff enough time to address and mail them.

Once these initial tasks have been accomplished, it's time to start looking ahead to the event and going over all the details. Consider the requirements of the speaker, the need for a film projector, decorations, exhibits, printed programs, food, drinks, heat and air conditioning controls, light switches, sliding panels for noise level control, seating arrangements, microphone and audio controls, lectern, water glasses, and so on. There are hundreds of minor items that can spell success or disaster. If everything runs smoothly, nobody notices. But if something goes wrong, everyone notices. That's why you take nothing for granted. Fuses do blow; extension cords are forgotten; speakers fail to show; the weather turns nasty; the programs aren't delivered. You have to have alternate plans for things you can anticipate, and you must be able to adjust rapidly to situations you didn't anticipate.

The more complicated the event, the more planning goes into it. While even a small luncheon takes some organization, a more significant occurrence demands far more attention.

A local tourism bureau that schedules a 3-day visit by travel writers must worry about transportation, housing, meals, printed materials, an attractive tour schedule, a lineup of appropriate local celebrities, the availability of equipment for the writers, a supply of the best hosts and guides, perhaps some film or slide shows, and a long list of other details. They may even pray for decent weather. Obviously, an occasion like this must go off perfectly or the effect is worse than never scheduling anything.

Inaugurating a new cruise ship has even more details, from the appropriate guest list and clearances to consideration of all of the engineering requirements. Someone must even worry about the traditional champagne bottle.

There are some events that may be common to both the small agency and the major carrier. A few are considered here.

## The Film Program

Film showings aren't original in the promotion of travel, but they are effective. They're also an inexpensive way to attract an audience.

Planning ahead for these shows means considering what films might be topical, seasonal, or otherwise appealing, and then booking them early. If possible, have the films in your office two or three days ahead of the proposed events. Most good films are in demand and, even if the distributor has multiple prints, it could be difficult to get yours when you need it.

How do you locate films?

Airlines and cruise lines, tourist offices, and major resort areas generally have films they're happy to loan out. In addition, there are production houses and distributors who publish their own catalogues. Get on their lists and you'll be furnished with an annual roster of available films. Trade publications like *Travel Weekly* publish periodical articles with a rundown of the new and award-winning travel films.

Some films have a rental charge; many are free, except for return postage. You'll be given a date for the return of the film, or for its transfer to another user.

While ordering the film, check for an appropriate place to have the showing. Some agencies—very few—have their own facility; others have a hall available in their shopping center or office building. If none of these alternatives is available, check for a local lodge hall, community center, hotel, motel, or even one of the facilities rented or loaned by local business firms. Be certain it's large enough to hold the anticipated crowd but not so large as to brand the evening a failure if fewer people show up.

Decide then what the program will be, and whether there'll be refreshments, and how you'll get your message across. These events can be as simple as an evening with a welcome, a couple of films, and a dismissal. Or they can be rather elaborate affairs, with films, cocktails, hors d'oeuvres, decorations, even hosts in native costumes. Sometimes the showings combine a film, folk dancing, a talk by a native of the featured country, and other activities.

When the films arrive, they should be previewed. This will provide an idea of the condition they're in and the subject matter. On occasion a film may be too commercial, too slanted, or inappropriate. Better to catch this before the showing, and either find a substitute for it or explain the content in advance. If the film is broken and needs splicing or other repairs, the local film studio or TV news department may be able to help you.

Showings, like any events, must be publicized, and this is where a little imagination helps. Instead of merely announcing "A Film on Fiji," planners should add a little "sell" to build an audience. Write "An exciting journey through some of the South Sea's most colorful islands, visiting the site where 'The Blue Lagoon' was filmed, watching the native Fijians perform a *meke,* sailing the waters through which Captain Bligh once navigated."

Hosts should arrive early the day of the event and check everything—screen, wall sockets, projector, film, extra projection bulb, extension cord, table for materials, microphone, speakers—everything.

They should greet people at the door, and help them meet other people. Name tags might be a good idea, using office personnel to fill them out, or letting them letter their own tags.

Be certain there are enough people to perform the necessary tasks. Someone to make out name tags? To serve punch and cookies? To run the projector? To introduce the films?

Try to keep the program under two hours. This is about the extent of the average attention span. Try to start promptly, avoid idle chatter, and wrap up on time.

Sunday afternoon is a good time for film showings—better certainly than a weekend night.

## Producing Films

Producing films is a province of the large carriers and tourism bureaus and tour operators. These are the sources from which agency programs are drawn.

Film work is extremely technical and will normally be handled by professional personnel. Travel representatives may work on the script, if they have a knack for this, and they could also supply some technical advice, but the shooting of the movie is in the hands of cinematographers. Those who pay the bills, however, have a right to make suggestions and critique results.

Many travel films look the same, or "feel" the same. They take the viewer from place to place, include attractive photography, a serviceable sound track, and narration that is commercial but uninspired. The best travel films have a solid central idea, something

**Fig. 11–2   Video cassettes are a new and effective sales tool for travel.** (Courtesy of Bill Ramsey Associates, Inc.)

different, something appropriate. Both kinds of film, if professionally done, may work.

## Travel Videos

During the last decade, travel videos have become increasingly popular. More than 700 million travel video cassettes were rented in 1985, sometimes for group programs, but often by people seeking information on a specific destination. While regular video outlets accounted for most of the rentals, some travel agencies also supplied these items to potential customers, and others made them available for in-house viewing.

Typically, a travel video will focus on a single destination and will include a scenic description, travel tips, plus data on hotels, restaurants, and attractions. The average cassette ranges in playing time from 10 to 60 minutes and some are part of a longer series. Most are periodically updated. These may also be used for programs and, when permitted, for travel TV shows.

## Cable Television

With the increasing availability of cable television and the multiplicity of channels which may be adapted to public use, many travel agencies are finding this a good outlet for promoting travel. Films and videotapes may work here, but so can straight talk supplemented by visuals. Viewers may be interested in current costs, travel conditions, or tips on clothing and economizing. Some agencies have used a tour of their facilities to bolster trade.

Costs are minimal compared with commercial television and the audiences, while smaller, are growing.

## Slide Programs

Multimedia slide shows with half a dozen or more projections are not practical for the average travel agency, although they may be affordable for tour operators and carriers. However, the problems involved in transporting, setting up, and operating these complicated shows often legislates against their use. Even with this technology, slides may not have the impact of film or video.

Less sophisticated slide shows, however, often make sense. They are flexible, informative, and can be tailored to fit a very specific need. Some are accompanied by live narration; some utilize audiotape. A tour manager, for example, may have slides taken on a previous trip and could show these to drum up interest in an upcoming journey. While a single projector could be used, improvements in this simple presentation technique may be made easily and inexpensively.

For one thing, you can attach a tape cassette to the projector to drop the slides automatically, at the right places in the script. The advantage of a cassette over a live voice is that you can add music and sound effects, and you can also be assured of more uniform voice quality. The live speaker, of course, also has advantages, like presence, and warmth, and the ability to adjust quickly to unforeseen problems or to answer on-the-spot questions.

The next step up is to use two projectors, with the cassette, and joined by a dissolve unit, which blends one picture into the other, making for a smoother and more artistic flow, rather than the familiar click. To use this combination, you must plan your slides accordingly, using every other one in the alternate projector, or, at least, knowing which one you want on the screen at any given time.

Above all, make the slide show move. There have been so many jokes about folks showing their vacation slides, the audience is already twenty percent desensitized. So keep it brisk, interesting, and short.

It's possible, too, to take both a slide show and a film show to another locale. Many companies use briefcase-sized self-contained slide units that project right on the side of the case. These can be carried into an office or board room and set in motion at a push of a button. For commercial accounts in particular, this would be a fine portable tool. The film projector takes more time to set up and you need a board room or something similar. If given the opportunity to show a film, arrive early and check all details before summoning the audience.

## Other Visual Aids

Don't neglect the value of such items as flip charts (large or small), descriptive brochures, tape cassettes or records, wall posters, and other items. Some of these don't function well alone, but, in concert with other tools, they perform a real service.

## The Speech

Like writing letters, public speaking is a job that may fall to the chief executive officer of a large travel corporation or the manager of a small agency. Local service clubs may provide the platform, or a national convention, a local television panel, or a governmental committee hearing. Being reasonably articulate is always a plus.

Not everyone is gifted as a speaker. It's important that you know your own limitations, and don't try to accomplish things you're not equipped to do. People who can't tell jokes, for example, shouldn't tell jokes. Nothing says every speech must start with a joke. Be natural; be yourself.

The first thing to consider about any speech is the content. Even the best delivery can't atone for a weak message. Have something to say.

When you know what you're going to talk about, you should determine whether your aim is to entertain, instruct, or persuade. Your approach will differ in each instance.

Then organize your speech, starting with the central idea, then listing the main points under that idea, then developing each point, and then developing the conclusion. After these items are complet-

**Fig. 11–3** Everyone likes to hear about travel, and an illustrated talk—if not too long—is generally welcome.

ed, go back and write transitions between the ideas, flesh out the paragraphs, and write your introduction. After these are all done, put them in the proper order, with the introduction first, and write for the style in which you plan to deliver the speech.

It's wise to keep any speech short—under twenty minutes. If illustrated with good slides, you can extend this time, but short is better than long.

Consider your audience makeup. Young or old or a mixture? Experienced travelers or neophytes? Economy minded or deluxe? The toughest audience to address is one that is composed of all types of people, from children to senior citizens.

Decide what system you are going to use for notes. Will you use small cards with topic headings? Or type the entire speech out? Or memorize it and go without any notes? Reading a speech is disastrous. Perhaps the best system—if you can handle it—is an outline on cards that guides you but does not constrain you.

Consider, too, the physical layout of the area where you'll speak. Sometimes a speaker arrives just before he's due to speak and discovers that he's in a large hall, with no loudspeaker system, and half the people screened from his view. Unless you have time to adjust, this can be disconcerting. Test the equipment in advance, too—the mike, lectern light, slide carousel switch.

Above all, the speaker must convey an image of control, even ease. A relaxed delivery or a compelling approach will carry people along. Even when the speaker is not terribly gifted, an audience will still be impressed with content and personality.

*Kinds of speeches.*  Each speaking opportunity may be different. Addressing the local Rotary Club calls for one sort of style, while describing tour opportunities to a small group of prospects requires another. Radio and television interviews call for short, informative responses and, when possible, a little humor. Conventions and workshops suggest a more dynamic presence.

There are times when agency or corporate personnel must make presentations to groups to secure new business. Since a lot may be on the line on these occasions, adequate rehearsal is a must, and there must be a comfort level for the presenter in terms of the material and the accompanying visuals. The speech must be tightly edited and the speaker should exhibit a high level of competence and enthusiasm. It also helps to be aware of the surroundings, of other presentations which may be made, and to anticipate possible questions.

## OTHER PROMOTIONAL IDEAS

What the intelligent travel agency manager should do is learn to think in terms of promotional ideas. After all, when you are dealing in service, there is considerable similarity among agencies in terms of offerings, prices, and other constants. The difference comes down to little things, like employee attitude and ability and the capacity for merchandising identical items.

Perhaps it's the use of a carousel rack instead of the long wall full of brochures. It might be the use of gift items with the agency name inscribed—items like flight bags, golf bags, garment bags, baby kits, business card files, desk organizers, luggage tags, document holders, correspondence portfolios, and many other giveaway pieces. Perhaps it's merely a distinctive luggage tag for tour members, or an iron-on decal, or a gift pencil.

Some suppliers specialize in selling small gifts to agencies for their tour members—wrinkle-free aerosol spray, a travel toothbrush with built-in toothpaste, sewing kits, travel games, or money belts.

Other PR ideas might include a touring travel desk, situated in high traffic areas on set days. Perhaps Monday at a university; Tuesday at a major industrial locale; Wednesday at a shopping center; Thursday at a hospital; and Friday at a military installation.

Not everyone may feel comfortable doing this, but a Boston agency manager dresses up in a variety of costumes, from Mickey Mouse to the Statue of Liberty, to bring traffic to her office. A Montana agency, located adjacent to a lake, hires a local woman to appear periodically as a mermaid.

In 1986, when travel to Europe was off, all sorts of promotions were tried, from direct appeals to Americans by spokespersons like Prime Minister Margaret Thatcher of England, to reduced prices, to giveaways.

## UNIFIED EFFORTS

Public relations is essentially a management function and the practitioner expends considerable time researching, analyzing, and advising. However, there is also this marketing aspect to travel PR in which all elements coalesce to produce sales.

All of this calls for planning and coordination. Professionals think in terms of campaigns. There are goals and themes and specific targets. Results are predicted and evaluated. This means that the public relations effort supports the advertising, and that all elements reinforce the central marketing mission.

A state tourism campaign, for example, might involve a commitment of dollars to a regional or national television schedule, print advertising in magazines and newspapers, a drive-time radio schedule, outdoor advertising, a few special events to generate publicity, feature stories in target publications, circulation of printed materials, and a number of other items. All would be scheduled for maximum effect.

It's worth repeating that the public relations phase of promotion can be extremely helpful without the expenditure of a large portion of the budget.

# CHAPTER HIGHLIGHTS

❏ Public relations efforts, which differ according to the size of the travel unit, involve research, planning, implementation, and evaluation, all with the profession's management concept.

❏ Public relations is more than publicity or advertising.

❏ There are numerous current roadblocks to communication, from the proliferation of messages to the ineptness of the communicator. Of these, the lack of any client benefit is the most significant.

❏ The basis of good public relations is human relations.

❏ Research and planning precede every PR decision, and community relations should always be considered.

❏ Publicity is merely a tool of public relations, but it's an important tool. Familiarity with news potential is necessary, along with skill in writing the news release.

❏ In addition to the news release, the travel article is another PR plus, and the feature story approach to writing can be learned, with practice.

❏ Among the many ways to approach a feature lead are the question, quotation, challenge, descriptive sentence, narrative, and first person style.

❏ Newsletters serve an internal morale function and may also be an effective tool for regular clients and potential clients.

❏ Special events require detailed planning, from setting the date to evaluating results.

❏ Among the visual aids used on-site or as part of an event are films, video cassettes, slides, and television. All require a certain amount of expertise to produce.

❏ Public speaking is a skill that should be cultivated by everyone in the travel industry, to be used at special events, presentations, hearings, television interview shows, and elsewhere.

❏ A variety of other promotional ideas may also be used in travel, from the giving of small gifts to more unusual activities, like dressing up in period costumes.

❏ Advertising, public relations, and other promotional aspects must be coordinated as part of the overall campaign.

■    ■    ■

# ❏ *EXERCISES*

1. Look at the travel ads in your local paper or in a magazine. Select one and come up with an idea for a public relations event to support this tour or concept.
2. Using the travel pages of a newspaper or magazine, find five different feature leads and categorize each.
3. Assume you have been asked by one of the national hotel chains to come up with a newsletter. Select the chain, create a name for the newsletter, and list the table of contents for the first issue.
4. List half a dozen features that might be used in subsequent issues.

# ❏ *CASE PROBLEMS*

*1. Take the following set of facts and turn them into a complete news release, remembering to include all elements shown in this chapter.*

❏ *March 17, 1988, St. Patrick's Day Party*
❏ *Globe Travel Agency, 24th and Hickory, Akron, Ohio*
❏ *From 4–7 p.m.*
❏ *This is an annual event.*
❏ *Irish coffee and brown bread will be served.*
❏ *Kevin Sheehan, who will lead a trip to Ireland for Globe in May, will show slides of his most recent tour of the Emerald Isle. He is the former mayor of Akron, and was born in County Cork, Ireland.*
❏ *Russell Seabrook, manager of Globe Travel Agency, said all are welcome and that dress is informal.*
❏ *There will be a drawing for several prizes, including clay pipes, a Donegal tweed coat, and two free tickets to the upcoming Irish Rovers concert.*
❏ *This is the fourteenth straight year Globe has had a St. Patrick's Day Party, and the sixth tour that Sheehan has led for Globe.*
❏ *Stewardesses from Aer Lingus, Ireland's national airline, will present all who attend with Irish shamrocks.*

❏  *Russell Seabrook said that visitors may also tour Globe's offices. And he said that new brochures from the Irish Tourist Board will be available.*

*2.  Outline a feature you might do on Saint Patrick's Day, and tell how you would work the special event in #1 into the copy. Write the lead paragraph and the final paragraph. Indicate what art or photography you would use to accompany this story.*

# THE ADVERTISING CAMPAIGN

No single ad, no feature story, no special event does the whole pro-motional job. It would be naïve for a travel manager to insert a small ad in a daily newspaper and then sit back and wait for the clients to turn up. Successful promotional efforts are the result of campaigns, a blending of many factors to produce a unified effect. That's why research and objectives are important. You set out to accomplish a specific thing, then implement the activities necessary to bring this about, and then you evaluate your program and performance.

## PLANNING THE CAMPAIGN

As with any enterprise, planning ahead—often far ahead—is the first step in a campaign. Laurence Stevens, writing in *The Travel Agent,* suggests preparing a schedule of the products you know you'll promote during the coming year.

> *Prepare a schedule of what product you intend to advertise on a certain date; example: February 1: Cruise; February 8: Hawaii; February 15: Florida; February 22: Mexico; February 29: Europe OTC, and so on. You know your own market best, so plan the timing of your product advertising accordingly. By the end of January you should have pre-pared your complete advertising schedule through the end of April, and have made tentative schedules for May, June, and July.*

Stevens' planning advice also includes allocating file space for promotional ideas, including those supplied by tour operators and cruise lines; better utilization of co-op advertising, where tour opera-tors furnish materials that the agency then personalizes; better analysis of past performance, in order to profit from errors and lapses.

Here are some practical steps to take when planning any campaign.

1. *Determine the current marketing situation.* This means an analysis of *all* the factors affecting your ability to market an individual travel product. You look at the nature of the item, the receptivity of the potential audience, the competition, past performance, current factors that could enhance or inhibit sales, and anything else that will influence your ability to deliver that service to that prospect.

2. *Establish some goals.* You should have some idea of what you hope to accomplish through your campaign. This may be expressed in numbers of tour members who need to be signed up, in number of visitors to be lured to a city, in an increase in the occupancy rate, in the number of inquiries to be generated, or in some other measurable form. You may have other promotional goals, too, like making clients aware of new office hours, or introducing them to an expanded flight schedule, or pinpointing your agency as the expert on Hawaii. If the budget is large enough and the personnel sophisticated enough, results could even be broken down by media.

3. *Constructing the budget.* Once you have an idea of what you need to accomplish, then you can work on what it will take to get the job done. This balance is rarely ideal since most agencies and small hotels or tour operators have to be a little thriftier than they would like to be. They utilize a number of methods in arriving at a budget—some of them good, and some merely guesswork. They could build a budget around what they consider necessary to the success of the campaign; or could construct it on the basis of competitors' efforts; or take a percentage of the anticipated profit to advertising; or they could break it down on a per sale basis, figuring the cost of advertising into every tour ticket sold.

   Too often, however, the budget comes out of a consideration of "what we did last year" without much discussion of the wisdom of such a selection process.

   Since many travel firms are relatively small enterprises, there is no need for an elaborate marketing plan, such as major corporations would compose, but a realistic, well-thought-out plan is a must.

   If a shrewd manager wants to get the most for the dollar, it makes sense to budget wisely within the planned marketing framework. Specific amounts should be assigned to areas like newspaper advertising, direct mail advertising, promotional activities and other budget items. This is called a marketing mix, and the goal is to achieve the best blend of expense to produce maximum sales at minimum cost.

Let's say a medium-sized firm decided to allot $15,000 annually for all of its promotional activities. This amount might be spent in this fashion:

- ❏ Newspaper advertising—Sunday travel section— 533 column inches at $15 per column inch ........ $8,000.00
- ❏ Quarterly newsletter to clients (printing and postage) ................................................................. $3,400.00
- ❏ Other direct mail ............................................... $  600.00
- ❏ 60 radio spots at $30 per spot (two short campaigns) ........................................................ $1,800.00
- ❏ Special events, production, miscellaneous .......... $1,200.00

$15,000.00

This, of course, is only one way to allocate funds. Some managers may decide to go heavier on direct mail or to eliminate radio. Others may want to add television, but this calls for a larger budget.

The point is, they should use a variety of approaches, putting them together in a proportion that works for them.

Budgets for airlines, hotel chains, and cruise lines run into the millions of dollars. They employ advertising agencies to advise them on the most effective media buys. They are also able to spend more money on special events, like parties for travel agents or travel writers. These larger travel entities also get more heavily into television and magazine advertising. Typically, the cruise line, for example, would huddle with its ad agency team, discuss with them the line's goals and approximate budget, and the advertising agency would then respond with the creation of a campaign and a detailed budget containing their recommendations on how the allotted funds should best be spent.

State and local tourism bureaus normally work this way, too. For most, the budgets are smaller than those of major carriers or hospitality firms, but larger than the typical travel agency. Some states have promotional budgets that run into the millions; others struggle along with $300,000 or so. Part of this depends on the size of the state (or city) and part depends on how much reliance is placed on tourism. Wyoming, with the Tetons and Yellowstone, may spend an amount disproportionate to its population.

Note that these budgets cover not only advertising, but all the costs attributable to promotions. The newsletter must be included, the open house, the week-long excursion for travel editors, and the four-color annual report.

4. *Development of media strategy.* This phase could wait until after the campaign theme was conceived, since the theme might have an influence on the media chosen, but media are frequently selected first, based on past experience about their individual effectiveness. They would program so many newspaper ads; money for production and mailing of direct mail; perhaps some radio, television, or outdoor; and, on occasion, a category of miscellaneous for such things as parties or film rental and the like.

The media mix should relate to established campaign goals. Those media that have performed best for this sort of travel product in the past should get preferential treatment; the remaining media (if they decide to use them) share the remaining budget.

5. *The creative phase.* While these other decisions are taking place, someone should also be working on the creation of the message. The creative people work on the overall theme, the copy platform, and the way this theme will be worked into print, broadcast and other media, and how this will be reflected in printed materials and publicity.

6. *Integration of all phases of marketing.* Not only must the budget consider the multiplicity of items which fit under promotion, but these things must also be blended together to complement one another. They have to be scheduled so they dovetail logically and effectively.

Perhaps the campaign includes a media blitz during a key period, having the outdoor boards appear at the same time as the radio and television schedule. Perhaps the direct mail is planned to reach prospects right after an intensive print period. Perhaps radio and print lead up to some massive special event, like the launching of a ship or the addition of several branch offices.

**Fig. 12–1   Same layout, different audience and copy. The Princess Cruise campaign, featuring *Love Boat* star Gavin MacLeod, speaks to travel agents (left) and cruise prospects (right).** (Courtesy of Princess Cruises)

Personnel, too, should be involved and should be aware of the media and publicity schedules. Branch offices, if they exist, should be given the time to organize their own local strategy.

7. *Implementation of the campaign.* At some point the campaign starts and it should run smoothly, without hitches. This means good initial planning, but it also means constant supervision to see that the television spots were mailed on time, that the direct mail house has completed the prospect package, that the proofs for the print ads have been approved and returned. Agency managers and advertising agency staff keep an eye on things, noting how the print ad looks and where it is placed, monitoring the television schedule, checking on coupon responses (if these are part of the campaign) and simply overseeing things to ascertain how the goals are being met.

8. *Analysis of results.* Campaigns should be thought out completely before they are launched, checked while they are in operation, and evaluated after they are over. Every attempt

should be made to make the analysis as dispassionate and objective as possible. There is no sense in kidding yourself about results, merely to salve an ego. If you fail, you fail. Profit by the experience and try to discover what went wrong. Don't repeat the mistake.

In evaluating a campaign, remember that there are other reasons for failure besides the advertising and promotion. The travel product could be at fault, either because it was overpriced, not competitive, advertised at the wrong time, or improperly conceived. The strategy might have been wrong. Perhaps planners over-reacted to competition, pitched an appeal to the wrong audience, or started the ad campaign before their offices were geared up to respond. Planners might also have failed in selection of media, neglected follow-through, or developed a premise that lacked credibility.

## HYPOTHETICAL CAMPAIGN

Again, the difference between what a tour operator or major resort might do and what a small travel agency might accomplish are worlds apart. Goals and expectations are different, and the budgets are certainly different.

A resort area might want to launch a campaign aimed at attracting the young executive and spouse. They could commit half a million dollars to this particular goal, investing it in magazines, like *Fortune* and *Time* and *U.S. News & World Report,* which have a readership profile that fits the target audience, in some travel sections in major metropolitan newspapers (like *The New York Times*), and in direct mail aimed at a select list of prospects.

An airline serving Hawaii might spend as much on a luau for travel agents and writers as a small travel agency spends in a year on newspaper ads.

Let's assume a midsized agency decides to conduct its own theater tour of London and Great Britain, featuring four days and four plays in England's capital city, plus visits to a Shakespearian performance at Stratford-on-Avon and a light opera festival in Bath. Here's one way that campaign might develop.

1. All details of the tour would have to be settled. Hotels, ground transportation, meals, play tickets, airfare, and other considerations. This might all be turned over to a tour opera-

**Fig. 12–2   Both of these ads are directed to travel agents and, although similar, the copy and layout reflect a slightly different approach to each magazine's readers.** (Courtesy of Princess Cruises)

tor or the agency could put together the package itself, select-ing a tour director and English coach company.

2. Once the elements of the tour are in place, the tour must be priced, building in costs for the tour director, funds for ex-tras, and profit for the agency. A theme will be selected and media budget determined.

3. The tour itinerary is then roughed out, polished, and put into brochure form. This printed piece may be of the agency's own creation or may be part of a shell provided by the tour opera-tor or carrier.

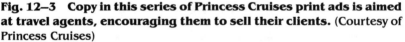

**Fig. 12–3    Copy in this series of Princess Cruises print ads is aimed at travel agents, encouraging them to sell their clients.** (Courtesy of Princess Cruises)

4.  Meantime, the agency would have been thinking about special groups that could be interested in the tour. Local drama societies, college students, those with season tickets to the community playhouse, clients who have taken similar trips to New York, and other cultural organizations. A determination would have to be made as to how far, geographically, they would extend this offering. A satellite city would certainly want to include suburbia and any smaller cities within a reasonable radius, assuming there was not any competition that was more conveniently located.

5. An advertising campaign would be planned, focusing heavily, perhaps, on newspapers. It would be geared to coincide with mailings to the groups cited in #4. If radio and television are to be used, these media would also be scheduled to achieve maximum impact. Other media might also be used, like ads in local play programs or college newsletters. Some one thing should be the focus of the advertising, like price, the titles of the plays, or the reputation of the tour manager.

6. This tour could also be helped by special events. There should be at least one gathering of prospects, allowing them to meet the tour manager, go over the itinerary, see film or slides on England, sample tea and English biscuits and, most importantly, to visit with others, ask questions and, hopefully, sign up.

7. If budget and circumstances allow, the agency could even be decorated with British symbols and tea could be served to all visitors. A local university professor might have a free lecture on British theater. Some publicity material from England might be turned into local news releases or features. The tour manager could appear on local radio or television talk shows. Any appropriate avenue for promoting the tour could be explored.

8. While the campaign is on, the travel agency will keep track of interest level and of those who sign up. This latter group must be kept informed and enthusiastic (using special events, mail, and phone), and those who inquired must be cultivated so that they become tour members. If any phase of the media campaign seems to be dragging, it could be altered or cancelled. Successful advertising might be expanded. The agency should know its goals in terms of tour members. If they are lagging behind expectations, they will want to beef up their efforts. If they are exceeding expectations, they may set new goals and change the strategy accordingly.

9. After the deadline for signing up is reached, figures are supplied to the carrier, hotels, tour operator and others, and last minute details are checked. There may be a final get-together for those heading to England and staff members will likely go to the airport to see them off.

10. Once the tour is completed, the tour manager provides a report and the entire experience is analyzed. The agency will want to know what things worked and which things didn't and why. Did the agency make money? How much? Was it

worth the effort? Were clients satisfied? Did the tour manager perform satisfactorily? What about the hotels, ground transportation, theater seats, quality of the plays, meals? Every element is reviewed, conclusions drawn, and, hopefully, lessons learned.

Even within the confines of the small agency, campaigns could vary. One might be a hurry-up affair following a local university's selection for a bowl game. Another might be aimed at correcting the impression that using a travel agency costs extra money. Still another might be designed to position this agency as *the* expert on cruises.

For the larger travel firm or the hospitality industry, the variations are even more pronounced. Regardless, they all require goals, planning, allocation of funds, implementation, and evaluation.

## CHAPTER HIGHLIGHTS

❏ No one activity can do the entire promotional job; a campaign of some sort is required.
❏ The campaign embodies an analysis of the marketing situation, setting of goals, development of a budget, creation of media strategy, creation of theme and content, integration of the varied elements of marketing, implementation, and evaluation.

■          ■          ■

## ❏ *EXERCISES*

1. Using travel magazines as your source, select one member of the travel industry, review this firm's advertising, and calculate the theme and goals of this campaign. You'll have to go through a number of publications in order to determine what the firm has in mind.
2. Take any product with which you are familiar through advertising and describe the campaign for it, including as many different aspects (print, radio, TV, direct mail, outdoor) as you can. Also mention the different approaches in individual ads or commercials.
3. What are the advantages of an advertising campaign compared with a series of unrelated ads for a product or service?

4.  Pick a hotel, restaurant, or tour and identify this entity as your client. Assuming you were going to run a campaign for one month for this client in your immediate area, and assuming you could buy twenty television spots (thirty-second spots) throughout that month, list the times or shows you would select for these spots and explain why. Obviously, the target audience will be determined by you once you make your initial selection.

## ❏ *CASE PROBLEMS*

*1. Select your favorite tourist area, or, at least, one you know something about. Assume you are an advertising agency account executive who has the responsibility of promoting this tourist area. You are meeting with the creative team in your agency, all of whom have only a general knowledge of the area. You have to give them some direction as to what you feel should be featured, who the audience for the campaign might be, what approach might work best, and how you think the budget might be allocated in terms of media buys (like heavy on TV or newspaper or whatever).*

*Identify this area and outline the points you will make to your colleagues in the agency. If any of your directions or choices require explanation, supply this information, too.*

*2. Assume that your college football team (or one from a nearby university) has been selected to play in the Sugar Bowl in New Orleans. You are the manager of a medium-sized travel agency and you decide to put together a package that will include four days in New Orleans, including round-trip air, hotel, tickets to the football game, sightseeing, and one or two special dinners or events. Let's further assume that you are located approximately 1,000 miles from New Orleans, in the Midwest. You have only one month before the bowl game, so you have to act fast. There is no time for any in-depth research.*

*What are some of the first things you'll want to consider? What target audiences will you single out? Besides the regular media routes, are there other ways you can advertise and publicize this tour? How would you determine your budget for promotion? How would you evaluate the success or failure of this enterprise?*

# THE HOSPITALITY
# INDUSTRY

The travel industry has a number of dimensions, and each of them promotes itself in a somewhat different fashion. There are services that plan tours, conduct tours, that transport business and leisure travelers, that entertain, and there are those that house individuals and groups. Hotels, motels, restaurants, and resorts are part of what is called the hospitality industry, a facet of the travel business that concentrates on accommodating the traveler once he or she gets to a destination.

The *Hotel and Travel Index* lists some 36,000 properties around the world. Obviously, there are many more units: hotels and motels that may not make the directory for one reason or other, plus everything from rent-a-cottage and farmhouse stays to an array of bed-and-breakfast (B & B) choices. The non-hotel/motel options are likely to promote themselves largely through specialized directories, brochures, plus occasional magazine and newspaper listings. They also produce brochures on postcard mailers and rely to a considerable extent on word-of-mouth and repeat business.

There are, for example, directories listing B & B and cottage rental by area and published by national tourist boards. Some smaller directories cover a geographic region or a special facility type. In addition, local tourist boards may be relied upon to have information on these places. Travelers to a certain locale can purchase these lists for a nominal fee.

For those looking for more unusual accommodations, there are also books, usually with a modest price tag, that focus on specialized facilities, like *Historical Houses Castles & Gardens,* a publication that carries advertisements and information on hundreds of manor houses and habitable castles in Great Britain and Ireland, or Derek Johansen's *Recommended Hotels in Great Britain,* a colorful annual that features the author's selections among manor houses and small hotels, or the *Relais & Chateaux Guide,* which blends product advertising with descriptions and pictures of properties, along with map inserts giving locations. Some directories may charge for inclusion; others scrupulously avoid this.

Overall, advertising and promotion for the specialized accommodation is minimal and selective. For one thing, these units do not operate on volume because they haven't the space. Mass media appeals make no sense for most of them.

Hotels and motels, especially those that are large or part of a chain, represent a different promotional problem entirely.

## HOTELS AND MOTELS

Worldwide there are approximately 9 million hotel rooms available and, in the United States, more than 56,000 hotels. It's a competitive

**Fig. 13–1   Each facility and each locale positions itself a little differently, accenting things like location, amenities, service, or price.**

business. Experts figure the American leisure market at between 40–50 million, while business travelers number about 2 million but travel more often. Both types must be sold a slightly different promotional package. Another challenge for the industry is the growing number of businesswomen traveling, amounting to almost 30 percent of the expense-account hotel trade. For these individuals, security may be a concern, and in-room bars may negate the need to walk alone into the hotel bistro.

Urban hotels also have to consider their community impact and responsibility. Hotels help attract conventions and other visitors, they provide unique facilities, they pay taxes, and they hire local people. In the Pittsburgh area alone, some 37,000 people are employed in the hospitality industry.

While various aspects of the hotel business are important—like the restaurant and the rental of meeting rooms—the main income is derived from room rental. During a peak season, hotels might average an occupancy rate of close to 85 percent, but this falls off to an average of slightly more than 50 percent in the off season. Building traffic during these low periods is always a marketing goal. Some hotels cooperate with the city in producing festivals, outdoor shows, and other attractions to lure visitors in these lax times.

The type of guest will vary according to season and location. In urban areas—say the hotels in downtown Chicago—50 percent of the guests would be business travelers, 35 percent individual travelers, and the remaining 15 percent would represent corporate groups contracted with a particular hotel.

Unlike travel agencies, a great many hotels would be affiliated with an advertising agency or have their own in-house advertising/public relations department. Major hotel chains would be clients of major ad agencies. This is big business. In 1986, Hyatt spent half a million dollars advertising a pair of its Acapulco hotels alone.

Another relatively recent phenomenon in the hotel business is the growing number of management and development companies that buy and operate hotels but with very little fanfare. These managers would exercise some control over the marketing and promotional phases of the operation. They could also tie up with some hotel representation firm to handle reservations. While this relationship has its advantages, the individual hotel has to remember it may be one of a few thousand hotels being represented and it is also at the mercy of the expertise and personality of the representative who responds to the call. The large chains, of course, have their own 800-number reservation centers.

## Research

At the very least, hotel managers should know *who* stays at their hotels. If they don't, they must initiate market research on the subject. Fortunately, a lot of information is available.

First, there are syndicated services that give general information or census data that can provide support and extension of other facts. Then there are customized services, requiring the hiring of professional pollsters. Finally, there is considerable in-house information, like registration cards and inquiries.

One New York hotel, a budget type, used its registration list and wrote or called those listed. From this effort they devised a profile of their customers, discovering that these people were married, over 35, with incomes between $20–$40,000 and probably came from the East Coast or the Southeast. They concluded that those with incomes under $20,000 don't travel much and those with incomes over $40,000 probably stayed at better hotels.

After pulling together a customer profile, a hotel (or hotel chain) might then check out the various media to see who delivers this sort of prospect most efficiently. Some planners take this even further, deciding on what factors they want to measure, seeing how various media handle each, then adding these up and dividing by the number of factors to arrive at a figure signifying the best media buy.

Another formula hotels sometimes use to measure performance is to divide the percentage of rooms sold by the potential (which should be realistic) and then multiplying the result by 100. Thus:

$$\text{Performance Index} = \frac{\% \text{ Sold}}{\% \text{ Potential}} \times 100$$

If the hotel is performing less than 100, it's not living up to its potential.

Hotels and motels may also research other topics, from client-requested amenities to additional sources of convention or meeting bookings.

Once they have the data, they can decide on a course of action. Will they change the price ranges, change the package, or alter the promotional effort? Will they add or subtract staff? Expand, merge, or sell off properties? Remember that advertising and public relations can't do it all, but, if these can be identified as areas that need improvement, then planners should focus on them.

## Informal Data

Many hotels collect informal comments on their facilities, asking guests to fill out cards before leaving, or to mail in after they return home. Various publications also solicit remarks from readers on their favorite hotel experiences. While these statements are not scientific, they could prove helpful when writing advertising copy or when trying to address certain strengths or weaknesses of the property.

Subscribers to *Travel Weekly,* who are on the road far more than average, are periodically queried about their favorite hotels and what they liked about them. What surface are common areas of concern plus some special features, usually in the realm of service.

The *accommodations* themselves are praised for being "roomy" or "warm" or "plush." A few guests specify the variety and choices in rooms and others note the decor, furnishings, and cleanliness. Oversized tubs get raves and so do bathrooms with 24-karat gold fixtures.

There are those who are impressed by the lobbies and courtyards and gardens. "There were grand pianos and pianists everywhere," one woman remarked.

*Location* is a factor. Close to shopping and theaters. Remote and far from traffic. Handy to places like Disneyland or Washington, D.C. governmental offices. Motels advertise their proximity to the interstate highway and others may brag about the string of restaurants close by. Skiers want accommodations close to the lifts and gamblers may look for a place not far from the track.

The quality of the hotel/motel *restaurant* is often mentioned, with words like "good and plentiful" and "gourmet" emerging with regularity. Guests may single out the ethnic cuisine, the lunch on the terrace, the table linens, a generous wine steward, or the room service breakfast.

After they have talked about architecture, scenic setting, and closeness to the beach, it seems that the *staff* and the *extra touches* stand out. One hotel sends a reservation desk person to the room with the guest and bellboy, just to see that all is okay in the room. Another hotel, which transports its guests to the airport, even helps arrange seat assignments on the plane. Despite the fact that it's no longer a novelty, visitors continue to appreciate items like the bathrobes, slippers, toiletries, and shoe polish in the bathrooms, or the turndown service on the beds along with the bit of chocolate. Fast check-in and check-out are praised and, at one hotel, so is the 24-hour security person on each floor. Guests react favorably to unique gestures like moving the dining room tables to the water's edge for dinner, or supplying fresh fruit in the room, or emulating the European custom of serving tea and coffee in the lobby. In one mountain property, the practice of kindling the fire in the evening and relighting it again in the morning, before the guests arise, is cited. One guest even commented favorably on the doorman in beefeater garb and the elevator operators decked out in oriental style.

All of these innovations have public relations and promotional angles. Other hoteliers who gather this information may then apply variations of their own. You may spend thousands, even millions, on a massive ad campaign, and then it's the little things the guests recall.

## Target Audiences and Communicating with Them

The hospitality industry has four main target audiences:

❏ Potential guests
❏ Travel agents
❏ Local and national groups
❏ Restaurant patrons (where applicable)

There are other audiences. Large hotel and motel chains must consider their own internal staffs, using newsletters, meetings and incentives to keep them loyal and enthused. Certain hotels may also look to the community as a special public, or the government, or other members of the industry. These entities are reached more by public relations programs than by advertising or marketing techniques but, at any given time, they could be important. An impending bit of damaging legislation could, for example, turn the state legislature into a prime audience.

Normally, however, the number one target would be the prospect. Hotel and motel chains spend the bulk of their promotional efforts selling the image of their facilities, figuring that, if the name is regarded favorably, the individual will think of that option when traveling. The individual Holiday Inn may advertise in the local paper and yellow pages and may also involve itself in the community, but the best thing it has going for it is the reputation of the chain. Certain hotels, especially those in large cities, may campaign on their own for guests. The Milford Plaza in New York fits this latter category, with its 1987 theme centered around the "lulla*buy* of Broadway." A thirty-second television commercial apes the Broadway musical style, with dancing and singing hotel staff, and the print ads mirror this concept, emphasizing the $46 rate for room, breakfast, dinner and cocktails. Holiday Inn may focus on a more generic theme, like a good night's rest or the uniformity and reliability of facilities.

As with any campaign theme, whatever the hotel/motel comes up with should spotlight some unique, or apparently unique, difference; should be credible, even provable; and should be creatively presented. The approach may differ in different magazines and for

**Fig. 13–2  Price is the focus of this ad whose musical theme is echoed in the hotel's television commercials.** (Courtesy of Best Western Milford Plaza)

different clientele, but most advertising still relies on the basic psychological appeals cited earlier.

A Best Western ad, directed to seniors, mentions "dependable lodging on a retirement budget" while the Club Romantique in Florida headlines its promotion for honeymooners with "A little romance is all you need . . . everything else is included." Hotel Sofitel continues to focus on its image as a facility that operates on the European model and the Harber Court Hotel in Baltimore rides a current trend, telling prospects "they deserve it." Howard Johnson introduces a new Alabama unit with discount coupons and the Sheraton singles out a Nile cruise to give the chain a more exotic look. The Clarion hotels simply announce, "We'd love to have you stay with us."

This same sort of homey image has a different twist in the Helmsley of New York ads that invariably feature president Leona M. Helmsley, "the face that launched 8000 rooms." Using an exec as a celebrity has its risks; the public could tire of seeing the same face. On the other hand, this approach gives the impression the president is concerned about every detail of the hotel's operation. The copy supports this, talking about padded headboards and choice of pillows and two-sided extension mirrors in the bathrooms. Mrs. Helmsley, who also praises her husband, Harry, in some ads, insists in another series that she runs the hotels "the way I run my home." These ads attempt to blend opulence with personal attention, and one publication may contain as many as four different print versions.

Hyatt, too, may opt for multiple ads in a single in-flight magazine, calling attention to some resort properties in half-page ads, backed by a 2-page spread listing more than 80 American locations and captioned "Thinking of You." Another angle, in *Fortune* magazine, centers on the luxury and exclusivity of Hyatt's Regency Club. The firm's ad in an Atlanta city magazine might take still another tack, emphasizing local and regional uses of the hotel.

Since travel agents are in the position of recommending hotels, they are also an important promotional target. Besides supplying agents with printed materials, inviting them for a complimentary visit, providing discounts on regular room charges, and sponsoring periodic events, hotel chains may be in evidence at travel exhibits and in the pages of trade journals.

Advertising in trade publications may sometimes reflect themes of the consumer campaigns but, more often, they are aimed directly at the agents, discussing commissions, satisfaction, repeat business, and other practical matters. While factors like location may be featured, the bottom line, overtly or subtly, is the economic impact on the travel agency.

Quality Inns tells readers of *Travel Weekly* "How to Become America's Best Paid Travel Agent" and The Registry Hotel Corporation uses 72-point type to announce "15% Commissions." Lincoln Hotels positions itself as "unquestionably the finest hotel you *never* heard of" and the Radisson stresses growth, "While You're Reading This Ad, Another New Radisson Hotel is Being Planned."

"Book Them at the Drake" commands an ad for that New York hotel, while Novotel assures travel agents they will "fret no more" and the Hyatt plays up the fact that travel experts named them "America's Best Hotel Chain."

To reach local groups (for meetings, luncheons, and weekend stays) and national groups (for conventions, tours, business meetings, and the like) hotels and motels probably rely much more on personal contact and the mails. Some may not solicit this kind of business at all, but most are interested in some form of group bookings. Special rates often apply and there is added revenue from meals and other facilities. What the hotel tries to sell are things like convenience, ample room, parking, good food, accommodating staff, price, and other features. Meeting, group, and convention planners are a little like travel agents in that they're interested in others having a rewarding experience.

Not every hotel or motel has its own restaurant. Some of the smaller and the suite-only facilities offer nothing but coffee and rolls. Other hotels that may have restaurants may cater to guests only or may not advertise extensively to the drop-in trade. Some hotels, however, are noted for their cuisine. That attracts guests as well as diners and may help augment income. Much of their advertising may be on-site (with dresser top or elevator posters) or local (using newspapers, city magazines, radio, and television) or outdoor boards. Occasionally, a restaurant may appear as part of the hotel's appeal in a national ad, and there are always the special printed programs for art groups or other prospects. Typically, these restaurants focus on ambience, quality or specialized cuisine, or even the presence of a noted chef. A famous kitchen is always a help in selling groups.

Research is important in this area as well. Group and individual profiles are extracted whenever a hotel plans some new sort of program. Weekend vacations, for example, came partly as a result of needing to compensate for the lack of business travelers over the weekend and partly because research shows that 73 percent of

American vacations are 3 days or less, usually over a weekend. Research also shows that the major clients for weekend stays are people wanting to get away and relax, or couples—usually married, or those who like to party. Knowing these things greatly improves every aspect of the marketing strategy, including the advertising.

## Special Selling Tools

Besides the little touches that people remember, or even the major architectural additions (like a pool and waterfall in the lobby), hotels employ other marketing devices. Many are equipped to permit teleconferencing as bait for business meetings and some have frequent-stay programs, like the airlines frequent-flyer programs, giving regular guests cash awards, merchandise, upgrading in terms of rooms, travel, and other benefits. Hotels also tie into airlines' frequent-flying promotions, resulting in both free air travel and hotel space. Besides group rates, many hotels provide corporate rates, arranged in advance with large companies, allowing corporate travelers up to 50 percent off regular room charges. Incidentally, travel agents aren't always happy with this arrangement, since not all such deals are commissionable.

Other promotional ideas:

❑ Fitness centers, offering either complete workout equipment or pool and sauna or both.
❑ Twenty-four-hour restaurant.
❑ Weekend specials offering everything from 50 percent off rooms to reduced rates for rental cars and books of discount coupons for shopping and entertainment.
❑ A series of fashion shows.
❑ Murder mystery or other theme weekend.
❑ For groups: free coffee breaks, show tickets, complimentary suite, use of AV equipment, and other enticements.

The Campbell Inn, near the San Jose Airport in California, cleans car windshields of guests in the morning, marks the current page in the room *TV GUIDE,* and even delivers meals from area restaurants to guests who don't want to go out. In the 13 hotels in Atlantic City that feature casinos, a number are adding child care, bowling, miniature golf, and other attractions for the nongambler.

These promotions reach out to travel agents, who book only about 25 percent of the hotel space (as against 65 percent of the car rentals and 75 percent of the airline tickets). To help increase this

**Fig. 13–3   Reflecting its international character, Preferred Hotels' brochure repeats initial information in 6 languages.** (Courtesy of Preferred Hotels WorldWide)

activity, some hotel chains run sales contests, rewarding those who book the most space with free rooms or trips or cash. Stouffer Hotels let the top 5 producers (among the 5,000 travel agents who participated in their Magnificent Minute competition) spend 60 seconds running through the Maritz Merchandise Warehouse in St. Louis, grabbing anything they wanted in that time period. The Ramada Hotel in New Orleans awarded $10,000 to the winner of its sweepstakes.

Do these things work? Stouffer reported a 111 percent increase in travel-agency hotel bookings during the course of their recent contest.

## Media

Hotels and motels, like travel agencies, spend more money in newspapers than any other medium. They like the immediacy, flexibility, and relatively low cost of newspapers. A hotel may use the business section to reach the business traveler, but stay with the travel section for the leisure traveler.

Direct mail and other printed materials (for mailing, display, or location in travel agencies and chambers of commerce) are essential, and so is a listing in the Yellow Pages. Highway signs or urban boards may also be used, along with some radio and television. In general, only the larger chains do any appreciable TV advertising.

## Ratings

There are all sorts of rating systems for hotels, using stars or the alphabet, or some other designation. Most of these are the result of some association's opinion or critic's appraisal. These help establish a reputation and, since word-of-mouth is important, may have value far beyond the text they appear in. Often the same hotels surface.

In 1985, *Advertising Age* readers selected the Hyatt hotels as their favorite, followed closely by the Marriott chain. That same year, *Business Travel News* (which surveyed travel managers and agents), came up with Marriott as leader, then Hyatt. Also appearing in both lists were Westin, Sheraton, Holiday Inns, Four Seasons, Ritz-Carlton and Hilton. Making these lists may later serve as the basis for an advertising campaign or series of printed materials.

## Hotel Variations

There are the familiar metropolitan hotels and the auto-oriented motels, but the hospitality industry also offers variations. There are airport hotels, for example, which range from quite good to barely habitable. There's also the new generation of small hotels, a la New Orleans, with plush and often expensive suites and a host of delicate extras, from French soaps to tortilla soup and chocolate ancho ice cream. Airport hotels concentrate on the business traveler, counting on those wanting to save meeting time or those delayed by weather, while the ornate small hotels cater more to the luxury trade.

# RESORTS

Some of the marketing approaches for resort properties resemble those of hotels. The appeals may center on everything from setting to salon, and resorts also seek out groups, meetings, and conventions.

There are differences, however. Resorts sell pleasure, not quick checkouts or security. Read the headlines. "It's Better in the Bahamas." "Some People Have All the Fun." Words like "unwind" and "relax" get overworked. Copywriters have to think of myriad ways to describe beaches: sugar white, coral, secluded, sundrenched, pristine.

Travel agents also figure more prominently in resort bookings than they do in the standard hotel scene, so they become an even more important marketing target.

Resorts can be seasonal, and some of them have to make almost all of their income in a few months. Ski resorts come to mind. Others, while open year-round, may attract their largest audiences in the winter months. A cool January or a snow-free December can hurt resorts, depending on their location.

While resorts share some of the same advertising space as hotels, such as newspapers and magazines, they do better in the publicity area because they have a more exciting story to tell. Resorts have only 12 percent of the rooms available in the hotel and motel industry but they account for nearly a fourth of the revenue. Demand for resort rooms is growing faster than demand for regular hotel space.

A lot of promotion dollars go into resort advertising and public relations. A new property in the Dominican Republic recently spent more than a million dollars in advertising during its initial year of operation. Some spend much more. Besides the promotional expense, most resorts find they have to ante up a lot of money to expand and improve facilities, just to stay competitive. America's more than 400 ski resorts spent over $200 million in 1986–87 on expansion. Some added ice skating, health clubs, saunas, and pools, realizing that skiers, who average 5 days at a resort, will not ski every day. And, if these ski resorts relax, they could be overtaken by European countries, from Switzerland to Yugoslavia, who are pouring money into promotion and developing attractively priced packages. Even Cyprus allotted a modest $20,000 to promote their skiing!

Except for not considering the business traveler a major public, resorts would also have a varied client profile. There are Sun City ads for senior citizens, focusing on warm weather and low price. For the young or the newly married, there are themes like Sandals of

Montego Bay, announcing that "one price covers everything—except your suntan" and that "all you need is love." Golfers are asked to "Play the Legends" or to try the "unharried and unhurried fairways" at Seabrook Island Resort in South Carolina. The adventurous may be interested in a dude ranch or backpacking or scuba diving.

You could nearly divide resort promotion into two categories—those that promise relaxation and pampering, and those that feature numerous activities, from sports to live entertainment. There are also the spas and health resorts that are big on massage, saunas, whirlpools, beauty care, mineral springs, and perhaps even aerobics, yoga, or the services of a medical team. They combine an invitation to shape up with an appeal to complete relaxation. Mexico headlines weather, sports, culture, and archaeology. After a decline in traffic, Bermuda is marketing itself as a "lifestyle experience" and supplementing its ad campaign with a new 25-minute film. The Caribbean throws in music, yacht charters, and a sensual image.

Growing in popularity is the complete or all-inclusive resort, offering everything from boutiques and disco to sports and computers. Club Med, which initiated the idea more than 35 years ago, spots its "villages" around the world, from Tahiti to Thailand—more than 100 locations. They advertise in upscale magazines, on television, through direct mail, and they produce a lavish 100-page brochure depicting their offerings. Their client list is on the way to a million members.

As mentioned earlier, resorts get a boost from the travel page features in the newspapers, from the features in travel and other magazines, and even from television programs like "The Lifestyles of the Rich and Famous." The articles are often specific, identifying superior restaurants and carrying prices for accommodations and entertainment. Recently, the practice of selling hotel/resort videos has caught on. These cassettes, usually running 15 minutes and costing about $15, capture tours, cruises, and about 50 different programs on Hawaii, Mexico, and the Caribbean. Another promotional ploy is to bind special sections on a resort area into travel trade journals and, of course, to supply travel agencies with posters, brochures, and decorative materials.

As with other forms of hospitality advertising, communications addressed to travel agents talk in terms of commissions or client satisfaction. "Your Clients Will Want to Go Straight to the Point" reads an ad for Point Pleasant Resort in the Virgin Islands, while others tout "up to 20 percent" in commissions.

**Fig. 13–4  Adopting a rebus layout design, Phillips combines information on its seafood cuisine with details on its hotel.** (Courtesy of Phillips Corporation)

# RESTAURANTS

Consumers are familiar with restaurant advertising. Local newspapers invariably carry it. Some ads merely sell name and location, while others list menus, prices, and entertainment. Locally, good restaurants help build their own reputations, but restaurants hoping to attract travelers have to be bolder. You'll see their ads in in-flight magazines (North Beach: The Dining Experience in San Francisco), or consumer travel magazines (Enjoy the Prime of Your Life: Lawry's, Chicago), or trade journals (Shannon Castle Banquets: Treat your clients like royalty and reap princely rewards), or in your hometown daily (Enjoy Sunday Brunch at Calveccio's; only $7.95). Hotels generally place guides in rooms, telling guests about local restaurants, and the Yellow Pages in the phone book contain listings and ads. Some radio and television commercials are aired, normally only locally. You might also notice local billboards, especially in or near airports.

Restaurants also benefit from a variety of rating services. These are listed by state and city, include information about cuisine and prices, and may even feature a rating scale. While these lists are frequently reliable, they still represent a limited taste and may not match the appetite of the individual visitor. That's why word-of-mouth and recommendations from hotel staffs remain important. There are also guidebooks, like Simon & Schuster's *The Best Restaurants in America* and *Mariani's Coast-to-Coast Dining Guide* and others, including many city or state guides. Listing in these and other guidebooks can rarely be manipulated but a good product and proper promotion can't hurt.

Restaurants also have their special publics, like luncheon groups, clubs, tours, and meetings. Personal or phone contact may be used for the larger groups with special menus or prices utilized to attract the former.

# CHAPTER HIGHLIGHTS

❑ Hotels and motels vary in size and purpose and their promotional budgets and efforts reflect this.

❑ Competition among the nation's 56,000 hotels is intense, and the key to success is room occupancy.

❏ Larger hotel chains will undoubtedly employ an advertising agency, and they may also be run by a management and development company.

❏ Research in the hospitality industry seeks to develop a customer profile or to measure performance, and it combines polling with the use of existing data, including the hotel's own records. Various external rating services also provide information and prestige.

❏ Target audiences in the hospitality industry usually include potential guests, travel agents, groups, and restaurant patrons. There are also a number of secondary markets.

❏ Advertising themes in this industry may be aimed at a specific audience or may concentrate on a single item, from price to quality.

❏ To gain an edge or clientele, hotels/motels may add special services like an all-night restaurant or weekend packages or fitness centers or special events.

❏ Newspapers are the principal medium used by the hospitality industry, but direct mail is also important and larger chains employ all of the media, including television and outdoor.

❏ In recent years, some other housing formats have been introduced, from bed and breakfast to luxury suites, and from airport hotels to castle stays.

❏ Resorts cater more to pleasure, promoting either a relaxing lifestyle or a long activities menu—or both. They also get considerable mileage out of publicity from feature stories or television programs.

❏ Restaurants are normally local advertisers, with a few carried in publications that reach travelers and with some using a wide range of media, from Yellow Pages to outdoor. Rating services are a public relations plus for this segment of the hospitality industry.

■          ■          ■

## ❏ EXERCISES

1. Select your favorite restaurant, local or otherwise, and write three words or phrases you feel describe its uniqueness.
2. Visit a local or regional hotel. See what brochures they have describing themselves or their community. Do they have a

printed meeting or party planner they supply to groups? Is the restaurant a factor in their marketing?

3. Check with the local Chamber of Commerce. How active are hotels and motels in supplying information to them? How often do they get queried about accommodations?

4. Look in the newspaper travel section of magazines to which you subscribe. Find three ads for resorts. What do you think the target audience is for each ad? What aspects of each ad attract you and which ones repel?

## ❏ CASE PROBLEMS

*1. Take a hotel that you know, either in your area or some other familiar region. Assume this hotel wants to book a state-wide meeting of the Professional Photographers Association. Some 250 members of this group are expected to attend and about half will bring their spouses. You are the PR person for the hotel and your boss asks you to write a memo to him/her listing your ideas for a marketing approach to this group. What do you have to offer them? What special things might you include to beat out other hotels in the state?*

*2. You are the owner of a ski resort and, during the past two winters, snowfall has been light. Even with the use of snow machines, you haven't been able to produce the best snow for skiing. You are looking around for other ways to make your resort appealing and to build back your clientele. What might you add? Are there any new target audiences you could approach? What marketing tools would you use (keeping in mind that the budget is fairly tight)?*

# CARRIERS AND TOUR OPERATORS

An essential part of the travel industry is transportation, and those businesses that move people from one spot to another also look for ways to promote themselves. They have to fill seats, book cabins, and rent cars. Some of their efforts, like those of hotels, are directed at potential consumers, some at groups, and some at travel agencies.

There are differences among these suppliers. Business travelers are a key public for the airlines, but not for cruise lines. The same distinction might be made between rental cars and coach or train travel. Clients may also be distinguished by age level and income. Advertising, too, varies, depending somewhat on budget and somewhat on goals.

This chapter examines some of the principal carriers and their marketing efforts, and also looks briefly at tour operators and their campaigns.

## AIRLINES

In the last fifty years, air travel has made remarkable improvements. In the 1930s, the smaller, propeller-driven planes were often uncomfortable, had limited range, couldn't fly over or around storms, experienced delays, and were without the food and service now routinely supplied. Today, despite complaints, airlines keep pretty well to their schedules, provide a generally smooth flight, and offer movies, a choice of music, bar service, and food. Passengers still ride them to get someplace, unlike a cruise where the trip itself is the treat, and the competition for these travelers is hotter than ever.

Following deregulation in 1978, the number of airlines in America nearly quadrupled. Many of these newcomers were soon struggling, hit by increased costs, strikes, and the constant fare wars.

# Four things to remember when booking Ireland.

AER LINGUS

DELTA

NORTHWEST

PAN AM

It's never been simpler to plan trips to Ireland. Take your choice of four major airlines or choose from several charter operators. Take your pick of departure times and places.
For reservations call your favorite airline. For information on Ireland call the Ireland Information Center at **1-800-223-6470**.

## IRELAND
The unexpected pleasures.

Irish Tourist Board, 757 Third Ave., New York, N.Y. 10017 (212) 418-0800

**Fig. 14–1 This symmetrically balanced ad (with headline and logo in green ink) is a product of the Irish Tourist Board, supplying the names of principal carriers to Ireland.** (Courtesy of Eoin Kennedy, TPO, Irish Tourist Board)

Many folded. Today, five airlines and their partners (American, United, Texas Air, Delta, and Northwest) handle 80 percent of the Revenue Passenger Miles. When you realize that 90 percent of the nonauto travel between cities is by air, this adds up to considerable income—more than $12 billion in the first half of 1986. This combination of available monies and narrowing list of suppliers spells competition, and competition means a battle to cut costs, offer incentives, and devise winning marketing plans.

Before deregulation, the differences cited by airlines might have been the quality of their food or the uniforms of the stewardesses. Braniff painted its fleet and United laid claim to the friendly skies. After deregulation, with mergers, hundreds of special rates, new routes, and a series of incentive programs, the differences became more marked. Better than 4 out of every 5 passengers today are flying on some sort of discounted ticket. Travel agencies complain that booking airlines is chaotic, even with the help of computers.

People's Express came in with rock bottom fares, for those who would settle for a certain amount of uncertainty and a no-frills approach to in-flight service. American Airlines decided to go after

**Fig. 14–2   Delta Air Lines features a typeface layout and a professional service theme to reach travel agents.** (Courtesy of Delta Air Lines Inc.)

the business traveler, combining this campaign with seasonal pitches to the regular tourist. United provided half-fare coupons for a month after a damaging strike. Continental offered to upgrade coach tickets on other airlines to first class on its planes. Airlines advertised wider seats, a broader choice of destinations, and, often, lower fares. Some, like Southern Airlines, before its collapse, pushed "single-class travel," criticizing other airlines that separated their passengers, and Regent Air Corporation even picked up travelers in a chauffeur-driven limousine.

When lower fares became the dominant theme for nearly all airline campaigns, Texas Air spent $50 million on an image campaign to position Continental (one of the lines they own) as a quality line, with exceptional service and real value. Their theme line was "Up Where You Belong," and the advertising buys were heavily oriented toward television.

While television spots characterize Continental's thrust, United, two years earlier, rediscovered the value of direct mail, after their month-long pilot strike. A series of mailings were sent to United's Mileage Plus membership list, trying to regain or retain the loyalty of their regulars. A poll of former passengers revealed that fidelity to United has eroded and this was their response. While the results weren't perfect, direct mail did help halt the trend.

Perhaps the most common innovation in terms of competition was the "frequent flyer" program that allowed passengers to total up their mileage and cash appropriate totals in for additional trips or other gifts. This program is not without its critics, and it has caused some problems for firms employing the frequent traveler. Those who do little traveling sometimes resent the benefits accrued by their colleagues. The promotion has worked, however, and at least one travel agent, noting its success, devised his own plan for those who use his agency, awarding them points redeemable for catalog merchandise.

The promotions multiply. Eastern offered passengers low fares on their late night cargo planes and found thousands of takers. McClain Airlines, out of Phoenix, positioned itself as a one-class-only airline, catering to business passengers. "Class Without Cost" is its theme, and McClain blended radio, outdoor, transit advertising, and a heavy dose of print to push this concept.

Airlines often package their own tours and bring together other elements, either by contract or merger. United Air Lines, for example, could fly you to your destination, rent you a Hertz car, and put you up in a Western Hotel—while their corporation existed. These combinations may also share ad campaign costs, although most such ads are geared for the specific audience for that specific service.

Some airlines squeak by and do little advertising beyond newspapers and a few outdoor boards, but the major lines are also major advertisers. You see their logos emblazoned on tail sections on TV commercials, and you glimpse their full-color ads in a wide range of magazines. These lines also buy billboard space, and may even be credited on TV game or entertainment shows for providing cast transportation. Most of them publish their own magazines, and behave just like other large corporations. Still, each continues to try to discover some singular niche that will provide a marketing edge and distinguish one airline from another.

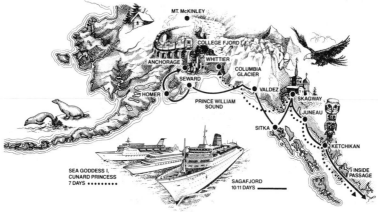

# THE SIGHTSEER'S ALASKA: ALL THE WAY TO ANCHORAGE.

## ONLY CUNARD'S 'GLACIER ROUTE' OFFERS YOUR CHOICE OF SAILING STYLE—CLASSIC, YACHT-LIKE OR INFORMAL.

By continuing to Anchorage—instead of turning back at Juneau or Skagway like most other cruise lines—Cunard shows you more of Alaska's greatest sights, including 4½-mile-wide Hubbard Glacier; 250-foot-high Columbia Glacier; and six-glacier College Fjord.

From May through September you see them all, plus the fascinating ports of the Inside Passage, in 10 or 11 days on the classic cruise ship Sagafjord or in seven days on the yacht-like Sea Goddess I or the informal Cunard Princess. Embark in either Vancouver or Anchorage.

On Sagafjord, you enjoy the classic cruise experience—highly personalized service; unhurried, single-sitting dining; and free access to the famed "Golden Door Spa at Sea."® Ten days, from $2,030; 11 days, from $2,250.

Appealing even to those who might never have cruised, Sea Goddess I offers the freedoms and pleasures of a private yacht shared by never more than 58 couples with similar backgrounds and tastes. Dine when and with whom you please, or opt to be served course by course in the privacy of your suite-room. Seven days, $4,000.

On the informal Cunard Princess, stroll spacious sightseeing decks. Take in the casino, piano bar or Observation Lounge. Dance in the nightclub or in the smashing Indoor/Outdoor Center. And as on Sagafjord, dine amid panoramic views. Seven days, from just $1,270.

**Cruise/tours of 12 to 19 days include Midnight Sun Express.**

Cunard's four tempting cruise/tours feature rail travel from Anchorage in

the luxury of a private, glass-domed car. (No exhausting overland bus rides!) Ask your travel agent about our low-cost or no-cost airfare, available from 79 cities.

Rates per person, double occupancy, dependent on departure date; taxes extra. Sagafjord and Cunard Princess registered in the Bahamas; Sea Goddess I registered in Norway.

# CUNARD

QUEEN ELIZABETH 2 • SAGAFJORD • VISTAFJORD • SEA GODDESS I • SEA GODDESS II • CUNARD COUNTESS • CUNARD PRINCESS

**Fig. 14–3 Besides an eye-catching layout and informative copy, Cunard supplies a map for Americans weak on their geography. (Courtesy of Cunard)**

## CRUISES

Thanks to our changing lifestyles, some renewed promotional efforts, and to the popularity of television shows like "Love Boat," cruise patrons have tripled in number since 1970, amounting to between one and a half and two million passengers and accounting for $5.5 billion in cruise line revenues. To accommodate this increase, ten new ships were launched between 1982 and 1985, adding 15,000 more berths. More christenings or reconstructions are in the works.

Choice of accommodations is wide ranging, from under $200 a day to well over $3,000 a day. Sailing venues are also varied, from the inland waterways of Alaska to the Greek Islands. Warm weather ports remain the favorites, making places like the Caribbean and South America key sales areas.

With all this growth, however, the market has barely been tapped. Only 5 percent of Americans have signed up for cruises, and two-thirds of the potential market are relatively unfamiliar with the joys of this vacation option. To corral this vast untouched segment, cruise lines, in recent years, have tried to correct the impression that sailing to Aruba and St. Thomas will be dull. Campaigns rely heavily on shipboard activities, lavish meals, and headline entertainers, along with frequent ports of call. Young Americans are lured by the love-boat-style promise of romance and older Americans are subject to deck chair, dining, and congeniality appeals.

As with other sectors of the travel trade, marketing themes may emphasize price, itineraries, the ship's design and facilities, the crew's experience and accessibility, sightseeing, cuisine, or entertainment. Many cruise lines describe their passenger profile as an affluent, active professional between 40 and 60 years of age. American Hawaii Cruises promotes family travel, and American Cruise Lines has made a special effort to interest meeting and convention groups. Other lines may focus on a youthful clientele, on charter potential or, almost always, on the travel agent.

Media buys also vary. Norwegian Caribbean Lines pioneered the use of network television, a medium still not utilized by most cruise companies. Newspapers and magazines (especially those with an affluent readership) are common sources of advertising coverage, and every major line is big on attractive printed materials. Cruise lines also select markets carefully. Since many specialize in delivering specific tour areas to passengers, they may narrow their promotional efforts to those areas matching the profile of their best prospects.

**Fig. 14—4    The popularity of cruises spurred the creation of a special cruise addition of Instant Travel Art.** (Courtesy of Louis Mercurio Associates)

Not only do ads for cruises dominate many magazines; they are also among the more attractive and compelling presentations. Cruise lines lend themselves to spectacular photography and it's always easier to wax poetic in copy about the sea than it is to sell the ambience of a weekend in some urban setting.

In trade journals, like *Travel Weekly* and *Tour & Travel News*, special sections are frequently included on cruises. Some are part of the regular extensive coverage of the subject and some are full color inserts. "Save on Early Reservations" cautions one ad. "Three Extra Days of Vacation Free" advises another. "Cruise Tahiti!" suggests a third, adding that, from certain cities, the air is free. As with other trade ads, the focus is on client concerns or commissions.

Travel agents contend they prefer selling cruises to tours. The task is simpler, more profitable, and more fun, according to them. Despite this, researchers for cruise lines discovered that agents were often reluctant to suggest cruises unless queried by the prospect. Part of this shyness stemmed from the belief that only older, more affluent people would be interested. To counteract this stereotypic attitude, cruise lines push familiarization trips for agents along with reminders that selling cruises takes less time than selling land packages.

A quick glance through a magazine like *Cruise Travel,* a new publication devoted entirely to this segment of the industry, reveals the scope of the marketing themes and the imaginative character of the prose. An inside front cover spread for Royal Caribbean explains: "Our Ships Don't Have Sails, but They Could Put the Wind Back in Yours." The ad copy begins: "The water slides by in blue-white ripples, punctuated now and then by the leap of a flying fish. The breeze, as it skims past you down the open deck, seems to carry all your worries right out to sea." American Cruise Lines invites readers to "discover a more pampered way of life" and Carnival Cruise Lines plays up their "eight great meals and snack a day" plus casinos, night club shows, parties, current films, and "romantic moonlight." With a little thought, every line can come up with something special to sell. Mediterranean cruises may emphasize history and Alaskan cruises focus on adventure. Big ships write about comfort and diversion while small lines brag that they can take you places larger lines can't, perhaps even right up on the beaches.

Themes also change to meet opportunities or correct misconceptions. When prospects begin to think cruises are only for the affluent, then price and value become promotional items. To counteract the activity-laden pitch of some lines, others emphasize that their cruises are free of "regimented play." If potential passengers seem turned off by fears of seasickness or other discomforts, advertising may play up the size and performance of its fleet and the experience of its crews. The Holland American Line makes a point of its "no tipping required" policy, a rarity among cruise lines.

A few cruise lines use spokespersons. Kathie Lee Johnson adds an appropriate perkiness to the TV and print ads for Carnival Cruise

Lines and who better than *Love Boat* captain Gavin MacLeod to tout the pleasures of Princess Cruises? Other lines may showcase their entertainment headliners.

Keep in mind, too, that there are other sea-going options, from tramp steamers to inland ferries. Many of these advertise only in directories or in specialized publications, or they may settle for listings and occasional posters. After all, if you want to reach the Isle of Arran in Scotland's Firth of Clyde, you'll want to board one of Caledonian MacBrayne's ferries, so the trip is purposive rather than festive. So the promotion is also practical, centering on schedules and prices and routes, although some mini-cruises for pleasure may be featured.

Cruise lines also tie into package tours, combining their trips with flight schedules, hotel bookings, car rentals. Some tours that reflect the problem of available time offer flights one way and return cruises. Others pair up with hotel chains and land packages to deliver a more extensive and varied trip.

## TRAINS

The Golden Age of train travel in America is definitely past, but trains are still carrying passengers in this country and, in Europe and elsewhere, this form of travel remains healthy. American railway passengers are carried on Amtrak, a government-subsidized system, which may never be profit-making. Periodically, the government threatens to get out of this business entirely but that action is curtailed by concern for those who would otherwise find it difficult to travel, and by the realization that costs of closing down the system and, in an emergency, starting it up again would be horrendous. Amtrak is the country's sixth largest carrier, transporting more than 20 million passengers to almost 500 destinations.

Early promotional campaigns for Amtrak asked for time to get things in shape, then told potential riders things were getting better, then moved into an advertising mood that combined nostalgia with on-time scheduling. When traffic fell off in 1982, Amtrak repositioned itself as a service that could compete favorably with other means of transportation. Their "All Aboard Amtrak" campaign in 1983 cost more than $20 million, and it was preceded by modernizing of equipment, addition of amenities like improved food service and more comfortable suites, improved reservation and ticketing methods, and an effort to guarantee on-time performance. Amtrak

**Fig. 14–5  Nice sequence, leading from head to coupon, in this ad aimed at a variety of tour types.** (Courtesy of Eurailpass)

also began to cooperate with airlines and cruise ships to develop package tours and added pricing options.

Some of the train's advertising points remain standard: ability to walk around while traveling, the closeness to the landscape, and the opportunity to meet other people. New copy platforms might take in the uniqueness of the experience, or what Amtrak called the "magic" of the ride. There are attempts to evoke memories for former train passengers, reminding them how much fun it used to be and how much better the accommodations are now. The system is even into escorted tours, video entertainment, bingo, trivia, and movies.

The world is full of romantic train journeys. The Orient Express, originally a route between Paris and Istanbul, now unites London with Venice as well. A luxurious journey with gourmet meals and ornate surroundings, this trip caters to an upscale clientele. Swiss trains take advantage of scenic landscapes and Japanese trains emphasize speed. Canadian train lines build in stays at some of the grand old railway hotels and the Trans-Siberian Railway appeals to the more adventurous and patient traveler. There are trains that cross Australia's barren Outback and a new rail program that winds through the Scottish Highlands.

While this mode of travel is not inexpensive, there are a number of discount ideas, like rail passes that cover all the travel you can do within certain time periods. The most famous of these is the Eurailpass which offers 15 days of travel for under $350 and three months of unlimited travel for about twice that amount.

## MOTOR COACH

Travel by bus has always had to battle a negative image revolving around discomfort, lack of cleanliness, absence of a glamorous atmosphere, and the time it takes to get from place to place. Motor coach execs point out that people who lodge these complaints probably haven't ridden a bus in years. Motor coach travel is far more comfortable, partly because of better seating design and partly because of improved heating and air conditioning. Greyhound features attractive terminals, unlimited travel passes, discount fares, even food and beverage service. A few tour companies offer deluxe service, with carpeted motor coach interiors, more than twice the passenger room, all window seats (which turn 360 degrees), and a driver/escort.

Almost two-thirds of all bus passengers are on charter trips, many of which are economical and flexible, allowing for side trips and choice of hotels and restaurants. These are in addition to the company's own prepackaged tours which may combine transportation, meals, and lodging.

While the over-50 age group remains the best target audience for motor coach tours, destinations sometimes attract a younger crowd, to ski excursions, for example. Destinations are enhanced by seasonal advantages (like Fall Foliage Tours of New England) or by special events (Tulip Time or Windjammer Festivals or an Old Time Fiddlers' Competition).

**Fig. 14—6   Motor coaches not only advertise their services but also serve as moving billboards themselves. Touring coaches, however, rarely do this.**

Greyhound, at the top of the motor coach heap, budgets in excess of $20 million annually for advertising, often broken down by audiences, with special appeals to Hispanics, college-bound students, the military, and the elderly. Trailways, which offered discounts to the members of the American Association of Retired People, used direct mail to reach senior citizens and, like Greyhound, allowed children to ride free. Motor coach carriers are also conscious of public relations value as the campaign to transport runaways home free-of-charge testifies.

## CAR RENTALS

Although Hertz and Avis continue to dominate this market, there are many newcomers to the field, from National and Budget with their competitive fares to Rent-A-Wreck which eschews the later model vehicles and rents out vintage cars.

Three themes seem popular in promotional campaigns: bargain rates, quality transportation, and speed and ease of renting and returning. O. J. Simpson and Arnold Palmer combined to demonstrate the simplicity of a Hertz check-out and later paired up to emphasize the low rental prices in specific locales. Hertz has continued to play up its Number One rating, even though Avis hitchhiked on that boast, proclaiming that, because they were second, they tried harder.

Business travelers are a major source of rental car income (even though more and more leisure vacationers are flying and renting), so you might expect to see car rental firms advertising heavily in publications that reach this market. The major companies, of course, are in all media, but they make certain they reach their prime prospects. In *Fortune* magazine, amid the welter of appeals for investment houses and office computers, Avis tells readers they're "red hot" with "supervalues" and that they won't keep business clients "cooling their heels," and Dollar Rent-A-Car pitches its corporate discounts. In *Business Travel News* Alamo Rent-A-Car offers its "corporate alternative" featuring competitive guaranteed rates and unlimited mileage, while Hertz is touting "Lincolns for Pennies" and Budget is matching models and prices with the big boys.

Almost invariably, consumer advertising for rental cars showcases price, often in the boldest, largest type, and trade publication copy combines client and cost appeals. "Your Clients Will Want to 'Fly the Coupe' $36.95 a Day," proclaims Thrifty Car Rental, while Budget stresses its worldwide plan in a series that compares prices in specific locales.

One relatively recent wrinkle in the car rental field is the increase in tie-ins with other travel suppliers. Thrifty Rent-A-Car Systems teamed up with Texas Air, Eastern, Continental, and Days Inns of America Inc. to help each other market services. Dollar affiliated with Rodeway and Hertz joined Air France to help promote business travel to that European country. Sometimes these partnerships stretch ad budgets, sometimes they provide traveler incentives.

All the major car rental companies operate internationally, competing with firms in those countries. Fly/drive packages are common, as are commercial and corporate rates, frequent traveler bonuses, and other plans. Vehicles range from subcompacts to luxury limos and Europe also does a brisk trade in minibuses, trailers, and chauffeur-driven cars.

Besides the traditional advertising media, car rental companies all rely on listings in everything from the Yellow Pages to local entertainment guides and their desks are in evidence at airport terminals and major hotel lobbies.

# TOUR OPERATORS

If you've ever taken a Caravan Tour, you'll be assured of receiving their annual catalogue detailing current offerings. Tour companies look for repeat business.

Two principal targets of tour operators are tour prospects, reached through newspapers, direct mail, and magazines; and travel agents, contacted by sales personnel, phone, direct mail, and in their trade journals. Other audiences might be corporate or incentive groups, organizations, and other suppliers who may represent potential for a tie-in.

Tour companies also get a word-of-mouth reputation, from travel agents and from consumers. A good experience may not only result in repeat business but may also influence other prospects. A negative experience can start a reverse reaction.

There are thousands of tour combinations, from African safaris to three days in Disneyland. What people are looking for are tours that take them to places they want to see, in safety, and at a reasonable price. What travel agents want are offerings that will appeal to their clientele and ones that will turn a profit.

There are the more recognizable names in this service area—Olsen, Caravan, Tauck, Pan Am, Maupintour, TWA Getaway tours, and other industry leaders—and there are others with less familiar names but a strong series of offerings—The Cortell Group, C.I.E., Trafalgar, Westours, Thomson, Brendan, Globus, Mayflower, Grand Circle, Four Winds, and hundreds of additional companies. American Express and the American Automobile Association have their own tours and their own following. Individual countries also have smaller, but capable, tour companies, like Lismore in Ireland and England.

Because it is by far the most effective marketing tool, tour operators make certain that travel agents are kept informed and are supplied with adequate materials. Agency literature racks display tour folders; agency shelves and counters and cabinets contain client copies of tour information; agency walls display tour posters. A lot of money is spent by operators on printed materials.

A typical tour brochure might fit in a #10 envelope but the major companies also produce more extensive publications. Pan Am's Holiday/Europe book for 1987 ran to 132 pages; Caravan's for the same year totaled 72. Both lead off with a few general pages, describing hotels, introducing escorts, capsulizing special features or company philosophy. Caravan promotes quality and value; Pan Am writes about flexibility, number of destinations, and group rates. Typically, the text then shifts to descriptions of the tours, including highlights, day-by-day itinerary, dates, and costs. Travel tips and tour restrictions complete the book.

All media may be used for tours, but not always in the same kind of mix, and not always by the tour operator. A local travel agency may decide to use a tour operator for a trip it has in mind, or just opt to sell one of the package tours. Either way, the agency may contract for the advertising itself or co-op the charges. These ads would appear in the local paper, probably in the Sunday travel section, and would be supported by printed materials and, sometimes, by a limited radio schedule. Individual tours would rarely be marketed on television, although a tour area, like Hawaii, could be advertised as a joint venture of an agency and an airline.

Tour operators do advertise in the trade publications, letting travel agents know what offerings they'll have and how they will help the agencies make money. In consumer and travel magazines, the aim is often to get the prospect to send for more detailed literature.

Tour operators also sponsor parties or receptions for travel agents and they produce films and sometimes give illustrated lectures. Representatives may meet with travel writers or editors to help plant stories, and the practice of providing familiarization tours to agents and writers is widespread. Articles in trade journals could be the work of tour operator staff members and the more active operators also do a lot of personal visiting. Foreign operators usually plan selling trips to America, visiting those places where experience tells them the best prospects and the most productive agencies are located. They may even bring entertainment and put on a show for those who can be identified as interested in their packages.

## CHAPTER HIGHLIGHTS

❏ Five airlines handle 80 percent of the Revenue Passenger Miles, but there is a lot of competition for travelers, resulting

in large advertising budgets and a number of different discount deals.
- ❏ Frequent-flyer programs and tie-ins with other travel services are common.
- ❏ Cruises continue to grow as a travel option, but only 5 percent of Americans have ever taken one. All media are used in promotion, with newspapers dominating.
- ❏ Travel agents prefer selling cruises to tours, and find them easier to market.
- ❏ Although the affluent are the best prospects, cruise lines are working hard to expand the range of clientele.
- ❏ Amtrak carries more than 20 million passengers annually but, without subsidies, couldn't afford to operate. They market the uniqueness of the train experience, along with on-time arrivals.
- ❏ Motor coaches have done a lot to change their downbeat image, but the public hasn't yet caught up with these improvements. This form of transportation remains, primarily, an option for the older traveler or the very young.
- ❏ Car rental companies have proliferated, and generally compete on price and quality of equipment.
- ❏ Tour operators may be large or small, but their prime audience is the travel agent, and their chief tools are printed materials.

■          ■          ■

## ❏ EXERCISES

1. Find the theme line for five airlines (like the "friendly skies" for United) and critique each for its appropriateness and effectiveness.
2. Bring in three print ads for three different cruises to three different areas. Determine from the copy approach who the target audience is. What psychological appeal is used? How effective do you find each?
3. What do you feel—personally—are the plus and minus factors of a train trip? Of a motor coach tour?
4. Come up with an idea for a tour that would appeal to a special group of people like science fiction fans or members of a gourmet food club. Use your imagination. How would you market this tour?

# ❑ *CASE PROBLEMS*

*1. Keeping in mind that only 5 percent of Americans have ever taken a cruise, and that the potential for other travelers is considerable, you, as a travel agency tour manager, want to expand your market which, in this case, is in your own city. First, you want to find out why people haven't taken a cruise. Conduct ten brief interviews among friends or acquaintances who have not been on a cruise, asking them why and what it would take to change their minds. Using this information, and assuming it to be representative of your target audience at large, drawn up a brief, one-page plan for meeting these obstacles.*

*2. Assume that an airline that does not currently service your area has been given permission to add your closest airport to its flight schedule. You are in charge of public relations for this airline and you want to make a big show of your inaugural flight from the new city. What sort of event might you schedule? Describe the elements of this event. What persons or groups would you invite? How would you arrange for publicity? Are there any other considerations?*

# 15

# NATIONAL, STATE, AND LOCAL TOURISM PROMOTION

While individual airlines, cruise lines, and hotels may have their own economic agendas, each with a bottom line of profit for the specific venture, larger entities like countries, states, and cities also have a stake in the tourist dollar. All of them commit funds to attract visitors to their area, because visitors mean sales of goods and services, jobs, and taxes. Some regions start off with more physical assets than others, but all try to market whatever they have to sell.

Each of these geographical entities does what any other member of the travel industry attempts. They conduct research, develop a profile of their best prospects, analyze their own offerings, create a theme, and then market their program. Generally, the smaller the unit, the more narrow the focus and the smaller the budget, but even the medium-sized cities avail themselves of professional advertising and public relations expertise.

## PROMOTING THE COUNTRY

For many nations, tourism rates in the top three sources of income; in some cases, it is the chief revenue producer. Whenever a natural disaster, terrorist attack, unfavorable exchange rate or other negative factor intervenes, the country's economy immediately shows the effect. Even a false but widely circulated rumor can take its toll on travel.

Even when things are normal, members of the travel industry within any country put a certain amount of pressure on the government to do whatever is necessary to enhance the influx of tourists.

This may involve anything from improving roads to stabilizing the political situation. Where tourism is a factor, these pleas are heard. If rumors spread that visitors may be hassled by police or robbed by bandits or cheated by merchants, these ills must be corrected. Even the finest marketing program can't function under these handicaps.

Besides the activities in which a government tourism bureau might personally engage, the individual nation's hotels, airlines, cruise lines and hotels/resorts may also be doing their own marketing, hopefully tied to the overall theme. The Irish Tourist Board (Bord Failte) and the Irish International Airline (Aer Lingus) share the responsibility of attracting tourists to Ireland, and they are aided by hotel chains, tour operators, and some special attractions. Much of this combined advertising and promotion would focus on the Irish landscape, the Irish people, and the Irish culture.

Americans must keep in mind that they are not the only people who tour. The Japanese, for example, are world travelers. Consequently, Americans may see only a small portion of the advertising done by other countries. Spain tries hard to bring British tourists to its warmer winter climate, and the Fiji Islands beckon visitors from Australia and New Zealand.

Fiji also keeps its tourism eye on America. Starting in 1984, Fiji launched Project America, with the aim of doubling visitors to the island nation. In the early 1970s, some 50,000 Americans would trek annually to Fiji but that number was more than halved when some airlines began to skip Fiji as a stopover. The country also suffered because of cyclone damage to some key hotels, political unrest and, undoubtedly, because of competition from the much closer islands of Hawaii. Fiji's promotional budget has been a modest million dollars or less, matched by a similar amount from private sources. In addition to advertising and mailing of printed materials and promotions with travel agents, Fijian representatives have been more in evidence at travel conferences and trade seminars, and, to build clientele lists in New Zealand, they sent their Fiji Police Band on tour.

Finland, which experienced a drop in visitors from the United States in 1986, due largely to concerns about the Chernobyl fallout, countered by opening a new office in Los Angeles. Finnish authorities consider Californians prime prospects because of their sophistication about travel and their willingness to try something new—like reindeer-driven sleigh rides.

Capitalizing on the success of the film, *Crocodile Dundee,* and on the publicity caused by Australia's contest for the America Cup and its prime viewing area for Halley's comet, the Australian Tourist

Commission poured $30 million into an advertising campaign to reach Americans. Half of that went into three years of television buys and nearly $7 million were committed to the production of a pair of commercials starring Paul Hogan, the star of *Crocodile Dundee.* The campaign generated a million and a quarter inquiries from the United States and helped boost tourism from America some 40 percent. Picking up on the TV image of Australians as a cheerful, friendly people, a series of print ads played on Australian slang in the headlines and also emphasized the warmth of citizens Down Under.

Because of the dropoff in tourist traffic to Europe in the summer of 1986, various nations came up with programs to recoup some of the losses. Great Britain offered free trips and lodging as prizes, trimmed fares and room rates, showcased its theater offerings, and publicized the wedding of Prince Andrew to Sarah Ferguson. France unveiled a package that included a chauffeur-driven limo and discount shopping. Germany teamed with Avis for some economical fly/drive bargains. Hilton Hotels offered 25 percent off their room rate, and Aer Lingus marketed two-for-one travel coupons.

For 1987, some European countries doubled their tourism budgets in order to gain back some of their lost revenues. The European Travel Commission, an umbrella organization, ran a late March ad supplement in *The New York Times, Chicago Tribune,* and the *Los Angeles Times.* The Italian Government Travel Bureau raised its tourism budget to more than $4 million, and Greece, which suffered from negative reports on its airport, outspent Italy, using celebrities with Greek roots to provide testimonials. Switzerland and Belgium, with more modest budgets, are both engaged in cooperative ventures with their national airlines, advertising in magazines like *The New Yorker* and increasing the number of familiarization tours and travel agent workshops. Germany also included *The New Yorker* in its publication list, along with *Travel & Leisure, Gourmet, Signature, The New York Times Magazine* and others.

Besides advertising, many European nations were also heavily into trade shows, special programs for American travel agents, and visits to American media with the aim of generating favorable publicity.

Themes varied. Bord Failte advertised, "Ireland, the Unexpected." Thailand built its campaign around unusual events like its water festival, Royal Barge Procession, and Elephant Round-Up. Hong Kong called itself "the most exciting city on earth" and Yugoslavia became "Europe's Most Beautiful Value."

The United States, too, a relative amateur in the field of tourism promotion, began to expand its activities in the 1980s. For one thing, this country realized it had an imbalance in tourist dollars, with almost $9 billion more going out than coming in. Even with this discrepancy, America garnered over $14 billion in 1985 from foreign visitors and this influx supported over 300 thousand jobs. The nearly 22 million people who came here that year trooped to New York City, Los Angeles, San Francisco, and Miami as their choice destinations, with the British and Germans favoring our beaches and the French enthused about New Orleans. Many foreign visitors also appreciated the long hours stores are open, the number of free museums, and the helpfulness of American citizens.

This country gets a boost from movies and television that reach around the world, causing others to want to see America. Visiting here also becomes something of a status symbol, a proof that you are a seasoned traveler. In general, Europeans focus on our East Coast and the Japanese prefer Hawaii and California. All foreign visitors react favorably to the diversity and energy of America, to the natural and manmade scenery, and, overall, to the bargains available in dining and accommodations.

To help improve our tourism programs, some states, like Florida, have opened offices abroad, and some state tourism bureaus have dispatched delegations to target nations. Print advertising, television, and circulating films have been used to some extent, along with printed materials, but the typical budget of between $10–$15 million doesn't allow for much latitude. Even then, Congress occasionally makes moves on even this minimal amount.

Something new is always happening in tourism. Oil changes the travel habits of some Middle Eastern countries, or educational opportunities bring students from Africa. Now some tourism seers are projecting an increase in visitors from China, calculating that their modernization program may produce a higher standard of living and a more liberal attitude toward foreign travel. Those who have hosted Chinese visitors call them perfect tourists, people who have traveled little and are interested in everything.

For the moment, Canada holds a wide edge in number of tourists to America and time spent here. Western Europe follows, then Asia, South America, Mexico, and the Caribbean. Visitors from the South Pacific, Central America, the Middle East, Africa and Eastern Europe, although increasing, still amount to only about 600,000 people.

So there is ample room for growth, and America, more conscious of the economic impact and more sophisticated in its approach, is doing a better job of meeting competition. Good thing, too, because Europe, for example, is now able to offer ski vacations in the Alps at a cost comparable to ours, and off-season bargains are also being marketed more aggressively, like cut-rate shopping and theater weekends.

## STATE TOURISM

Not too many years ago, state tourism was restricted to the few "vacation" states and to certain seasonal promotions. Other areas produced brochures and answered inquiries but had no fully developed promotional packages. When these states did market them-

**Fig. 15–1 Kentucky selects a recognizable theme for its print campaign.** (Courtesy of Kentucky Department of Travel Development)

# South Carolina.

# It's a lot of great vacations.

Whatever kind of vacation you're looking for, you'll find it in South Carolina.

And to help you plan your vacation, we'll send you the new South Carolina Trip Kit—free! It'll tell you about things to do and places to stay. And there are maps to show you how to get there once you get here.

Wherever you go in South Carolina, you'll find a lot of great vacations. Just clip the coupon to find out how they can all be yours.

**NEW South Carolina Trip Kit**

FREE SOUTH CAROLINA TRIP KIT

Name _____

Address _____

City_____ State_____ Zip _____

South Carolina Division of Tourism, Room 685, Box 78, Columbia, S.C. 29202

**Fig. 15–2  Almost every tourism bureau offers free literature in its ads.** (Courtesy of South Carolina Division of Tourism)

selves, their messages seemed all too familiar. They all had friendly people and fishing and shopping and nice places to eat. Today the 50 states do better, isolating and emphasizing unique attractions, employing professional assistance, setting goals, and checking results.

Naturally, tourism expenditures vary. Illinois and New York lead the list with annual budgets of around $10–$15 million and, at the opposite end of the spectrum, are states like Mississippi and North Dakota with reported advertising expenses hovering around $100,000. Massachusetts, Alaska, Florida, and New Jersey have budgets between $5–$10 million, while Pennsylvania spends more than that and California, Tennessee, and Michigan less. In the $3 million range are states like Colorado, Ohio, North Carolina, and Virginia. Georgia, Missouri, Minnesota, Arizona, and Utah come in at between $2–$3 million, and the rest of the states spend less, reporting anything from a million-plus to a few hundred thousand dollars.

Before the age of computers and other means of quickly identifying inbound traffic, state tourism officials would count the license plates at popular attractions and draw up some assumptions about the source of visitors. Today, hotel registrations can be quickly tabulated, as can credit card information. Surveys are taken and some people still note license plates. Colorado knows, for example, that its best recruiting states are California, Texas, and Illinois, while Illinois draws heavily on its Midwestern neighbors and Kentucky. Hawaii's quartet of best target states includes Texas and Illinois along with California and Washington, while Japan, Canada, Australia, and New Zealand are their principal sources of foreign visitors. Louisiana pulls from the East and West Coasts, plus Texas, Ohio, Illinois, and the southeastern states, and from Canada, Germany, England, and France.

In 1986, when misfortune struck the European tourist scene, domestic promotional activity soared. The 50 states combined to spend about $216 million to lure tourists to their borders, focusing on cheap gasoline prices, the value of the dollar, and attractions that ranged from anniversary activities to new dog tracks. Besides looking to outsiders, some states also concentrated on their own citizens. California and Illinois, two big spenders, produced campaigns to convince natives to explore their own territory. Bill Cosby praised New Jersey and Johnny Cash lauded Tennessee in a pair of commercials. Kansas ads sighed, "Ah, Kansas!"

State budgets are often given a boost by corporate or travel industry dollars. These may appear in the form of co-op advertising, may be direct gifts, or may be used to subsidize something like travel writers' visits, billboards, or printed materials. They know that, of the billions spent in the United States by tourists, a high percentage will be of direct and indirect benefits to them.

What are some of the states doing?

New York, which popularized the heart shape on bumper stickers, is still merchandising the love symbol and the apple, but they have a new symbol, too: the refurbished and much-discussed Statue of Liberty. Their promotion isn't all focused on Manhattan. State

**Fig. 15–3   Colorful brochures are a key element in state tourism promotion.**

**Fig. 15—4  Two print ads in a very effective New York campaign call attention to the varied scenic attractions.** (Courtesy of Department of Tourism, State of New York)

tourism encompasses Niagara Falls, the Catskills, the Finger Lakes, and the Adirondacks. They sell nature, history, and turn-of-the-century luxury resorts.

Missouri's theme in 1986 was "Wake Up to Missouri," and their marketing goals were:

❏ To increase the overall perception of Missouri as an attractive vacation destination.
❏ Gain an increasing number of travelers from markets in nearby states and from Missourians vacationing in their home state.
❏ Promote all parts of Missouri as equally as possible.
❏ Extend the time visitors stay in Missouri and increase their number of visits per year.

Working with a little more money than the previous year, Missouri expanded its advertising reach, running in more places both earlier and longer. Their nearly $2 million budget bought the state a 10-week television schedule in 21 markets, radio in these same markets plus statewide markets, a heavy effort in spring newspaper advertising, and participation in preprinted newspaper inserts. Color ads in trade journals supplemented this regimen, along with cooperative efforts with trade groups soliciting foreign visitors. Missouri also promoted discount coupons, merchandising items like sweatshirts and tote bags, made gifts to group travel planners, produced a calendar, newsletter, travel guide, fact sheet, group tour manual, as well as periodic news releases. Half a dozen information booths cover entry points to the state and Missouri made good use of volunteer experts who are part of its Tourism Team of Missouri.

Alaska, which calculated that more than three-fourths of its visitors came to see relatives, ran a campaign within its borders to get residents to invite guests during fall, winter and spring, the state's off season. Skiing, birdwatching, and hot air ballooning were among the attractions cited, plus events like the annual Fur Rendezvous in February.

Michigan got great mileage out of hosting the convention of the Society of American Travel Writers, a function that cost $250,000 to stage but which brought in thousands of inches in print and dozens of minutes on network television.

After 14 years of advertising under the theme of "Virginia is for Lovers," that state switched to an "exciting times" line in 1983, then moved back to its successful romantic designation two years later.

Illinois built its promotion around the variety of state events, from Go-Kart Races to Steamboat Days, and they also used the high-profile Chicago Bears in their ads. Texas, limping along on a minimal advertising budget, managed to crank up publicity for its sesquicentennial celebration, while neighboring Arkansas, also noting its own statehood sesquicentennial, created a "Company's Coming" campaign that even invaded the Lone Star State. North Carolina won a 1987 Magazine Publishers Award for the best print ad with a colorful photo of decorative quilts hanging in front of an old barn—further proof that tourism advertising often showcases ad agency talents. Ohio switched from spending two-thirds of its tourism budget internally to spending about the same percentage out-of-state. Once disdainful of the peace-shattering effect of tourism, Colorado now markets that mountain ambience, moving from 42nd to 13th in the rank of state tourism budgets. Arizona sells sunshine; Lousiana promotes jazz and food; Mississippi plays up its antebellum splendor.

Tourism in Florida has been a real growth industry, evidencing some $20 billion in tourism-related income in 1986. Some cities in Florida witnessed a 70 percent hotel occupancy rate. Part of this success may be attributable to the exceptional job of research conducted by Florida's Division of Tourism. Over $300,000, exclusive of salaries and expenses for a quintet of professional staffers, was committed to research.

California, positioning itself as a year-round vacation state, has over 5,000 travel agencies within its borders and about 8 percent of the Fortune 500 companies. They also have Hollywood, Disneyland, the San Diego Zoo, the old Spanish missions, mountains, and seascapes. You can gawk at movie stars or watch migrating whales. These incentives allow California to advertise a little less than its traffic and potential might demand.

Some states, in addition to teaming up with regional businesses and travel firms, also team up with each other. Seven states tout themselves under the banner of the Rocky Mountain West and southern states may occasionally assemble within the pages of a special section on their region.

So there are gainers and losers. When California successfully convinces its natives to stay home, Hawaii feels the pinch. A good year in Colorado may spell improvements for gateway states like Nebraska. Even though the industry is divided into thousands of tiny domains, everything significant, worldwide or nationwide, may have an impact on the smallest element.

**Fig. 15–5 Play on words and illustrations catch the eye in this ad. Note type used in logo.** (Courtesy of Greater New Orleans Tourist and Convention Commission, Inc.)

**Fig. 15–6   Many individual cities focus on their special attractions.**

# CITIES GET INTO THE ACT

Okay, we know about New York and Phoenix and Los Angeles and Honolulu, but Detroit and Omaha and Tucson and Syracuse also want to have their say. No city is ignorant of the value of tourism. Some have an easier time than others in identifying their strengths, but almost all cities have *something* to talk about. Perhaps a famous person was born there or a colorful festival is held there. Perhaps, like Omaha, the city can proclaim "Big City Spice; Small Town Price," calling attention to the cost of an evening out for two, including drinks, dinner and a symphony concert, all under $70. Perhaps, like Miami, advantages accrue from the hit television series, *Miami Vice,* and move that city from its image as a community on the skids to that of a hot and glittering metropolis. New construction helps, and so do the myriad Florida events, and so does the exemplary cooperation between government and the tourism industry.

A convention center in Philadelphia is expected to boost that city's tourism reputation. Tucson has gone after the trade by doubling its room space, adding resorts and dude ranches and watching its airport terminal expand 100 percent. Atlantic City completed its 12th and 13th casino hotels in 1987 and has plans for 5 more. Non-gambling properties have risen alongside the casinos. Tampa, Florida, already popular as a convention site, is trying to edge into the leisure market, capitalizing on its proximity to Disneyland, beaches, and some principal resorts. Boulder, Colorado, markets cultural events; Boston ("Bright from the Start") blends in its pitch history, quaint customs and thoroughly modern facilities and entertainment. Memphis, in its ad campaign, encourages visitors to "start something great" while Atlantic portrays its impressive skyline in print.

Let's look at two totally different marketing problems and the responses to them.

Estes Park, Colorado, relies on tourism. It's one of those communities whose population multiplies significantly in summer, and whose residents, even without the help of surveys, can tell you if the tourist season is healthy or not. More than half their visitors are between the ages of 30–50 and earn between $25,000 and $50,000 a year. A third of them are professional people, and nearly half the annual visitors are first timers. To reach them, Estes Park spends around $150,000 in newspapers, magazines, and on television. The impact isn't outstanding but city fathers reckon they get an excellent dollar return for every advertising dollar spent. What do they

**Fig. 15-7** Typically, tourism departments supply a family of printed materials to meet a variety of needs.

promote? Their location, adjacent to Rocky Mountain National Park and proximate to one ski area; their amenities, lots of area motels, ranches and the Stanley Hotel; shopping, mainly of the gift kind; events, like the rodeo and bicycle races and dinner theaters.

For Omaha, Nebraska, the challenge is a little different. It's not perceived as a resort area, and it competes with Kansas City and Minneapolis for distant traffic. Research convinced its local tourism bureau, which is funded by a portion of the hotel/motel occupancy tax, that the best prospects for a weekend in the city were those who lived within a radius of 150 miles of Omaha. Others might be lured by the major race track, by a visit to Boys Town or the Strategic Air Command, or by the chance to see relatives and friends. Besides focusing on the relatively low cost of having a good time in Omaha, the city has also used its promotional budget (under $500,000) to convince outsiders how much the largest city in Nebraska has to offer. One ad is headlined: "A Few Words for Those People Who Think the Height of Culture in Omaha is a Good Steak" and another asks: "Most people would rather spend Saturday night in New York than Omaha. But how about the rest of the week?" Both ads play up the quality of life, the richness and variety of artistic offerings—and those steaks. Films, a slide show, limited radio and television schedules, strategically placed newspaper and magazine ads, a rack full of printed materials, and even a special events hotline complete the promotional package.

Big cities spend millions on promotion; small ones spend thousands, perhaps only hundreds. They work with their Chambers of Commerce and travel agents, with their hotels and attractions, with travel writers and editors, and they also do what they can to enthuse their own citizens about the glories of their community and the necessity of informing others.

## ATTRACTIONS

Although state and local tourist bureaus may plug special attractions within their borders, these places also market themselves. Disneyland and Disney World don't wait to be mentioned by others. Neither does Sea World or Knott's Berry Farm or Opryland. These attractions produce their own materials, generate their own publicity, and create their own advertising schedules. The Disneyland centers benefit from their television show and channel. Mount Rushmore takes advantage of acres of photographic coverage. Holly-

There's nothing that could make your next Florida tour more memorable than a visit to Busch Gardens. It's a roar down the raging Congo River Rapids. It's a safari across our Serengeti Plain. It's all the fun, and the romance, and the mystery found only at Busch Gardens,Tampa. It could be as close as you'll ever get to Africa. For more information about Busch Gardens, just call us Monday through Friday at (813) 977-6606. Or write to Busch Gardens, Group Sales Office, P.O. Box 9158, Tampa, FL 33674.

**Fig. 15—8 A humorous approach is used to attract visitors to a theme park.** (Courtesy of Busch Gardens, Tampa, Florida)

wood's glittering image is evoked by programs like "Entertainment Tonight" and the staggering amount of publicity attending the restoration of the Statue of Liberty helped all tourist attractions in New York.

Besides cooperating with government tourist entities, attractions may also affiliate with other appropriate organizations. Opryland and American Airlines make such a team, share space and time in the media, and share costs of hosting travel agents and meeting planners.

## OTHER TRAVEL UNITS

This text covered only the major aspects of the travel and hospitality fields. There are other members of the industry who also promote themselves. Travel schools, for example, or travel books. Travel organizations, like the American Association of Travel Agents, and

**Fig. 15–9   Each sort of attraction builds its own audience—Hawaiian surf; Buffalo Bill Museum in Cody, Wyoming; or a vintage car exhibit at a Texarkana fair. Each also promotes itself differently.**

travel publications, like *Travel/Holiday* or *Travel Weekly*. There are travel accessories, travel insurance, and travel consultants. Some areas have meeting planners and convention specialists.

There is also a wealth of travel clubs, from Club Med to teachers' organizations, groups sponsored by financial institutions, senior citizen travel clubs, organizations devoted to swapping condos, and those that specialize in ethnic groups, the handicapped, or a whole range of hobbyists. All of them advertise, favoring promotions in their own publications or direct mail.

Tourism is, and will remain, big business for the United States. More than $250 billion is added to our economy from tourism each year, and four and a half million people have jobs in the industry, resulting in salaries of nearly $50 billion. Local, state, and federal governments realize almost $25 billion annually in tax revenues.

And that doesn't count things like good will and enjoyment and a hundred other intangible byproducts of tourism.

That's why learning how to properly promote this immensely appealing natural resource is worth study.

## CHAPTER HIGHLIGHTS

❏ Tourism is a major part of the economy in many countries and government divisions collaborate with the travel industry in promoting visits.

❏ Foreign countries also promote themselves in America and elsewhere, increasing their budgets recently to make up for a falloff attributable to terrorism.

❏ The United States is a relative newcomer to overseas promotion, but has committed more and more resources and is being rewarded by an increase in tourists, primarily from Canada and Western Europe.

❏ All 50 states are involved in tourism, some spending $15 million or more and others getting by on $100,000 or so. Each engages in some research and tries to determine its chief selling points and its principal audiences.

❏ Virtually all tourism bureaus are clients of an advertising agency, and they also cooperate with tour operators, travel agents, carriers, and the hospitality industry.

❏ Hundreds of cities conduct their own promotional programs, sometimes spending millions, more often spending thousands. They also cooperate with larger travel units and try to market some unique aspect of their community.

❏ Special attractions are often part of state or local promotion, but, to some degree, they also promote themselves.

❏ A variety of other divisions of the tourism industry, from travel schools to travel clubs, rely on advertising and public relations.

■          ■          ■

## ❏ *EXERCISES*

1. Talk to someone in your local or state tourism office. What are their goals? What research do they do? What is their current theme and how was it developed? What do you think of it?

2. Find three ads for state tourism in travel magazines and critique each for image and impact.
3. What foreign country do you feel does the best job of promoting itself? Explain your reasons for this choice.
4. Which American city that you haven't visited would you like most to visit and why?

## ❑ CASE PROBLEMS

*1. Pick a foreign country—any country—and assume these people form a target audience for potential visits to your state. What will attract them to your state? How will you capture this theme in your campaign? How do you plan to reach these people (consider other things besides advertising)?*

*2. Again, focusing on your own state, and assuming you were interested in getting a larger number of under-30 tourists, what would be your focus? How would you work these ideas into a campaign? How would you reach your target audience?*

# GLOSSARY

**AIDCA**   An acronym designating conditions to be achieved by an advertisement; i.e. Attention, Interest, Desire, Credibility, and Action.

**accordion fold**   A method of folding paper so that it opens like the pleats in an accordion.

**account executive**   An advertising agency person who works directly with the client on an account.

**advertising**   Controlled, paid promotion of goods and/or services through the use of mass media, with the aim of influencing purchase or attitude.

**advertising agency**   A firm that specializes in the production and placement of advertising.

**advertising mix**   A blend of various media in order to conduct an intelligent and effective advertising campaign.

**agate line**   A unit of measurement in ads which is one column wide and 5½ points (1/14 of an inch) deep.

**airbrush**   A method of retouching artwork through the use of a fine spray.

**asymmetrical balance**   See **balance.**

**audience**   A segment of the public to whom an advertising or promotional message is directed.

**audio**   The sound portion of a TV script.

**audiotape**   A tape that records and reproduces sound, used in radio commercials, television, or film.

**avails**   This term refers to the times and programs which are "available" in the broadcast media.

**balance**   A condition in layout or design in which the weight of opposing elements seem to equalize each other. When the elements are in near perfect formal balance, this is called **symmetrical balance;** when the elements are not equally divided on both sides in a layout or illustration, but still project balance, this is called **asymmetrical balance.**

**Benday** Applying shading to a line drawing by the use of adhesive screens.

**bleed** If the printed image extends to the trim edge of the page, it is called a bleed.

**blow up** A larger version of an illustration, particularly a photo.

**body copy** The basic printed information in an ad, making up the "body" of the ad.

**boldface** A heavier and darker type.

**booklet** A small book, made up of eight or more pages, bound together, usually stapled.

**broadside** A large folder, which may unfold to any size from 25" × 19" to 38" × 25". Usually concentrates on a single theme. Sometimes used as a poster.

**brochure** Another term for a booklet or folder.

**brochure shell** A partially printed folder which can be localized by the addition of specific printed material.

**CPM** Refers to the cost of delivering 1,000 readers, viewers, or listeners to an advertiser. The letters mean Cost Per Thousand.

**caption** Copy accompanying and explaining illustrations. In newspapers, the caption traditionally went *above* the illustration.

**center spread** The right and left hand facing pages in the center of a publication.

**chromakey** An optical effect in television.

**circular** An inexpensive leaflet used in direct advertising.

**circulation** The number of copies of a newspaper or magazine that are distributed; or the number of homes regularly tuned to a radio or television station.

**classified advertising** Usually small print ads, listed by category, and often without illustrations.

**clip art** Pre-prepared art delivered by an art service, which can be clipped and used in advertising or other print media.

**close up** In television or film, a shot that focuses tightly on a subject. If a close up of a person, this is a head shot.

**cold list** A mailing list that is untried by a particular advertiser, so that he has no idea what returns to expect.

**cold type** Type produced without the use of hot metal, using either photocomposition, a special typewriter or a computer printer.

**collateral materials** Refers to noncommissionable media used in an advertising campaign, frequently printed materials, like brochures.

**color separation**   The process of breaking down a full-color illustration into the primary colors. Could also be a black-and-white negative of one primary color.

**column inch**   In measuring ads, this would be one inch on whatever column width the publication offers.

**commercial**   Another term for a broadcast advertisement.

**commission**   A fee paid to advertising agencies by the media, typically 15 percent, or to travel agencies by suppliers.

**comp**   A "comprehensive" layout, one that is in next-to-final form, and good enough to show to a client.

**continuity**   A radio, TV, or film script.

**co-op advertising**   A form of cooperative advertising where a supplier and a dealer (or a tour operator and a travel agency) share the cost of running an ad.

**copy fitting**   The science of determining what space will accommodate a certain amount of copy.

**copy platform**   The basic idea for the copy which comes out of the thinking and planning states.

**coverage**   The percentage of individuals or households in a specific area that are reached by certain media. In broadcast, this term is sometimes used to designate the effective reach of the signal.

**crane shot**   In film or television, an overhead shot, using a mechanical extension, or crane.

**crop**   The practice of cutting off portions of an illustration for mechanical or artistic purposes.

**cursive**   Typeface resembling handwriting but with disconnected letters.

**cut**   In letterpress, a term for an illustration or the engraving made from this illustration. In broadcast, a direction to remove material, or cease filming.

**cutline**   Copy accompanying and explaining an illustration. Traditionally *beneath* the illustration. Cutline and caption are now used interchangeably.

**dateline**   An indication at the beginning of a news release of the date and place of origin of the story.

**design**   The arrangement of the various parts to produce an artistic whole.

**dingbat**   A decorative device in printing, like a dot or a star.

**direct mail**   A form of advertising which reaches the individual consumer directly, usually via third class mail.

**direct sound**   The recording of sound at the same time as the filming, producing synchronized sound.

**display**   A type larger than 14 point, used in headlines and other places requiring emphasis. Also a form of advertising distinguished from classified advertising by the use of illustrations, white space, headlines, and other attention-getting devices.

**dissolve**   In film and television, a means of moving from one scene to another by momentarily blending both on the screen.

**dissolve unit**   An attachment to a pair of slide projectors which gives the effect of dissolving one slide image into the other.

**dolly**   A method of getting closer to a film or TV subject by rolling the entire camera forward (or, if you dolly out, backward).

**double fold**   A folder folded twice, to produce 6 panel surfaces.

**drive time**   The morning and evening traffic rush hours, when radio time (particularly AM) is most expensive.

**dub**   A copy of a video- or audiotape.

**dummy**   The layout for a brochure or booklet or magazine.

**duotone**   A photograph reproduced in two colors, usually black and one other color.

**echo chamber**   A sound studio device for adding timbre to a voice.

**engraving**   A printing plate either hand etched in reverse, or transferred from photographic or other copy through the use of acid.

**FTC**   Federal Trade Commission

**fade**   In television, an optical effect where the scene either emerges from black (FADE IN) or goes to black (FADE OUT).

**family of type**   One design of type in a complete range of sizes.

**fees**   Charges made by service firms (such as advertising agencies) for noncommissionable activities.

**film clip**   A short bit of film, used for TV news, or to promote some institution or event.

**finish**   The texture of paper.

**flat rate**   A standard rate for space or time, without any discounts for volume or frequency.

**flop**   To print a picture so that it's the mirror image of the original.

**flush**   To set printed copy even with other copy. *Flush left* means that the left edge of the copy is aligned, but the right edge (*ragged right*) may not be. A solid even box of copy would be *flush left and right*.

**folder**   A leaflet that is folded.

**font**   A complete assortment of type characters in one face and size.

**format**  The layout and style of an ad, publication, or printed page. (Nine basic formats for ads, for example, are given in the text.) Format also refers to the way elements in a broadcast program follow in sequence.

**frequency**  In advertising, the number of times an advertising message is delivered within a period of time. Also refers to the character of a broadcast signal.

**galley proof**  An initial proof, or copy, of an ad, or printed piece.

**gatefold**  An extended folded page that folds into the booklet like a gate.

**gravure**  One of the less common methods of printing, where the ink is retained in depressions for transfer to paper, rather than the upright surfaces being inked as in letterpress.

**gross rating points**  A rating method used in television and out-of-home media.

**gutter**  The inside margins of facing pages in a newspaper or magazine.

**halftone**  In order to capture the continuous tones of a photo when reproducing it, the photo (or illustration) is photographed again through a screen, and a printing plate made of the result. This is called a *halftone.*

**harmony**  Refers to all elements of a creative work, including layout, working together to produce an attractive result.

**house agency**  An advertising agency owned (or controlled) by the person(s) doing the advertising.

**ID**  Short for *identification,* a 10-second spot announcement on radio or television.

**in-house agency**  See **house agency.**

**insert**  A page (or pages) printed separately, and then bound into, or inserted into, a publication.

**institutional advertising**  Advertising aimed at building an image rather than the immediate sale of a product or service.

**inverted pyramid**  A reportorial style in which all essential facts are at the beginning of the story.

**italic**  A form of type that slants to the right.

**jingle**  Musical treatment of a commercial on radio or television.

**junior board**  The smallest size of outdoor billboard.

**justified margin**  Spacing out a line to make it full all the way to the right margin.

**keying**   Placing a specific number or letter in an ad in order to check the source of responses.

**layout**   The arrangement of various elements within an assigned space.

**leading**   A metal strip (or strips) used to add space between lines. If no leading is used, the copy is "set solid." In cold type, a space.

**leaflet**   A sheet of direct advertising, usually folded, not stitched or bound.

**learning**   A relatively permanent behavioral change brought about by some experience.

**letterpress**   A method of printing using raised surfaces.

**letter spacing**   Opening up spaces between characters, for effect, or to fill a line.

**libel**   Published slander that defames an individual.

**lightface**   A thin line type, as opposed to the heavy boldface type.

**line conversion**   A method of producing a special artistic effect by converting a photograph to a line illustration.

**list broker**   A person who sells or rents direct mail lists.

**lithography**   A method of printing from a flat surface, using the principle that grease and water don't mix.

**live**   A performance filmed simultaneously, as against being taped for later showing.

**local advertising**   Advertising paid for and signed by a local advertiser.

**logo**   Stands for logotype, the signature of an advertiser, including name and/or design, probably cast in one unit.

**lottery**   A contest involving chance, consideration, and prize.

**lowercase**   The small letters as against capital letters. *See also*: **uppercase.**

**mail order advertising**   A form of advertising designed to sell goods and services through the mails.

**make good**   A refund, or re-run, of an ad or commercial, when an advertising medium errs in scheduling or presentation.

**make ready**   Adjustments in a printed form to achieve the desired printing impression.

**marketing**   A combination of activities designed to efficiently move goods from manufacturer to consumer.

**marketing mix**   Bringing together elements like product, price, distribution, selling, and advertising into a single workable program.

**market segment**  A limited portion of the total consumer market.

**market share**  That percentage of the potential market which has been captured by an individual brand.

**markup**  The difference between cost and selling price.

**mat**  A papier-mache or composition form made from a plate.

**media**  The various communication forms—print, broadcast, outdoor, and so on.

**media mix**  A skillful blend of various advertising media in a campaign.

**medium closeup**  TV shot of head and partial torso.

**milline rate**  The cost of reaching a million readers with a line of advertising. Arrived at by multiplying the line rate by a million and dividing this result by the publication's circulation.

**montage**  The combination of several pictures or parts of pictures blended into a single unit. In television or film, the blending of several scenes.

**morgue**  The name given to the file room at newspapers and other media.

**motivation**  The root cause of much behavior.

**national advertising**  Advertising by a manufacturer or wholesaler, usually without any local store information; or advertising in a national publication.

**negative**  A reversed tonal image of an original photograph.

**newsletter**  A report issued periodically by a firm or organization to keep employees or the public apprised of current news about the institution.

**off camera**  An action or sound, including a voice, which occurs without being shown.

**offset**  Lithographic printing where an inked image is transferred from a flat plate to a rubber blanket to the paper.

**open rate**  The basic rate, subject to discounts for frequency of advertising.

**optical effects**  Film transitions (dissolves, wipes, etc.) which are added after the final cut.

**out-of-home advertising**  Advertising that is seen by people outside their homes, like billboards, exhibits, transit posters, and the like.

**overlay**  Transparent sheets used over art or photos to indicate location or shape of special treatment.

**package**  A complete broadcast program involving script, talent, music, etc.

**pan**  Lateral movement across subject or scene by film or TV camera.

**pasteup**  In print production, the combination of illustration and type on a single sheet ready for engraving or photographing.

**perception**  An interpretation placed on sensory experience.

**persuasion**  A method of bringing about change or conviction.

**photocomposition**  A method of producing type via photographic impression.

**pica**  A convenient unit of measurement; approximately $1/6$ inch.

**point**  A unit of measurement for type size. There are approximately 72 points to an inch.

**point of purchase**  Advertising displayed at the location where the purchase of that product or service may be made.

**poster**  A large sheet of paper containing a message.

**preferred position**  A specified page or section of a publication, or a specific location on a page. A premium is usually charged for this privilege.

**preprint**  Advertising that is reproduced independently and then inserted in a publication.

**press kit**  A collection of news-related materials for the communication media.

**prime time**  In broadcast, the time when there is the heaviest listening or viewing audience.

**primary colors**  Red, yellow, and blue. (Or magenta, yellow, and cyan.)

**probability**  In surveying, a form of sampling that relies for accuracy on the random method of selecting respondents.

**proof**  A sample of an ad or other printed material, supplied to the client prior to publishing, so the client may check for errors.

**public relations**  A planned, organized communication effort designed to build and hold good will.

**publicity**  A communication about a company or organization released to the media as editorial matter.

**quota sample**  In survey work, a sampling of respondents with known characteristics.

**random sample**  In surveying, a form of probability sampling where each unit in the universe has an equal chance of being represented.

**rating** A term used in broadcast to define the percentage of homes or individuals tuned to a specific program.

**reach** The number of different homes or individuals reached by an advertising message or campaign during a specified time period.

**register** The exact alignment of two or more forms in printing.

**release** A form used to obtain permission to use a person's likeness or statement; also a media order for placement; also a news release.

**remote** A broadcast or telecast originating away from the studio.

**reprint** Copy of an ad after it has run, or copy of a promotional article.

**reproduction proof** A proof of high quality used in making negatives or plates.

**retainer** A fee paid in order to retain the services of a professional person or firm for a specified period of time.

**retouch** Improving an illustration mechanically prior to reproduction.

**reverse** A white on black print, like white type on a black background.

**ROP** Run-of-paper, meaning that the editor may place the ad anywhere in the paper, as opposed to preferred position.

**ROS** Run-of-station, meaning that the commercial may be inserted anywhere it fits during the broadcast day or week.

**rotary board** In outdoor advertising, a single board that is periodically moved from location to location.

**rough** A layout stage between a thumbnail and a comprehensive sketch.

**sans serif** Type without cross strokes above or below the main strokes.

**scale of values** The various gradations of gray between white and black.

**scratchboard** An illustration technique where ink is scratched off the paper stock rather than inked on.

**screen** Cross-ruled glass or film used to produce dots and create halftones.

**script** A radio, film, or television outline for a program, including the scenes to be shown and the words to be said. Also a specific typeface, resembling handwriting.

**sequence** In layout or design, a literal or felt progression from one element to another.

**series** The full range of sizes in one type face.

**serif**   Short strokes at the top and bottom of Roman type.

**shell**   See **brochure shell.**

**showing**   In outdoor advertising, the percentage of coverage by a campaign.

**signature**   The advertiser's name in an ad. Also a number of pages printed on a single sheet.

**silk-screen**   A printing process using a stencil-like method.

**single fold**   A leaflet folded once.

**slander**   Oral defamation of character.

**slide chain**   A device used by television studios to project slides on tape, or on a live telecast.

**slogan**   A more or less permanent advertising phrase.

**spec**   A term used to describe the "specifying" of type faces and sizes.

**spot**   A short broadcast commercial, one minute or less in length.

**spread**   Two facing pages, usually in the center of a publication.

**stats**   Short for photostat, a positive or negative photograph.

**stock**   Paper or cardboard.

**stock photo**   A photo which may be purchased from a commercial vendor.

**storyboard**   A layout or blueprint for a TV commercial, using sketches or photos to delineate the action, accompanied by the narration or dialogue.

**subhead**   A smaller, subordinate heading, used to extend the large headline, or to introduce subsequent blocks of copy.

**super**   A television effect where one image is projected over another on the screen, usually a title or logo or some other print message.

**symmetrical balance**   See **balance.**

**sync**   An exact matching of sound and movement, like speech with lip movement.

**tabloid**   A newspaper about half the size of a standard newspaper.

**tag**   An addition to a commercial in broadcasting, frequently a specific comment by a station announcer.

**tear sheet**   A newspaper or magazine sheet containing an ad which is furnished to the advertiser.

**testimonial**   An advertising message by an identified individual.

**thirty sheet**   The largest standard outdoor billboard, larger than the twenty four sheet poster because of the extra border.

**thumbnail**   A small, quick sketch, the beginning stage of a layout.

**tilt**   Vertical movement of the camera in film or TV.

**tint block**  A colored panel, often screened back to allow type to be overprinted and read.

**trademark**  A word or symbol that identifies a product or service.

**traffic**  In an advertising agency, the department that schedules work, and controls the delivery and return of advertising materials.

**transfer type**  Sheets of alphabets or phrases in different type faces and sizes which may be affixed to layouts or illustrations to produce headlines or simulate body copy. Also called *press type.*

**tri-vision**  An outdoor billboard with three moving panels.

**twenty four sheet**  See **thirty sheet.**

**type**  The mechanically produced letter. The four basic forms are: Roman, block, script, and ornamental.

**typo**  A typographical error.

**uppercase**  Capital letters. See also **lowercase.**

**velox**  A particularly sharp photographic print which is suitable for reprinting.

**video**  The picture portion of a TV program or script.

**videotape**  A tape containing pictures and sound of a television program.

**vignette**  A photographic treatment producing soft edges around an illustration.

**voice over**  Written VO. Narration where the narrator is not visible on the screen.

**wash drawing**  As opposed to a simple line drawing, a drawing that has shades and values, applied with a brush.

**weight**  A term used to designate the thickness of paper.

**white space**  That part of a layout which has no copy or illustration.

**widow**  A short line at the end of a printed paragraph.

**wipe**  An optical effect where one scene is *wiped* off the TV screen and replaced with another.

**zips**  Short for Zip-a-tone sheets, which may be applied to illustrations to create the effect of shading.

**zoom**  A change of distance in a TV shot, using a zoom (or "Zoomar") camera lens.

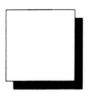

# INDEX